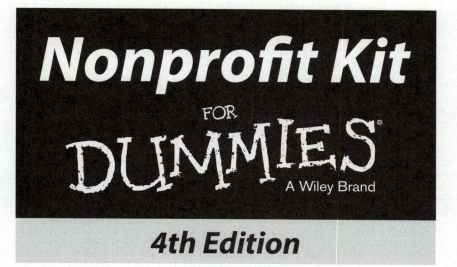

Nonprofit Kit

FOR DUMMIES®

A Wiley Brand

4th Edition

by Stan Hutton and Frances N. Phillips

FOR DUMMIES®
A Wiley Brand

Nonprofit Kit For Dummies®, 4th Edition

Published by: **John Wiley & Sons, Inc.,** 111 River Street, Hoboken, NJ 07030-5774, www.wiley.com

Copyright © 2014 by John Wiley & Sons, Inc., Hoboken, New Jersey

Media and software compilation copyright © 2014 by John Wiley & Sons, Inc. All rights reserved.

Published simultaneously in Canada

For general information on our other products and services, please contact our Customer Care Department within the U.S. at 877-762-2974, outside the U.S. at 317-572-3993, or fax 317-572-4002. For technical support, please visit www.wiley.com/techsupport.

Wiley publishes in a variety of print and electronic formats and by print-on-demand. Some material included with standard print versions of this book may not be included in e-books or in print-on-demand. If this book refers to media such as a CD or DVD that is not included in the version you purchased, you may download this material at http://booksupport.wiley.com. For more information about Wiley products, visit www.wiley.com.

Library of Congress Control Number: 2013949554

ISBN 978-1-118-60417-5 (pbk); ISBN 978-1-118-61247-7 (ebk);
ISBN 978-1-118-61249-1 (ebk); ISBN 978-1-118-61283-5 (ebk)

Manufactured in the United States of America

10 9 8 7 6 5 4 3 2

Contents at a Glance

Table of Contents

Introduction

*I*t may sound corny, but we feel a certain sense of mission when it comes to nonprofits. We've started them, directed them, raised funds for them, consulted for them, volunteered for them, given money to them, and written about them. We've worked with nonprofits in one way or another for more years than we care to remember.

Why have we continued to work for nonprofit organizations? Yes, we care about others and want to see the world become a better place — our values are important to us. But, to be honest, that's not the reason we've worked for nonprofit organizations for so many years. We believe the reason is that we can't think of anything more interesting or more challenging to do.

Starting a new program is exciting. Getting your first grant is thrilling. Working with the multifaceted personalities that come together on a board of directors is fascinating. Learning a new skill because no one else is there to do it is fun. Seeing the faces of satisfied clients, walking along a restored lakeshore, hearing the applause of audiences — all are gratifying.

That's why we do it.

About This Book

When we refer to nonprofit organizations, unless we say otherwise, we're talking about organizations that have been recognized as 501(c)(3) nonprofits and are considered public charities by the IRS.

We try to cover the gamut in this book — everything you need to know to start and manage a charitable organization, from applying for your tax exemption to raising money to pay for your programs. We include supplemental information on a CD (if you're reading a print copy of this book) and online (if you're reading an e-version of this book), including forms to help you create a budget, examples of grant proposals, and links to websites where you can find more help.

We also attempt to give you a bird's-eye view of the economy's nonprofit sector. When you look at financial resources, for example, nonprofits are much like the rest of the world: Most of the wealth is held by relatively few nonprofit organizations, a certain number of them are in the middle, and many, many more struggle to make ends meet.

We try to be honest about the difficulties you'll sometimes face. You probably won't be able to achieve everything you set out to accomplish, and you'll always wish you had more resources to do more things. Still, we can't imagine doing anything else. Maybe you'll feel the same way after you jump into the nonprofit world.

Foolish Assumptions

When writing this book, we made some assumptions about who may be interested in reading it. Here are some of the readers we imagined:

✓ You have an idea that will help solve a problem in your community, and you believe that starting a nonprofit organization is the best way to put your idea into action.

✓ You serve on a board of directors and wonder what you're supposed to be doing.

✓ You work for a nonprofit and need some ideas about fundraising, managing your organization, or working with your board of directors.

✓ You're simply curious about the nonprofit sector and want to find out more about it.

If you're one of these people, we're confident that this book will answer your questions and give you the info you're seeking.

Icons Used in This Book

We use the following icons throughout the book to flag particularly important or helpful information.

This icon means that you can find more helpful information and management tools on the CD that accompanies the print book or online through book support.wiley.com if you're reading an e-book or don't have access to a CD drive.

The Remember icon provides important information that you should be ready to put into practice.

You may not need this technical stuff today (and can skip over it), but — who knows? It may be invaluable tomorrow.

This icon is posted next to little hints and suggestions gleaned from our experience over the years.

Warnings are just what you think they may be. We alert you to information that can help you avoid problematic situations.

Beyond the Book

A lot of work goes into running a nonprofit organization. But the good news is that there's no shortage of information to help you set up programs, raise funds, apply for grants, recruit employees and volunteers, and do everything else you need to do. With that in mind, we provide additional materials to help in your efforts:

✔ We couldn't squeeze all the samples, forms, and lists of helpful websites into the book, so we provide them in digital form. If you're reading a print version of this book, the extra material is on the CD at the back of the book. If you're reading an e-book, use your web browser of choice to go to `booksupport.wiley.com` and download the files. (You can also use that URL if you have the print book but don't have access to a CD drive.)

We mention many of these files within the chapters; we also include a file of web resources for most chapters. All digital files are labeled with the chapter number and the order in which the element appears in the chapter. For instance, the first digital file in Chapter 2 is labeled File0201. For a complete list of digital files, turn to Appendix B at the back of the book.

✔ This book also comes with some access-anywhere goodies on the web. The free Cheat Sheet at `www.dummies.com/cheatsheet/nonprofit kit` provides

- A list of steps that are necessary for securing nonprofit status from the IRS

- A rundown of the roles and responsibilities of people who sit on the board of directors for a nonprofit organization

- 12 ideas for raising money for your nonprofit organization

✔ This book's Extras page online contains links to articles that enhance the content in the book. At www.dummies.com/extras/nonprofit kit, you'll find

- A quick review of a few parliamentary rules you can use during board meetings

- Pointers for writing an e-mail fundraising letter

- Tips for raising money on your website

- Additional resources you can turn to when you need more information about a specific aspect of running your nonprofit

Where to Go from Here

If you're new to the nonprofit world, we suggest beginning with Chapter 1, where you find fundamental information to get you moving in the right direction. If you're familiar with nonprofits already but want to better understand your responsibilities as a board member, you can find the answers you need in Chapter 6. If you're a new board member and want to understand the organization's finances when spreadsheets are passed out at board meetings, we provide guidance about both making a budget and understanding financial statements in Chapter 11. If you need help to publicize and market your programs, we offer some suggestions in Chapter 12.

If you're like many nonprofit workers or volunteers, you want to know how to get money for your organization. Chapters 13 through 18 cover this topic, so they're good places to begin.

Whether you are new to the nonprofit world or a seasoned professional, we think you'll find helpful and valuable information in this book to get you started or continue your good work.

As you're reading, you may note that some web addresses break across two lines of text. If you're reading this book in print and want to visit one of these web pages, simply key in the web address exactly as it's noted in the text, pretending the line break doesn't exist. If you're reading this as an e-book, you've got it easy — just click the web address to be taken directly to the web page.

Part I
Getting Started with Nonprofits

 Visit www.dummies.com for free access to great Dummies content online.

In this part . . .

- ✔ Peek inside the nonprofit sector and get a glimpse of the role that these organizations play in our society and economy.

- ✔ Get an overview of everything that goes into starting and running a nonprofit organization.

- ✔ Figure out what goes into a mission statement and get pointers on how to write one that will serve your organization well into the future.

- ✔ Discover what you need to do to incorporate your new nonprofit. After that task is completed, apply for tax-exempt status from the IRS.

- ✔ Make sure you maintain your nonprofit status by filing the required IRS reports.

Chapter 1

Tuning In to the World of Nonprofit Organizations

1t's a typical day in your hometown. Your alarm wakes you from a restful sleep, and you switch on your radio to hear the latest news from your local public radio station. You hear that a research institute's study reports that economic indicators are on the rise and that a health clinic across town is testing a new regimen for arthritis. Plato, your Golden Retriever/Labrador mix, adopted from the animal shelter when he was five months old, bounds onto your bed to let you know it's time for breakfast and a walk. Plato is followed by Cynthia, your 4-year-old daughter, who wants to help you walk Plato before she's dropped off at her preschool housed in the community center. You remember that you promised to bring canned goods to the food bank that's next door to Cynthia's school. You haven't even had your coffee yet, but already your morning is filled with news and services provided by nonprofit organizations.

You know that your public radio station is a nonprofit because you listen three or four times a year to its pledge drives, and you volunteer a few hours each month for the food bank, so clearly it's a nonprofit. But you may not know that the research institute is probably a nonprofit organization, just like the health clinic where the arthritis research is being tested and the animal shelter where you found Plato. It's likely that Cynthia's preschool and the community center where it rents its space are nonprofit organizations, as well. Whether we realize it or not, all of us — rich, poor, or somewhere in between — benefit from the work of nonprofit organizations every day.

Nonprofits receive revenue from a variety of sources in order to provide services. Because most nonprofits serve a defined need in the community, tax-deductible donations are an important revenue source. Sometimes nonprofits charge a fee for what they do. Other nonprofits may enter into contracts with your city or county to provide services to residents. Usually, nonprofit organizations get their income from a combination of all these revenue sources.

The nonprofit sector isn't a distinct place — it isn't some plaza or district that you come upon suddenly as you weave your way through your day. It's more like a thread of a common color that's laced throughout the economy and our lives. No matter where we live or what we do, it's not easy to get through the day without being affected by the work of a nonprofit organization. So, in this chapter, we help you understand exactly what a nonprofit organization is and how to start and manage one.

So What's a Nonprofit Organization?

People hear the term *nonprofit organization* and picture Mother Hubbard's cupboard, as in awfully bare with a zero bank balance. But in fact, some nonprofit organizations turn very tidy profits on their operations, and that's good, because cash flow keeps an enterprise humming, whether it's a for-profit business or not.

Comparing for-profits to nonprofits

The main difference between a for-profit and a nonprofit enterprise is what happens to the profit. In a for-profit company like Exxon Mobil Corporation, Microsoft, the Walt Disney Company, or your favorite fast-food chain, profits are distributed to the owners, including shareholders. But a nonprofit can't do that. Any profit remaining after the bills are paid has to be plowed back into the organization's service programs, spent to strengthen the nonprofit's infrastructure, or kept in reserve. Profit can't be distributed to individuals, such as the organization's board of directors.

What about shareholders — do nonprofits have any shareholders to pay off? Not in terms of a monetary payoff, like a stock dividend. But in a broad, service sense, nonprofits do have "shareholders." They're the people who benefit from the nonprofit's activities, like the people who tune in to public radio or enroll their children in a nonprofit preschool. These people are often called stakeholders because they are committed to the success of the nonprofit.

A sector by any other name

Not everyone thinks that *nonprofit sector* is the best term. That's because of the array of organizations with different types of nonprofit status. Some of these organizations are formed to benefit their members — such as fraternities and labor unions — and don't share a broad public-serving intent. Another reason *nonprofit sector* may not be the best choice of terms is its negative connotation. After all, what's worse than not making a profit? But, as we point out earlier, and we remind you again in later chapters, not making a profit isn't the determining factor. Alternative terms that you may hear include the following:

✓ **Voluntary sector:** This term emphasizes the presence of volunteer board members and the significance of voluntary contributions and services to the work of 501(c)(3) organizations. In this definition, the organizations alone don't represent the meaning of *nonprofit;* the definition includes the vast web of their supporters who participate as volunteers and donors.

✓ **Independent sector:** This term emphasizes the public-serving mission of these organizations and their volunteers and their independence from government. (Independent Sector is also the name of a nonprofit organization that provides research, advocacy, and public programs for and about the nonprofit sector.)

✓ **Charitable sector:** This term emphasizes the charitable donations these organizations receive from individuals and institutions.

✓ **Third sector:** This term emphasizes the sector's important role alongside government and the for-profit business economy.

We use the term *nonprofit sector* throughout this book, but we want you to understand its limitations and be familiar with other commonly used terms.

Introducing the one and only 501(c)(3)

When we use the term *nonprofit organization* in this book, for the most part, we're talking about an organization that has been incorporated (or recognized in some way) under the laws of its state and that the Internal Revenue Service (IRS) has classified as a 501(c)(3) and determined to be a public charity. If the term 501(c)(3) is new to you, add it to your vocabulary with pride. In no time, "five-oh-one-see-three" will roll off your tongue as if you're a nonprofit expert.

Other kinds of nonprofit organizations *do* exist; they're formed to benefit their members, to influence legislation, or to fulfill other purposes. They receive exemption from federal income taxes and sometimes relief from property taxes at the local level. (Chapter 2 discusses these organizations in greater detail.)

Nonprofit organizations classified as 501(c)(3) receive extra privileges under the law. They are, with minor exceptions, the only group of tax-exempt organizations that can receive contributions that are tax deductible for their donors.

The IRS tax code describes the allowable purposes of 501(c)(3) nonprofit organizations to be serving religious, educational, charitable, scientific, and literary ends.

Check out File0101 for a more detailed list of the activities that 501(c)(3) nonprofits take on. Pop in the CD or click the link in the table of contents to view this file.

Being a nonprofit organization doesn't mean that an entity is exempt from paying all taxes. Nonprofit organizations pay employment taxes just like for-profit businesses do. In some states, but not all, nonprofits are exempt from paying sales tax and property tax, so be sure that you're familiar with your local laws.

Finding Your Mission and Entering the Nonprofit World

People form nonprofit organizations in order to work toward changing some condition in the world, either for a specific group of people or for society in general. The overall goal or purpose of a nonprofit is known as its *mission*. Taking the time needed to clearly outline a nonprofit's mission is time well spent because the mission guides the activities of the organization, helps the nonprofit's directors decide how to allocate resources wisely, and serves as a measure for evaluating the accomplishments of the group. We think developing a mission statement is so important that we devote an entire chapter (Chapter 3) to guiding you through this process.

It's also important to examine your personal mission before embarking on the path of launching a nonprofit. You're creating a legal entity that has responsibilities for reporting to both the state and federal governments. If the organization grows to the point where you must hire employees, you're responsible for paying regular salaries and providing adequate benefits. And although you can be compensated for your work as a nonprofit staff member, you can't develop equity in the organization or take away any profits at the end of the year. Chapter 2 has more information to help you make this important decision.

Setting up a nonprofit

Nearly all nonprofit organizations are established as corporations under the laws of a particular state. If you're located in Iowa and you plan to do most of your work in that state, you follow the laws in Iowa to set up the basic legal structure of a nonprofit corporation. Although you'll find some differences from state to state, in general, the process requires writing and submitting articles of incorporation to the state and developing *bylaws,* the rules under which the corporation will operate.

After your nonprofit is established under your state laws, the next step is applying for 501(c)(3) status from the IRS. This step requires completing and submitting IRS Form 1023. You need to specify in some detail the proposed activities of the new organization, and you're asked for projected revenue and expenses for the year in which you apply and two years into the future. To be honest, you can't complete this form in one afternoon. It requires substantial time and thought to develop the necessary material and should be reviewed by an accountant and legal representative before filing. We discuss the incorporation and IRS application process in Chapter 4.

Making plans and being flexible

After you start managing a nonprofit organization, you'll discover that planning is your best friend. Every task from budgeting to grant writing requires that you make plans for the future. And you need to do a substantial amount of planning before you're ready to send in your IRS application for tax exemption.

Don't be frightened by this recommendation to plan. The act of planning fundamentally comes down to thinking through what you're going to do as well as how and when you're going to do it. Your plan becomes the road map that guides you toward achieving your goals and your nonprofit mission. Planning is something that you should pay attention to every day.

You should always begin with a plan, but that doesn't mean that plans shouldn't be altered when the situation calls for it. Circumstances change; flexibility and adaptability are good traits to nurture if you're running a nonprofit organization. Chapters 7 and 11 cover planning and budgeting. Chapters 12 and 13 discuss planning for marketing and fundraising. Chapter 8 addresses how to evaluate your work and know if your plans are achieving the results that you want to see.

Bigger than a breadbox

The nonprofit sector is larger than many people realize. Here are some figures from the National Center for Charitable Statistics, based on IRS data, and the Independent Sector, regarding 501(c)(3) public charities in the United States:

✔ More than 979,000 organizations were registered as public charities with the IRS in 2010.

✔ Assets held by these groups in 2010 totaled more than $2.7 trillion.

✔ The number of public charities increased by 47 percent between 2000 and 2010.

✔ Approximately 75 percent of public charities in 2010 had annual gross receipts of less than $100,000.

Being Inspired and Inspiring Volunteers

The nonprofit sector is exciting. It encourages individuals with ideas about solving social problems or enhancing arts, culture, the environment, or education to act on those ideas. It creates a viable place within our society and economy for worthy activities that have little chance of commercial success. We think that it combines the best of the business world with the best of government social-service programs, bringing together the creativity, zeal, and problem solving from the business side with the call to public service from the government side.

We also find volunteerism inspiring. Everyone has heard stories of tightly knit communities where neighbors gather to rebuild a barn. That spirit of pitching in to help is the best part of living in a community in which people share values and ideas.

Many people live in places that contain groups from a wide variety of backgrounds. The nonprofit sector provides an array of institutions in which all people can come together, with both those who resemble them and others who are unlike them, to work toward the common good. Volunteerism enables everyone to pitch in to rebuild "the barn" in a wide variety of contexts.

Applying the term *voluntary sector* to nonprofit organizations came about for a good reason. In the United States, according to the Bureau of Labor Statistics, 61.8 million people volunteered at least once between September 2007 and September 2008.

When you're working in a nonprofit, you'll likely be supervising volunteers — and they'll likely supervise you. What we mean is that (with very few exceptions) nonprofit boards of directors serve as unpaid volunteers. And if you're the executive director, your supervisors are the trustees or board members of the organization. At the same time, you likely depend on volunteers to carry out some or all the activities of the organization. You may serve as a volunteer yourself.

The word "supervision" sounds harsh, and we don't mean to suggest that non-profits are or should be run with an iron hand. The board of directors does have ultimate responsibility, however, for the finances and actions of a non-profit organization, and, therefore, people serving in that capacity have a real duty to make sure that the organization has sufficient resources to carry out its activities and that it's doing what it's supposed to be doing.

We prefer to think of nonprofits as being an organized group activity. You need to depend on others to reach goals, and they need to depend on you. We talk about boards of directors in Chapter 6 and working with volunteers in Chapter 9. If your nonprofit employs paid staff or hopes to someday, Chapter 10 provides some guidance in hiring and managing employees.

Finding the Resources to Do Your Job

One distinctive feature of the nonprofit sector is its dependency on contributions. We devote many pages of this book — most of Part III — to advice about getting contributions through fundraising.

Gifts from individuals of money, goods, services, time, and property make up the largest portion of that voluntary support. This portion is also the oldest of the voluntary traditions in the United States and goes back to colonial times. Since the late 19th century, private philanthropic foundations have emerged as another major source of support, and more recently — particularly after World War II — the federal government and corporations have become important income sources. Earned income through fees for service, ticket sales, and tuition charges also can be an important revenue source for many nonprofits.

Seeing where the money comes from

Among private, nongovernmental sources of support, gifts from living individuals — as opposed to bequests from people who have died — have always represented the largest portion of total giving, but philanthropic giving by foundations and corporations has been growing. Table 1-1 gives estimates of the sources of private contributions in 2011. The best fundraising strategy for most organizations is to take a balanced approach that includes individual giving as well as grants and corporate contributions.

Table 1-1	Sources of Private Contributions: 2011	
Source of Income	*Amount of Total Giving in Billions*	*Percentage of Total Giving*
Individuals	$217.79	73%
Foundations	$41.67	14%
Bequests	$24.41	8%
Corporations	$14.55	5%
Total	$298.42	100%

Source: Giving USA: The Annual Report on Philanthropy for the Year 2011 (2012). Chicago: Giving USA Foundation.

Fundraising for fun and profit

Nearly every nonprofit organization depends on generous donors for the cash it needs to pay its bills and provide its services. Even if you have income from ticket sales, admission charges, or contracted services, you'll find that raising additional money is necessary to keep your organization alive and thriving.

You can see from Table 1-1 that individual giving is the largest single source of contributed income to nonprofit organizations. But you can't just sit waiting by the mailbox for the donations to begin arriving. Two basic rules of fundraising are that people need to be asked for donations and thanked after giving one. Chapter 14 focuses on raising money from individuals, Chapter 15 covers raising money with special events, and Chapter 18 discusses campaign fundraising, which is used when you need to raise extra money for your building or your endowment.

Grants from foundations and corporations make up a smaller percentage of giving to nonprofits, but their support can be invaluable for start-up project costs, equipment, technical support, and sometimes general operating costs. Keep in mind that the figures given in Table 1-1 don't apply equally to every nonprofit. Some organizations get most of their income from foundation grants; others get very little. Chapter 16 introduces you to resources to help you find potential grant sources. Chapter 17 takes you through the process of crafting a grant proposal.

Fundraising works better if people know you exist. That knowledge also helps get people to your theater or to sign up for your programs. Here's where marketing and public relations enter the picture. Chapter 12 helps you figure out what your message should be and how to circulate it to the world.

Make no mistake about it, fundraising is hard work, but if you approach the task with a positive attitude and make your case well, you can find the resources you need.

Chapter 2

Deciding to Start a Nonprofit

Maybe you've been thinking about starting a nonprofit organization for years, or maybe an idea to solve a social problem or provide a needed service recently popped into your head. It could be time to make your idea a reality. But before you file your incorporation papers, you need to understand the positive and not-so-positive factors that can make or break your new organization. Like opening any business, starting and managing a nonprofit organization isn't a simple matter.

Take a look at the economy around you. Are existing nonprofit organizations in your community thriving, or are they struggling to find financial and volunteer support? In addition, are you equipped to manage money and raise funds — which isn't always an easy task even when business is booming — and can you inspire others to work with you whether they're board members, staff, or volunteers?

In this chapter, we pose some questions that you should think about (and answer) before you begin the process of incorporating and applying for tax exemption. If some of your answers point to the conclusion that your idea is worth pursuing but that now isn't the right time to start a brand-new nonprofit organization, we suggest you consider using a fiscal sponsor. As we point out later in this chapter, the benefits of fiscal sponsorship are many.

When we use the term *nonprofit* in this book, we're referring to organizations that have been recognized by the IRS as public charities under section 501(c)(3) of the tax code. Later in this chapter, we describe some of the other kinds of nonprofits to point out the distinct attributes of these 501(c)(3) public charities.

Weighing the Pros and Cons of Starting a Nonprofit

Before you jump headfirst into making your nonprofit dream a reality, you need to understand some basic facts about nonprofit organizations. We begin with some of the pros:

- You'll receive exemption from taxes on most income to the nonprofit.

- For some types of nonprofits, you'll have the ability to receive contributions that are deductible for the donor.

- You'll gain the opportunity of receiving grant funds from foundations and corporations.

- You'll get the feeling that you're contributing to the solution of a problem or to the improvement of society.

Just about everyone would consider these facts to be positive, but they aren't the whole story. If you're thinking of starting a nonprofit to get rich or to avoid paying taxes, consider the following list of cons:

- Nonprofit employees' salaries are subject to income tax like all other types of compensation.

- You'll be required to file an annual report with the Internal Revenue Service (IRS). The complexity of the report increases as your nonprofit income increases. (See Chapter 5 for more information about reporting requirements.)

- You can't start a nonprofit organization to benefit a particular individual or family member.

- Competition for grants from foundations, corporations, and government agencies is tough, and so is getting donations from individuals. You'll be up against more-established nonprofits with successful track records.

- If you decide to move on to other pursuits down the road, you can't take any assets accumulated by the organization you've built with you.

The bottom line is this: Think carefully about your motivation for launching a nonprofit organization. Remember that nonprofit organizations are permitted special privileges because they're formed to benefit the public, not individuals.

Doing Your Homework First

Beyond thinking about the challenges you'll face in starting and running a nonprofit organization, you also need to apply some common sense. Nonprofits don't operate in a vacuum, and neither should you. Personal commitment and inspiration can take your organization far, but you also need to find out how your community will receive your particular idea. So before going full steam ahead with your nonprofit, investigate your competition, get community support, decide how to fund your organization, determine whether you're really ready to run a nonprofit, and develop a game plan. Read on to find out how to get your nonprofit off to a great start.

Checking out the competition

Just as if you were starting a business, you should examine your competition before starting your nonprofit organization. If you wanted to open a grocery store, you wouldn't choose a location next to a successful supermarket, because the market can bear only so much trade. This principle holds true for nonprofits, too. You may have the best idea in the world, but if someone else in your community is already doing it well, don't try to duplicate it.

On the other hand, if your area doesn't have a similar program, ask yourself why. Maybe your community doesn't have enough potential clients or audience members to support the project. Or maybe funders don't perceive the same needs in the community as you do.

Assessing the needs of your area is a good way to evaluate the potential market for your nonprofit's services. You may want to use some or all of the following methods to determine your community's needs:

- ✔ Telephone surveys or written questionnaires to a random sample of residents in your community
- ✔ Interviews with local foundation and civic officials
- ✔ Focus groups with people who are likely to benefit from the organization

For more details on assessing your community's needs, see Chapter 7.

Finding people to help you

Your chances of success increase if you begin with support from others, and the more help you have, the better. Sure, you can probably find an example of a single-minded visionary who alone battles through all sorts of adversity to establish a thriving nonprofit, but starting and running a nonprofit organization is essentially a group activity.

When starting a nonprofit, you need to find people to serve on the board of directors and to support your efforts with donations of money and volunteer time. The first people you usually identify as supporters are family and friends. How can they turn you down? In the long run, however, you need to expand your supporters to others who believe in the organization's mission (and not because you personally created it).

Some people hesitate to share their idea with others because they believe someone may try to steal it. We think this fear is largely unfounded. No matter what your idea is, you'll be better off if you invite others to join you in undertaking it.

To find people to help you and support your organization, take every opportunity to speak about your idea before civic groups, religious groups, and service clubs. You can pass out fliers or set up a booth at a volunteer fair. Set up a Facebook page and invite your contacts to spread the word. Talk to your friends and coworkers. Put on your salesperson's cap and convince the community that it needs your program.

If you're having a difficult time drumming up support, it may be a sign that you need to refine your idea or that others view it as impractical. You may need to go back to the drawing board.

Figuring out how you'll pay the bills

Funding your nonprofit organization is a big issue. Even if you begin as a volunteer-run organization and work from a home office, you still need funds for letterhead, supplies, equipment, postage, and insurance. You also have to pay filing fees for your incorporation and tax-exemption applications. Many nonprofit start-ups are funded by the founder in the beginning. Are you able to pay all the start-up expenses before revenues start flowing to your new nonprofit?

Putting together a budget can help you decide whether the start-up expenses are manageable for you. You'll be creating lots of budgets sooner or later, so you may as well get an early start. Flip to Chapter 11 for details on budgeting and other financial issues.

If you can't fund the operation by yourself in the early months, you need to make a compelling case that your new organization will provide an important service to the community and then convince donors that you have the knowledge and experience to provide it. You can solicit contributions from individuals before the IRS grants the organization tax-exempt status, as long as you reveal that your exemption is pending. (These contributions become deductible to the donor if you file for your exemption within 27 months of the date you incorporated and receive tax-exempt status.) Start-up grants from foundations or corporations are rare and next to impossible to obtain before the IRS recognizes your organization's tax-exempt status, so don't plan to receive any grants from outside organizations.

New organizations can avoid the awkward period between starting up and receiving tax-exempt status by beginning as a sponsored program of an existing nonprofit organization. This arrangement is known as *fiscal sponsorship*. We discuss fiscal sponsorship in detail later in this chapter.

You also can try out your program on a small scale before filing for tax-exempt status by partnering with an existing nonprofit organization to test the success and need of your idea. For example, if you want to start a summer arts program for low-income children, talk to a local church or community center that serves that population and ask if you can teach an art class one day a week for a month. This enables you to try out your idea, demonstrate the need, and set up benchmarks for success.

Taking a long, hard look in the mirror

Ask yourself whether you're the right person to start a nonprofit organization, and try to answer honestly. If your organization offers a service, especially in the health and social-service fields, do you have the educational background, qualifications, or license necessary to provide those services? In addition to being professionally qualified, you need to consider whether you feel confident about your management, fundraising, and communication skills.

When starting and working in a new nonprofit organization, you need to be able to stretch yourself across many different skill areas. You may be dressed to the nines one day to pitch your project to the mayor or to a corporate executive, and the next day, you may be sweeping the floor of your office or unplugging a clogged toilet. In other words, you need to be versatile and willing to take on just about any task that needs to be done.

When potential donors are evaluating grant proposals, they certainly look to see whether the organization's leadership has the background, experience, and knowledge necessary to carry out the proposed program. This doesn't necessarily mean that you need to be an experienced nonprofit manager, but try to assess your background to see how you can apply your experience to the nonprofit that you hope to start.

Planning — and then planning some more

If there were ever a time to plan, this is it. Planning is what turns your initial idea into a doable project. Planning is also a good way to find potential holes in your thinking. For example, you may believe that your community doesn't have adequate animal rescue services. You may be right, but when you begin to break down the idea of starting an animal shelter, you may find that the project costs more money or requires more staff or facilities than you first thought it would. When armed with that knowledge, you can adjust your plan as necessary or scrap the idea altogether.

To begin planning, write a one- or two-page synopsis of your nonprofit idea. In your synopsis, include why your organization should exist, what you're trying to do, and how you plan to do it. It's a good idea to outline both short-term and long-term goals and the resources needed to meet those goals. The list of resources should include money, volunteers, and an appropriate space to carry out your activities. After you've prepared your synopsis and list of resources, talk to as many people as you can about your idea, asking for help and honest feedback about your project. The purpose of this planning process is to think through your nonprofit idea step by step. (If you need help in the planning process, take a look at Chapter 7.)

Understanding Nonprofit Ownership

We once received a telephone call from a man who was shopping for a nonprofit. "Do you know if there are any nonprofits for sale in New Hampshire?" he asked. Although this question doesn't come to us often, it illustrates a misconception about the status of nonprofit organizations. No one person or group of people can *own* a nonprofit organization. You don't see nonprofit shares traded on stock exchanges, and any equity in a nonprofit organization belongs to the organization itself, not to the board of directors or the staff. Nonprofit assets can be sold, but the proceeds of the sale must benefit the organization, not private parties.

If you start a nonprofit and decide at some point in the future that you can't or don't want to manage it anymore, you have to walk away and leave the running of the organization to someone else. Or, if the time has come to close the doors for good, any assets the organization owns must be distributed to other nonprofits fulfilling a similar mission.

When nonprofit managers and consultants talk about "ownership" of a nonprofit organization, they're using the word metaphorically to make the point that board members, staff, clients, and the community all have a stake in the organization's future success and its ability to provide needed programs.

Benefiting the public

People form nonprofit organizations to create a public benefit. In fact, non-profit corporations are sometimes referred to as *public benefit corporations*. A nonprofit organization can't be created to help a particular individual or family, for example. If that were possible, we'd all have our separate non-profit organizations. You can start a nonprofit to aid a specific group or class of individuals — everyone suffering from heart disease, for example, or people living below the poverty level — but you can't create a nonprofit for individual benefit or gain.

Just because you're working for the public's benefit doesn't mean you can't receive a reasonable salary for your work. And despite the name *nonprofit,* such an organization can have surplus funds — essentially, a profit — at the end of the year. In a for-profit business, the surplus money can be distributed to employees, shareholders, and the board of directors; however, in a non-profit organization, the surplus funds are used to strengthen the organization or are held in reserve by the organization and aren't distributed.

Being accountable to the public

People are paying more attention to nonprofit organizations these days. A few media reports about excessive salaries and new concerns about how some nonprofits have spent donated funds have prompted donors, legis-lators, and the general public to ask more questions regarding nonprofit finances and management.

Although nonprofit organizations aren't public entities like government agen-cies and departments, their tax-exempt status and the fact that contributions are tax deductible require them to be more accountable to the public than a privately owned business is.

We discuss nonprofit disclosure requirements in more detail in Chapter 5, but at a minimum, federal law requires that nonprofits file a report (Form 990) every year with the IRS. The amount of detail required in the report depends on the size of the nonprofit organization. States have their own reporting requirements, so contact your appropriate state office to learn what is required. See File0402 for links to information about what is required in your state.

Nonprofits with annual gross receipts equal to or less than $50,000 can file the 990-N; nonprofits with gross receipts less than $200,000 and assets less than $500,000 can file the 990-EZ. Nonprofits with gross receipts equal to or greater than $200,000 or assets equal to or greater than $500,000 must file the long-form 990.

A word about excessive compensation

Although nonprofit employees have no absolute limit on the amount of compensation they can earn, the IRS does have the authority to penalize individuals (and organizations) who receive (or pay) excessive compensation. Whether the IRS considers benefits "excessive" depends on the situation. For instance, a staff member earning $100,000 annually from an organization with a budget of $125,000 may need to worry, but someone earning $100,000 from a nonprofit with a $5 million budget probably doesn't.

An employee who's found to be receiving excessive compensation may be required to pay an excise tax, and in dire cases, the nonprofit organization may lose its tax-exempt status. Chapter 5 offers more information on excessive compensation.

So when setting your nonprofit's executive director's salary, make sure the amount of compensation is justified by salary surveys of similar organizations. Also factor in the local cost of living, the size of the nonprofit's budget, and the type of services being provided. Community foundations, local United Way affiliates, and nonprofit consulting firms can offer salary guidelines to aid in the compensation decision.

Federal law also requires nonprofits to make their three most recent 990 reports, as well as their application for tax exemption, available for public inspection. State and local laws in your area may require additional disclosures. Posting your 990 reports and other required documents on the web is an acceptable way to meet disclosure requirements.

To get familiar with the 990 report, download a copy of it from the IRS website at www.irs.gov. You also can view completed 990 forms from other nonprofit organizations at GuideStar (www.guidestar.org).

Nonprofits Aren't One-Size-Fits-All

The words *nonprofit* and *charity* go together in most people's minds, but remember that not all nonprofits are charitable organizations. The most common examples are business and trade associations, political advocacy groups, fraternal societies, and clubs. Although these nonprofits enjoy exemption from corporate income taxes, people who donate to them can't claim a tax deduction for their contributions.

Most nonprofits, charitable or not, are incorporated organizations that are formed under the laws of the state in which they're created. Some nonprofits have other legal structures, such as associations or trusts, but these are in the minority. The IRS grants tax-exempt status to a nonprofit after reviewing its stated purpose. (See Chapter 4 for information about incorporating and applying for a tax exemption.) Nonprofit types are identified by the section of the IRS code under which they qualify for tax-exempt status.

In this section, we provide an overview of the types of nonprofit organizations and some of the rules and regulations that you'll be subject to if you decide to incorporate and seek tax-exempt status from the IRS. You may discover, for example, that your idea will have a better chance for success if you create a social-welfare organization — a 501(c)(4) — or a for-profit business.

Identifying nonprofits by their numbers

Nonprofit organizations can be formed under the IRS code for many reasons other than charitable ones. To give you a taste of the variety of these organizations, the following list summarizes various classes of nonprofit organizations:

- **501(c)(3):** These organizations are formed for educational, scientific, literary, charitable, or religious pursuits and also to test for public safety and to prevent cruelty to children and animals. Nonprofits in this category may be classified as public charities or private foundations; the source of support for the organization usually determines the classification. Foundations are subject to additional reporting requirements. This book focuses on 501(c)(3) organizations that are classified as public charities. Contributions to these organizations are tax deductible for the donor.

- **501(c)(4):** These organizations are known as *social-welfare organizations* because they're formed for the improvement of general welfare and the common good of the people. Advocacy groups tend to fall into this category because organizations with this classification are allowed more leeway to lobby legislators as a part of their mission to improve the general welfare. Certain employee organizations also come under this classification. Contributions to these organizations aren't deductible for the donor.

- **501(c)(5):** Labor unions and agriculture and horticulture organizations formed to improve conditions for workers are in this category. These groups also may lobby for legislation.

- **501(c)(6):** Business and trade associations that provide services to their members and work toward the betterment of business conditions are placed in this classification. This category includes chambers of commerce and real estate boards, for example. Again, lobbying for legislation is allowed.

- **501(c)(7):** This section covers social clubs formed for recreation and pleasure. Country clubs and organizations formed around a hobby come under this classification. These organizations must be funded primarily by memberships and dues.

- **501(c)(9):** This type of nonprofit is an employees' beneficiary association that's created to pay insurance benefits to members and their dependents. It must be voluntary, members must have a common bond through employment or a labor union, and in most cases, it must meet nondiscrimination requirements.

Several other 501(c)-type organizations are so specialized in nature that we won't go into them here. One of our favorites is the 501(c)(13), which covers cemetery companies.

Political action committees (PACs) and parties have their own special classification, too. They're recognized under IRS code section 527 and are organized for the purpose of electing persons to office. They have special reporting requirements and aren't required to be incorporated. Donations to these organizations are not tax-deductible.

To get the full flavor of the various categories of nonprofit organizations, check out the IRS website (www.irs.gov) or review IRS Publication 557.

Odd little rules and regulations to add to your file

Entire volumes have been written about IRS regulations and laws pertaining to nonprofits. But don't worry — we just want to give you an overview of some facts that may help you decide whether starting a 501(c)(3) nonprofit organization is your best choice.

IRS regulations can change from year to year, so be sure to look at the most recent version of IRS Publication 557 for the latest information.

Nonprofits and political activities

Nonprofits can't campaign to support or oppose the candidacy of anyone running for an elected office. However, the stipulations on lobbying for specific legislation are less clear. In the following list, we break down the rules so you know what you can and can't do, depending on what type of nonprofit you set up:

- ✓ **Social-welfare organizations and labor unions:** These organizations have more leeway when it comes to legislative lobbying than 501(c)(3) organizations do. In fact, lobbying can be their primary activity. Groups that lobby must inform their members what percentage of dues they use for lobbying activities, and they can't work toward a candidate's election.

- ✓ **Charitable organizations, or nonprofits that the IRS considers public charities under section 501(c)(3):** These nonprofits may participate in some legislative lobbying if it isn't a "substantial" part of their activities. The IRS doesn't define the term *substantial*, so it determines this question on a case-by-case basis.

- **Public charities:** These nonprofits can spend a higher portion of their budgets on lobbying activities if the organization chooses to elect the *h designation* (IRS Form 5768), which refers to section 501(h) of the IRS code. Electing the h designation requires more financial reporting to the IRS, but it allows the nonprofit to spend a greater percentage of its income on lobbying activities. The IRS allows more expenditures for *direct lobbying* (when members of the nonprofit talk with a legislator about an issue at hand) than for *grassroots lobbying* (encouraging members of the general public to contact legislators to promote an opinion about a piece of legislation).

- **Private foundations:** Although they, too, are recognized under section 501(c)(3), these organizations may not participate in any legislative lobbying. The only exception to this rule is when pending legislation may have a regulatory impact on the foundation.

Penalties for engaging in too much political activity can include loss of your organization's tax exemption. However, going deeper into the details of these laws and reporting requirements is really beyond the scope of this book. So if you're contemplating involving your nonprofit in serious legislative activity, consult an attorney or tax specialist for advice. More information is available at the Center for Lobbying in the Public Interest website at www.clpi.org.

The situation with churches

Churches are in a category all by themselves. The IRS doesn't require them to file for a tax exemption, nor does it require them to file annual reports to the IRS. Some churches, however, do apply for an exemption because their social-service programs often include anything from preschools to soup kitchens. These programs can then apply for foundation funding and government grants or contracts to help pay the costs of providing the services.

Church programs that haven't been officially recognized as being tax-exempt are highly unlikely to receive foundation grants or government contracts.

Taxes, taxes, taxes

Nonprofit organizations may be subject to *unrelated business income tax,* also known as UBIT. When a nonprofit earns $1,000 a year or more from a trade or business that's unrelated to its exempt purpose, this income is taxable. In addition, some corporate sponsorship funds may be subject to UBIT if they're perceived by the IRS as advertising dollars. IRS Publication 598 tells you all you need to know about this subject; visit www.irs.gov to take a look at this publication.

Some states exempt *some* nonprofits from paying state sales and use taxes. Check the laws in your state to see whether your organization is exempt from paying these taxes. The same is true of property taxes — it depends on your local jurisdiction. Your nearest tax assessor can tell you whether you have to pay property taxes.

Nonprofit employees must, of course, pay income tax on their salaries and other taxable compensation.

Nonprofits owning for-profits

Nonprofits can own for-profit businesses. We don't recommend it, because you're going to have enough on your plate, especially when you're starting out, but it is possible. The business is subject to all regular taxes, just like all other for-profit businesses. Profits from the business become assets of the nonprofit and must be used to further the organization's goals and programs.

Very small organizations

If your nonprofit has less than $5,000 in annual revenues, it doesn't need to apply for a tax exemption. You can even go a bit over $5,000 in a year if your average annual income over a three-year period is less than $5,000. When your income averages more than that amount, however, you have 90 days following the close of your most recent tax year to file for a tax exemption.

Even if your organization has revenues under $5,000, you may still need to file the IRS 990-N form. This form can only be filed online. Check the IRS website at www.irs.gov for the latest information about this requirement.

Nonprofit compensation

Nonprofit organizations have one common feature, regardless of their type: No board member, staff member, or other interested party can benefit from the earnings of a nonprofit. Instead, assets are forever dedicated to the purpose of the organization. If the organization dissolves, the nonprofit must transfer the assets to another organization that performs a similar function.

Just because assets are dedicated to fulfilling an organizational mission doesn't mean that people are required to work for nonprofit organizations for free. Nonprofits can and should pay reasonable salaries to their staff members, if they have any. But keep in mind the difference between paying a salary and splitting the profits at the end of year.

Comparing Nonprofits and For-Profits

Believing that nonprofit organizations have special advantages isn't uncommon. And to some extent, it's true. How many for-profit businesses, for example, get help from volunteers and generous donors? On the other hand, the advantages to owning your business exist, too. In this section, we discuss the similarities and differences between nonprofits and for-profits to help you decide which direction you should go.

How they're alike

We start with the similarities between the nonprofits and for-profits because, believe it or not, there are several. For instance, consider the following:

- ✔ Sound business practices are important to both organizations.
- ✔ Strong financial oversight, including budgeting for revenue and expenses, is a key factor for both organizations.
- ✔ Good planning based on good information is a critical factor in the success of both nonprofits and for-profits.
- ✔ Management skills, the ability to communicate clearly, and attention to detail make a difference whether you're working in a nonprofit or somewhere else.
- ✔ A little bit of luck doesn't hurt either type of organization.

A final similarity involves the term *entrepreneur,* which usually describes someone who starts a new business. But any person or group that sets out to establish a nonprofit organization is entrepreneurial as well. After all, you're starting out on a path that may lead to great success, and you'll assume some risks along the way. We hope that you won't risk your house or your savings account to get a nonprofit going, but you may have uncertain income for a while.

How they differ

Although for-profits and nonprofits require similar professionalism and dedication from their leaders, they differ when it comes time to interpret their bottom lines and successes.

The biggest difference between nonprofits and for-profits is the motivation for doing what you do — in other words, the *mission* of the organization. For-profit businesses exist to make money (you know, a *profit*). Nonprofits exist to provide a public benefit.

Evaluating the success of a for-profit endeavor is easy: Did you make money, and, if so, how much did you make? We're not saying this to cast stones at the capitalist system or to in any way disparage the millions of folks who work for profit-making endeavors. After all, the nonprofit sector depends on profits and wealth for its support. And of course, nonprofits have to balance the books, too. Even nonprofits prefer to end the year with more money than they had when they started. They just don't call it *profit;* they call it a *surplus.*

For a nonprofit to be successful, it needs to change some aspect of the human condition; it needs to solve a problem, provide education, or build a monument. Because the goals of nonprofits are so lofty and progress toward achieving them is often slow, evaluating nonprofit success is sometimes diffi-cult. See Chapter 8 for information about evaluating the results of your work.

Hybrid corporations: Neither fish nor fowl?

Some states have passed legislation that allows for the formation of corporations that can earn and distribute profits to shareholders but also must pay attention to the social and public ben-efits of their business. Efforts to create these new corporate entities, which blend the best of the nonprofit and for-profit worlds, arise largely from the corporate social responsibility move-ment, which has grown substantially during the last 25 years.

You may have heard the term *double bottom line,* a concept that basically means businesses should not only try to make profits but also work toward improving the social condition of their workers and customers and the environment in which they operate. To that end, many com-panies have corporate giving programs that support nonprofit organizations in their com-munities, as well as programs that encourage employees to volunteer for local charitable groups. In the case of the new hybrids, how-ever, corporate giving isn't optional; compa-nies are obliged to consider the social impact of their activities and work toward making the world a better place.

The following three corporate models fall into the hybrid category. As such, they all have one thing in common: In the eyes of the IRS, they're viewed as for-profit entities, and their income is taxable as in any for-profit business. That means if you wanted to make a donation to the work of a hybrid corporation, the IRS wouldn't allow you to claim your contribution as a chari-table gift.

✔ **Low profit limited liability companies (L3Cs):** The L3C model was designed to better attract capital investments from investors seeking a return on their money,

as well as program-related investments (PRIs) from foundations. (PRIs are loans from foundations, not grants.) Foundations can count the funds used to provide PRIs toward their charitable-spending require-ments as long as the charitable purpose of the project is approved by the IRS. The gov-erning documents of the L3C are designed to make this approval easier to receive. So far, the IRS hasn't approved blanket accep-tance of all PRIs awarded to L3C com-panies. Find more information about the L3C hybrid corporation on the Americans for Community Development website (www.americansforcommunity development.org.)

✔ **Benefit Corporations (B-Corps):** B-Corp organizations must adhere to certain accountability and transparency stan-dards and have positive impacts on society and the environment. The nonprofit organization known as B-Labs (www. bcorporation.net) is leading the B-Corp accountability standards and advo-cacy efforts toward encouraging state lawmakers to pass legislation establish-ing this corporate model. B-Labs com-pares the B-Corp movement to Fair Trade Certification, which ensures that products are produced in an equitable, environmen-tally sound manner.

✔ **Flexible Purpose Corporations (FPCs):** These are the newest form of hybrid corpo-ration and are similar to the B-Corp, except that they must have a more specific chari-table purpose. Accountability and trans-parency standards for FPCs are developed internally by the corporation rather than by an outside certifying agency.

Using a Fiscal Sponsor: An Alternative Approach

If you're simply interested in providing a service, maybe you don't want to waste your time with the bureaucratic and legal matters that can complicate a new nonprofit start-up. Or maybe you have a project that will end after a year or two, or you simply want to test the viability of an idea. Why bother to establish a new organization if it's going to close when you finish your project?

You may not need to start a nonprofit to carry out the program you're thinking of starting. Instead, *fiscal sponsorship* may be the best route for you to take. In this approach, your new project becomes a sponsored program of an existing 501(c)(3) nonprofit organization. Contributions earmarked for your project are tax-deductible because they're made to the sponsoring agency.

A fiscal sponsor is sometimes called a *fiscal agent,* but this term doesn't accurately describe the relationship between a fiscal sponsor and the sponsored project. The term *agent* implies that the sponsoring organization is acting on behalf on the project, when really the project is acting on behalf of the organization. After all, the project is technically a program of the sponsoring nonprofit.

This distinction may seem nitpicky, but it's an important one to keep in mind because you must satisfy the IRS requirements for this type of relationship. The 501(c)(3) sponsoring organization is responsible to both the funders and the IRS to see that the money is spent as intended and that charitable goals are met.

Fiscal sponsorship as a first step

Using fiscal sponsorship as a temporary solution while establishing a new nonprofit corporation and acquiring a tax exemption can be an effective approach for the following reasons:

✔ You avoid the tricky period when you have a nonprofit corporation but no tax-exempt status.

✔ You have an opportunity to test the viability of raising funds for your idea.

✔ You have time to establish an organizational infrastructure and to create a board of directors in a more leisurely manner.

✔ You can pay more attention to building your program services in the crucial beginning stages of your project.

✔ You have time to determine if your program is effectively meeting the needs you intend and can develop benchmarks to support the organization if and when you pursue your own 501(c)(3) entity.

Examining common details of a fiscal sponsorship relationship

Here are some important points to keep in mind if you decide to go the fiscal sponsor route:

- ✔ The mission of the fiscal sponsor must be in alignment with the project. In other words, if you have a project to provide free food to the homeless, don't approach your local philharmonic orchestra as a potential sponsor. Find a nonprofit that has similar goals in its mission statement.

- ✔ The board of directors of the sponsoring organization must approve the sponsorship arrangements. They are, after all, ultimately responsible.

- ✔ Both parties should outline a contract or memorandum of understanding, detailing the responsibilities of each. See File0201 for a sample fiscal sponsorship agreement.

- ✔ The fiscal sponsor customarily charges a fee for sponsoring a project — usually between 5 percent and 15 percent of the project's annual revenues, depending on the services it provides to the project.

- ✔ Some fiscal sponsors provide payroll services, office space, group insurance coverage, and even management support, if needed. Be sure to ask if these additional services are included in the fiscal sponsor's fee.

- ✔ Contributions to the sponsored project should be written to the sponsor, with a note that instructs that they be used for the project.

Some foundations are reluctant to award grants to fiscally sponsored projects, even announcing in their guidelines that they won't do it. One reason for this reluctance is their concern that the board of the sponsoring organization exercises less oversight toward fiscally sponsored projects than it does toward their agency's other programs. Those foundations also may be concerned that the sponsoring nonprofit is providing convenient access to 501(c)(3) status to entities engaged in activities that don't qualify for that tax status from the IRS. Not all foundations share these prohibitions, however. In fact, some are proponents of fiscal sponsorship as a way of supporting new ideas and timely programs. You can read much more about foundations and grant proposals in Chapters 16 and 17.

Finding a fiscal sponsor

You may be able to find a fiscal sponsor near you by using the Fiscal Sponsor Directory (www.fiscalsponsordirectory.org). Some nonprofit organizations are formed with the sole purpose of providing fiscal sponsorship services. Another place to search is at your local community foundation. Community foundations have wide connections in the areas they serve and likely are aware of qualified fiscal sponsors.

If your area doesn't have a community foundation nearby, contact the nearest United Way office or another nonprofit that provides referrals and ask for help in finding the right agency to sponsor your project.

You don't want to go with just any fiscal sponsor. You have to do your homework to find one that fits your needs. First determine whether the sponsor's mission covers the type of program you'll be offering. Then do a little research to find out whether the sponsor is trustworthy. For example, you can perform an Internet search for the fiscal sponsor's name. Does its name appear in news stories detailing nonprofit misconduct or other skullduggery? Ask others in your community, including individuals who are knowledgeable about nonprofit activities in your town. While you're at it, read its 990 tax form posted on GuideStar (www.guidestar.org) to see if it's financially sound.

When you're vetting a fiscal sponsor, ask the sponsor these questions to determine whether it's a good fit for your project:

- ✔ Have your board of directors and accounting and legal advisors approved the fiscal sponsorship?

- ✔ Do you charge for specific services, such as access to insurance programs, over and above your basic sponsorship fees? What additional services do you offer?

- ✔ Do you allow sponsored projects to hire salaried employees, and do you provide payroll services and access to health insurance?

- ✔ Do you provide coaching and mentoring in nonprofit management and fundraising?

- ✔ How frequently do you write checks to pay bills? What's the frequency and format of financial reporting for the sponsored program?

- ✔ Do you require projects to maintain a minimum annual income?

- ✔ Do you formally acknowledge gifts and donations?

- ✔ Do your potential foundation funders make grants to fiscally sponsored programs? Will your donors be comfortable donating to a fiscal sponsor?

The National Network of Fiscal Sponsors (www.fiscalsponsors.org) has developed guidelines for best practices in fiscal sponsorship. If you're considering using a fiscal sponsor, we suggest reviewing these guidelines to help you make a choice about which fiscal sponsor is best for your project.

Chapter 3

Writing Your Mission Statement

In This Chapter

▶ Identifying the key components of a strong mission statement

▶ Creating an effective mission statement with help from others

▶ Using your statement to make organizational decisions

A good *mission statement* clearly states a nonprofit's purpose — including who benefits from its work — and how it works to fulfill that purpose. The process of developing your mission statement is important because it can help you refine your ideas, test them with other people, and inspire those involved in the mission-writing process.

Mission statements can be one-liners or long declarations that go on for two or more pages. We suggest aiming for something brief but in between these two extremes. A mission statement contained in one line resembles an advertising slogan, and a long, rambling statement is rarely read or remembered, even by the board of directors and staff members.

Take some quality time to think about what you want to include in your mission statement because it defines what your organization hopes to accomplish. After you've decided on your organization's mission statement, you can use it as your go-to reference when making decisions about your nonprofit's activities. You'll also include your mission statement in your 990 tax report to the IRS, in brochures, and in grant proposals. You may even print it on your business cards or coffee mugs.

In this chapter, we give you some guidance about how to create a simple yet compelling mission statement.

Mission Statement Basics

The mission statement is an organization's center. We were tempted to use the word *heart* rather than *center,* but we think that's stretching the metaphor a little. We could also have said that mission statements are living, breathing organisms from which all organizational life flows, but that's really going too far. People are at the heart of and bring life to an organization. Mission statements just help give this human energy direction.

Can organizations operate without good mission statements? Yes, and some do. We're sure that some nonprofits out there haven't looked at their mission statements since the Clinton administration, and they're still doing good things. But social and environmental conditions have changed since the 1990s, and organizations have likely adapted to those changes. An organization's chances of success in making that adaptation are better if the nonprofit and the people associated with it know exactly why it exists, what they're trying to do, and how they're going to do it.

A mission statement should state what the organization's purpose is, how the purpose will be achieved, and who will benefit from the organization's activities. It may also include organizational values and vision. In addition, the mission should be

- ✔ **Memorable:** You want to carry it around with you at all times.

- ✔ **Focused:** You want it to be narrow enough to focus the activities of your organization but broad enough to allow for growth and expansion.

- ✔ **Easy to read:** Your statement should be written in plain language so folks don't need a set of footnotes to decipher it. Be sure to limit your use of adjectives and try to avoid jargon.

Clarifying your purpose

When thinking of your organization's purpose, think of your desired end result. What would you like to see happen? What would the world (or your community) be like if your organization were to succeed?

To say that you have to have a purpose seems almost too basic. Maybe you're thinking to yourself, "Of course I have a purpose. Why do you think I bought this book? I want to start a nonprofit to [*fill in the blank*]." But we bring up this point because clarifying the purpose is basic to a mission statement.

For example, you may know that you love cats and dogs and have always wanted to work with them, but that isn't the same thing as identifying a nonprofit organization's purpose. For example, a mission statement for a fictitious humane society might be: The mission of Friends of Animals is to provide temporary shelter for homeless puppies, dogs, kittens, and cats until responsible, loving homes can be found.

This sentence doesn't describe the humane society's facilities or how it recruits and trains volunteers, but it does clearly state which animals it serves and that it doesn't intend to foster them as long as they live but rather to place them in good homes. And if someone came to Friends of Animals with a ferret, a pony, or a tarantula, its staff would know to refer that person to another shelter.

Knowing and understanding your organization's purpose is essential to making important organizational decisions. It's also a fundamental tool to use when asking for money, recruiting board members, hiring and motivating staff, and publicizing your activities.

Zeroing in on your beneficiaries

If you've determined your purpose, you probably know the primary beneficiaries of your activities. Their needs — whether they're kittens or refugees — make your mission compelling. Defining who will benefit from your nonprofit helps to focus your organizational activities and is an essential ingredient in your mission statement.

Some organizations have a more general audience than others. If your purpose is preserving historic buildings, the beneficiary of this activity may be current and future residents of a city, a county, or even a state. It may also be the workers you train in the crafts needed to complete the building restorations.

Describing how you accomplish your goals

After you know your organization's purpose and its beneficiaries, the next step is deciding how you're going to make it happen. Mission statements usually include a phrase describing the methods your organization will use to accomplish its purpose. Think about the activities and programs you'll provide to achieve your goal. Take a look at these examples:

✔ To indicate how it will accomplish its goals, the Friends of Animals' mission may say, "This is accomplished by a dedicated staff of employees, volunteers, and board members."

✔ The mission of a national wildlife preservation organization, such as the fictitious Wildlife Preservation League, may state that its mission is to conserve and rebuild natural ecosystems, focusing on small mammals, other wildlife, and their habitats, for the benefit of future generations and the planet's biological diversity. How will the league accomplish its mission? The statement can explain that its national network of community-based nature advocates, educational programs, and advocacy projects on behalf of areas that sustain small mammal populations engage thousands of people of all ages in positive environmental experiences.

When describing how your organization addresses its purpose, you don't want to be so specific that you have to rewrite your mission statement every time you add a new program. At the same time, you want your mission statement to be concrete enough that people reading it (or hearing you recite it) can picture what your organization does.

Envisioning your future with a vision statement

Simply put, a *vision statement* is your dream — your broadly described aspiration for what your organization can become. Vision statements can describe a future desired condition as a result of the organization's activities, but they're more typically applied to the organization itself. Usually, the statement includes phrases like "the best" or "recognized as a leader."

Here's an example of a vision statement from a fictitious agricultural policy think tank:

> *The Agricultural Economics Institute will encourage excellence in its staff by providing opportunities for collaboration and professional development. The Institute's research projects and position statements on agricultural matters will be widely reported in the media and referred to in the setting of state and national agriculture policy.*

Some nonprofits include their vision statements in their mission statements, and others don't. We believe that holding a dream is a good thing, and we see some truth to the statement, "If you can't imagine doing something great, you probably can't do it." Still, we encourage you not to spend an excessive amount of time shaping your vision statement. Focusing on a clear purpose and concrete means for addressing it is more important.

Keeping your focus narrow at first and broadening over time

The narrower your mission statement, the easier it is to convey your organization's purpose and activities and to focus your attention and resources on achieving success. If you start out with a mission to benefit every man and woman on Earth, you're likely to frustrate yourself and your board. In this situation, you'd likely be trying to work at a scale that far exceeds your organization's resources.

Keep in mind, though, that you can always change your mission statement. As your organization achieves initial success and you determine that it's time to expand, you may want to review — and possibly broaden — your mission as a part of your organizational planning process.

Keeping your statement short and sweet

In keeping with our notion that a good mission statement is easily expressed, we tend to favor short, pithy statements over long, rambling ones.

We understand, however, that some organizations want to describe their aims and activities more fully than what can be captured in one or two short sentences. For those organizations, we suggest that you begin your mission statement with a short summary that states simply what your nonprofit hopes to accomplish, how it plans to do it, and for whom. You can print this succinct version on brochures or use it as an introductory statement on your website. Then you can prepare your longer statement, which includes all your organization's programs.

Writing the Mission Statement

You probably already have a good idea of your purpose (if you don't, check out the earlier section "Clarifying your purpose"). Now you have to refine that idea, state it simply in a few words, and officially get it down on paper. Frankly, it's easier to have just one draft and refine the statement's wording, but we highly recommend that you invite your board, staff, and volunteers to participate in identifying the statement's key content — your organization's goals, purpose, programs, and vision. The act of creating or refining a mission statement can motivate and even inspire them.

While inspiration may be your goal, as you gather your group's ideas and begin to write your statement, you need to make sure your written statement is clear. In the following sections, we recommend a process for inviting participation *and* achieving clarity.

Getting input from your group

Whether you're working with a newly formed nonprofit or a long-running institution, everyone on your board or planning committee needs to agree on the mission statement. We recommend holding a meeting to solicit their input. The biggest advantage to this kind of group activity is achieving full buy-in from everyone involved. After all, you want people to believe in and accept the organization's mission statement. If they don't, they likely won't stick around to help uphold that mission (or won't do a good job of upholding it while they're there).

For groups that are working to establish a mission statement for a new nonprofit organization, we recommend that you find an outside facilitator to guide the group through the inevitable discussions about priorities and the direction of the new organization. Finding a neutral person who can bring an outsider's perspective to the group's deliberations is extremely helpful. A facilitator also takes responsibility for managing the group so you and your colleagues can be full participants in the meeting. If you aren't near a *nonprofit support organization* (a nonprofit that helps other nonprofits with technical assistance), ask other organizations near you for suggestions.

Bring a few prewritten suggestions to the group meeting. Present them as drafts and ask for feedback. After an initial discussion among the group, give each member index cards or sticky pads and have them write down three ideas they feel strongly about keeping as a part of the mission.

After you collect everyone's written ideas, read them all aloud and — as a group — organize them so that similar ideas are grouped together. These notes should identify the key ideas that belong in your mission statement. Also be sure to ask whether anyone thinks an important idea is missing. If not, you're ready to assign someone to draft the mission statement.

Drafting the statement

A group process is essential to identifying the core ideas that belong in the mission statement, but when it comes to putting words on paper, we recommend that you choose your best writer and turn her loose.

We aren't fans of committee-written prose. We've sat in meetings where committees discussed adjective choices and the placement of commas without apparent end. The result of such efforts is usually murky writing that requires several readings to interpret the meaning. After a draft is on paper, feel free to bring it back to your group for their final thoughts and approval on content, grammar, and word choice. Until then, however, assign only one person to work on the draft.

When finalizing the wording of your statement, the best advice we can offer is to stay away from jargon and flowery rhetoric. Avoid the buzzwords that are currently popular in your field. In fact, this is good advice for any kind of writing — grant proposals, memos, letters, and so on. You don't want your audience scratching their heads and wondering, "What does that mean?"

Here's an example of a vague, unclear mission statement:

> *The Good Food Society works to maximize the utilization of nutritious food groups to beneficially help all persons in their existence and health by proclaiming the good benefits of balanced nutrition.*

You probably get the idea that this organization wants people to have better eating habits so they can enjoy better health. But try reciting this statement to someone you're trying to convince to contribute to your organization. Can you say tongue-tied?

Long, multisyllabic words don't make a mission statement more impressive. If anything, they have the opposite effect. Instead of using the preceding statement, try something like this:

> *Believing in the value of good nutrition, the Good Food Society aims to improve public health by providing information about the benefits of a balanced diet to parents of school-age children through public education programs.*

This mission statement may not be perfect, but it states the organization's values, its long-term goal, its targeted beneficiaries, and a general method for accomplishing the goal — all the ingredients of an effective mission statement (see the earlier section for details).

Imagine that you're riding in an elevator with someone who knows nothing about your nonprofit. You have 15 seconds to describe your organization's purpose and activities. Doing so is easy if you have a clear, short mission statement. Even if you have a longer mission statement, develop a 50- to 75-word spiel that you can recite from memory.

Living by Your Mission

You've brainstormed, drafted, and refined a short statement that clearly identifies your organization's mission. Congratulations! Now that you've put considerable thought and time into this exercise, what are you going to do with it? You'll use your mission statement in practical ways, of course. For instance, you'll likely

- Incorporate its description of the organization's purpose in your articles of incorporation (see Chapter 4).

- Include it in brochures, on your website, and in other marketing materials (see Chapter 12).

- Use it to help complete IRS Form 990 — the tax statement you'll file in one form or another each year (see Chapter 5).

Your mission statement also resembles the pin that holds the needle of a compass: You'll use it to chart your organization's direction. Here are some examples:

- When you have to make a decision about creating new programs or setting priorities, your mission statement should guide you as to whether they're appropriate for your organization.

- When your board and staff sit down to create a new three-year plan, they first need to revisit and commit to the mission statement. All other discussion about setting goals and refining programs should be tested for appropriateness against the statement.

- When you need to cut your budget and eliminate programs or activities, your mission statement should guide you to protect those programs that are core to your organization's purpose and vision.

Chapter 4

Incorporating and Applying for Tax Exemption

*1*f you want to provide programs and services as a nonprofit organization, you need to set up the legal structure for your organization and apply for its tax exemption. This process usually consists of forming a nonprofit corporation under the laws of your state and then submitting an application to the Internal Revenue Service (IRS), requesting that your organization be recognized as tax-exempt. You must take care of these tasks, which require attention to detail and ample planning, before you can begin to fulfill your mission.

In this chapter, we provide you with a guide to the incorporation and exemption process for a 501(c)(3) public charity. We also give you suggestions about where you can go for help. Keep in mind that we aren't attorneys and the information in this chapter isn't meant to be legal advice. Although many nonprofits are formed without the aid of legal counsel, we think that consulting an attorney is a good idea, even if it's only to review your work. After all, you're taking on legal responsibilities. Why not be certain that you've done everything correctly?

For quick reference, we've put together a checklist for forming a nonprofit organization (File0401). Pop in the CD or click the link in the table of contents to view this file.

Creating a New Entity — the Corporation

In almost all cases, the first legal step in creating a nonprofit organization is forming a corporation. A *corporation* is an entity or an organization that has legal standing. It's established by a group of individuals — the incorporators — under the laws of the state in which it's formed.

We say the first step is forming a corporation "in almost all cases" because exceptions do exist. In the United States, for example, associations, trusts, and sometimes limited liability companies can operate as tax-exempt nonprofit organizations. And charitable groups with less than $5,000 in annual revenues, as well as churches, aren't required to apply for tax exemption. In this chapter, we focus on the most common legal structure for nonprofit organizations: the corporation.

One advantage of creating a corporation is that the individuals who govern and work for it are separate from the abstract entity they create. Although board members can be liable for the corporation's actions if they don't exercise their duties and responsibilities carefully, in most cases, corporations protect individuals from personal liability. So you can think of a corporation as separate from the people who start it, because, well, it is.

When you establish a corporation, you're creating an entity that's expected to continue in perpetuity. In other words, the corporation you create goes on living after you decide to do something else or after your death. Corporations can be closed or dissolved, but you must take legal steps to do so. You can't just take down your shingle and walk away.

Looking to your state law

In the United States, corporations are created and regulated under the laws of the state in which they're formed. Although the way a corporation is formed from state to state has more similarities than differences, you do need to create your nonprofit so that it conforms to the peculiarities of your state. Some states, for example, require a minimum of three members to belong to a board of directors; others require only one. (Flip to Chapter 6 for more information about boards of directors.)

Check out File0402 for information about where to get specifics about incorporating in your state. Usually, the secretary of state's office handles incorporations. Some states have an incorporation package that includes the forms you need to file. You also can find state contact information on the IRS website at www.irs.gov.

Considering your corporation's governing documents

Think of a corporation as a tiny government with a constitution and laws. To set down the rules under which the organization will operate, you need to prepare the following important documents:

- **Articles of incorporation:** The *articles of incorporation* make up the document that creates the organization. It names the organization and describes its reason for existence. In the case of a nonprofit corporation, it specifies that the corporation won't be used to create profit for its directors. The articles are signed by the corporation's incorporators, usually three people, who may or may not end up being directors of the organization.

- **Bylaws:** A corporation's *bylaws* specify how directors are elected and the length of their terms, the officers and their duties, the number of meetings to be held, who is and isn't a member of the corporation, how many members or directors are required to be in attendance for a *quorum* (the minimum number of people required to be at a meeting so official business can be conducted, often a simple majority of members or directors) to be present, the rules for director attendance at board meetings, and the process through which the bylaws may be amended. They also may list the standing committees of the board and grant or limit particular powers of the trustees.

As you draft these documents (see the later sections "Writing the Articles of Incorporation" and "Developing Your Organizational Bylaws" for more specific information about writing them), remember that you're creating the legal rules under which your nonprofit will operate. You can change your articles of incorporation and bylaws by following the laws of your state (in the case of articles of incorporation) or the rules described in the bylaws.

Deciding whether to have members in your corporation

Corporations may have members. In fact, they may even have different classes of members — voting and nonvoting, for example. Generally speaking, though, having members in your corporation adds additional responsibilities to the governance of the organization. If you have members, for instance, you need to have membership meetings, probably at least one per year, and the members will be involved in choosing directors for the organization.

Depending on state law, you usually have the option to create membership conditions in either the articles or the bylaws. If you have a choice, we recommend adding these conditions to the bylaws, which are easier to amend than the articles of incorporation.

We don't advise having members unless you have a very good reason to do so. However, you may want to get as many people involved in your organization as possible, and having members is one way to achieve this goal. If your nonprofit is a neighborhood-improvement group, for example, including as many people as possible in the governance of the organization may be important.

Many nonprofit organizations have "members," who get membership cards and special rates on admissions to performances or exhibits. Don't confuse this kind of membership, which is a marketing and fundraising strategy, with legal membership in a corporation. You're free to start a membership program of this type without amending your bylaws or your articles of incorporation. See Chapter 13 for more information.

Choosing your corporation's name

Choosing a name for your new corporation may be one of the most important things you do as you set it up. A nonprofit's name is a little like a mission statement (see Chapter 3 for more on mission statements). Like your mission statement, your organization's name needs to suggest the types of programs and services you offer and the people you serve.

So if your programs provide home health services to people over 65, don't name your nonprofit something generic like Services for the People. Also stay away from names that are so abstract that they have no meaning at all. A name like the Reenergizing Society prompts more questions than it answers. What or who is being reenergized? How are clients being reenergized and why? Instead, use concrete, descriptive terms.

To avoid possible embarrassment, check the acronym that results from your organization's name. The Associated Workers for Union Labor, for example, isn't a title you want to abbreviate on your letterhead. After all, we don't know many people who'd want to associate with an AWFUL organization . . . .

Also be careful that you don't select a name that's easily confused with that of another organization. Before you decide on a name, do an Internet search to see whether any other companies or organizations already have that name. The state agency that accepts your application for incorporation has procedures for ensuring that two corporations in your state don't end up with exactly the same name. However, these procedures can't help you uncover organizations with the same name in other states or with names that are similar and could be confused with your name. To help ensure that you have a distinctive name, you may want to include the name of the city or region where your organization is located — Tap Dancers of Happy Valley, for example.

You also can search the Trademark Electronic Search System (TESS) found at www.uspto.gov to determine whether the name you have chosen is trademarked by another organization. If you want, you can register your own trademark with the federal government and with the state in which you incorporate.

If you incorporate your organization under one name and then decide that you aren't totally pleased with it, you can amend the incorporation papers you filed with the state. Often, however, organizations find it easier to register another name as a DBA, which stands for "doing business as." The original corporate name continues to be your organization's legal name, but you can use the DBA name on your letterhead, annual reports, and press releases — everywhere except legal documents. A county office usually handles this type of transaction. Check your local laws for more information.

Writing the Articles of Incorporation

For this section, we assume you have the articles of incorporation papers you need from the appropriate state office. (If not, use the state-by-state list on File0402 or the list of state offices at www.irs.gov for contact information.) That office may even have provided sample articles of incorporation and instructions about how to prepare your own. Pay close attention to the instructions and follow them step by step. The whole process may be as simple as filling in the blanks. Although you can amend articles of incorporation, it requires filing additional forms and paying more fees, so you may as well spend time getting them right the first time.

In this section, we give you some general guidance on drafting your articles. However, note that the sample articles we include here may not coincide exactly with your state's requirements.

IRS Publication 557 contains information about the language needed in the articles of incorporation, along with some sample articles. You can download this publication from the IRS website (www.irs.gov).

Crafting a heading

You must put a heading on your articles so people can identify them. The heading should be something like this:

Articles of Incorporation of the XYZ Theater Company, Inc.

Sometimes you're required to add a short paragraph after the heading, stating that the incorporators adopt the following articles under the [cite the state code number under which you're filing] of [give the state name].

Article I

You insert the name you worked so hard to choose here in Article I. Simply write a sentence like this one:

The name of the corporation is the XYZ Theater Company, Inc.

Could it be any easier than that?

Article II

Some states require that you affirm that your corporation is *perpetual* (meaning it's intended to exist forever). If your state requires that affirmation, put it in Article II. You can include something like this:

This corporation shall exist in perpetuity unless dissolved.

However, chances are that the state will give you the language to use if it's needed.

Article III

Article III is a good place to state the organization's purpose. This article is probably the most important because state authorities and the IRS review it to determine whether your organization qualifies as a charitable entity.

Remember that 501(c)(3) organizations must be organized for a charitable, religious, educational, literary, or scientific purpose. (See Chapter 2 for more on various classes of nonprofits.) You've already created your mission statement, right? If so, stating your purpose shouldn't be too difficult. (If you haven't created your statement yet, check out Chapter 3.) Using the XYZ Theater Company as an example, your purpose may look like this:

> *This corporation is established to provide theatrical productions of new and classic plays. It also will work to strengthen the theater arts, support emerging playwrights, and encourage persons to enter the acting profession by providing scholarships and grants to theater arts students and by promoting the benefits of dramatic entertainment to the general public.*

This article also must include a statement of exempt purpose under the IRS code, as in this example:

> *This corporation is organized exclusively for charitable, literary, and educational purposes, including for such purposes the making of distributions to organizations that qualify under section 501(c)(3) of the Internal Revenue Code or any corresponding section of any future federal tax code.*

You must state that no proceeds of the corporation will enrich any individual, except that reasonable compensation may be paid in exchange for services to the corporation. Finally, in this article, you must note that if the corporation is dissolved, any assets remaining will be distributed to another corporation that serves a similar purpose and qualifies as a tax-exempt, charitable organization under the provisions of 501(c)(3) of the Internal Revenue Code. You don't need to identify a particular nonprofit corporation; you just need to affirm that assets will be distributed to one serving a purpose similar to yours.

Article III may be the most critical for getting your nonprofit corporation established and, ultimately, approved for tax exemption by the IRS. If your state doesn't provide good examples of the language required in this article, ask a lawyer about the requirements in your state.

Article IV

All articles of incorporation identify the name and address of an *agent of the corporation,* someone to whom mail can be addressed. This address is considered the address of the corporation until changed. Include the person's name and street address. Post office boxes aren't allowed to be used as addresses.

The agent of the corporation doesn't need to be a director or incorporator of the corporation. This person can even be your attorney.

Article V

Put the initial directors' names and addresses in Article V. Most nonprofits start with three initial directors. If you're incorporating in a state that requires only one director, we still recommend having three. Because nonprofit organizations are formed to provide public benefit, demonstrating that several people are involved as volunteers may strengthen your application to the IRS for tax-exempt status.

Article VI

In Article VI, you list the incorporators' names and addresses. *Incorporator* simply refers to the person or people who are creating the corporation. Often, the incorporators and the initial directors are one and the same. Again, whether you need one or more depends on your state requirements.

Article VII

If you want your corporation to have members, you define the qualifications for membership in Article VII. You can define classes of membership — voting and nonvoting, for instance. If you don't want members, all you have to say is, "This corporation has no members." Better yet, refer the question to your bylaws, which are easier to amend if you change your mind. If that's what you decide to do, you can use this language:

> *Membership provisions of this corporation are defined in the bylaws.*

Corporate members aren't the same as the subscribers to a PBS station or the members of a museum or zoo, for example. Members of a corporation have the right to participate in governing the organization.

Article VIII

You may not need an Article VIII in your articles of incorporation. Some forms have a blank space here to add additional provisions. We don't recommend adding any unless you're sure you know what you're doing. Maybe your group is adamant that all future directors must be elected by 85 percent of the membership. Such a provision probably would ensure that you'd never elect new directors, but who knows? Use this blank space cautiously.

Signed, sealed, and delivered

After you finish writing your articles of incorporation, you must have the incorporator(s) sign them. In some states, you need three incorporators; in others, you need only one. If the articles need to be notarized, the signatures must be added in the presence of a notary public.

Most states charge a fee for filing for incorporation. If your state requires a fee, include a check or money order with the articles and any other required forms, and then mail everything to the appropriate state office. Usually you mail only the original articles to the state office, but sometimes a state office requires one or more additional copies.

Your next step is to wait. It's hard to say how long the response will take — it depends on the efficiency of the state office and the volume of incorporation papers it receives. For a surcharge, some states offer an opportunity to expedite processing.

Simply creating a nonprofit corporation doesn't make your organization tax-exempt. You also need recognition from the IRS (see the section "Applying for Tax Exemption" later in this chapter) before your nonprofit is a "real" nonprofit. You may need to complete a tax-exempt application in your state, too.

If your articles are in order and your corporate name passes muster (meaning that no other organization in the state has the same name), you receive a certified copy of the articles, stamped with an official seal. Guard this piece of paper as if it were gold. Make copies and put the original away for safe-keeping in a fireproof box. You've taken the first step toward starting your nonprofit. Congratulations!

Obtaining Your Employer Identification Number (EIN)

The first thing to do after you complete your incorporation is to apply to the IRS for an *Employer Identification Number,* or EIN. Even if you don't plan to hire employees anytime soon, you need this number for your application for tax exemption and for all your state and federal reports. The EIN is like a Social Security number for organizations; it'll be attached to your nonprofit forever.

Getting an EIN is easy and free. All you have to do is submit IRS Form SS-4. You can either download and print the form from www.irs.gov or complete the online application. You can even apply by telephone. As IRS forms go, this one is simple and straightforward and only one page long. If you apply by phone or complete the online application, we recommend that you download Form SS-4 beforehand to get an idea of the questions you'll have to answer.

Choose only one method to apply for your EIN. Don't send in IRS Form SS-4 and apply by telephone. You may end up with two EINs, a confusing situation for everyone.

The name of the applicant isn't your name; it's the name of your new organization. As with the incorporation papers, you need to identify an individual as the principal officer and include that person's Social Security number on the form. Here are some of the other items you need to fill out, line by line:

- **Line 9:** If your organization is a church or church-controlled organization, check that box in section 9a. If it's not, check the "Other Nonprofit Organization" box. Specify what sort of nonprofit organization you are. In most cases, "charitable" is sufficient. In section 9b, fill in the state where your organization is incorporated.

- **Line 10:** Most likely, your reason for applying for an EIN in line 10 is "started a new business."

- **Line 11:** In line 11, the date on your incorporation papers is the date the business was started.

- **Line 12:** This line asks for the closing month of your organization's accounting (fiscal) year. (See the later section "Dealing with financial information" for an explanation of a fiscal year.)

- **Lines 13 and 14:** These lines relate to the number of employees you intend to hire and your expected payroll tax liabilities over the coming 12 months. You can enter "0" and "No" if your organization doesn't plan to hire staff in the year ahead. If you do intend to hire people for whom you'll have to pay payroll taxes, you need to check IRS withholding tables (www.irs.gov) and estimate the amount of payroll taxes that will be due to the IRS.

- **Line 16:** This line asks you to check the box that describes your organization's principal activity. You can check "Other" here, but try to be a little more specific when describing your activities in the blank space. You may say "Charitable — Arts," for example.

The IRS estimates that you'll receive your EIN in four to five weeks if you apply by mail. You'll receive your EIN immediately if you submit the online application.

If you want to apply for an EIN by telephone, the person named as the principal officer on the SS-4 Form must call the IRS Business and Specialty Tax Line at (800) 829-4933. Be sure that you've completed the SS-4 Form before you make the call. An IRS worker takes your information over the phone and assigns an EIN to your organization. You must fax or mail the form to the appropriate IRS office within 24 hours of making the call.

Developing Your Organization's Bylaws

Bylaws are the rules by which your organization operates. As with articles of incorporation, different states have different requirements about what needs to be included in the bylaws, so make sure you contact the appropriate agency in your state to get the specific information you need.

Use the state contact information on File0402 to find the office in your state.

In general, bylaws guide the activities of your organization and the procedures of your board of directors — how many directors, how long they serve, how they're elected, what constitutes a quorum, and so on. Like the articles of incorporation, bylaws are divided into articles. However, because bylaws require more detail, the articles themselves are divided into sections (and subsections, if needed) to address various aspects of the articles.

You can always change bylaws. However, amending the bylaws almost always requires more than a simple majority; usually two-thirds of the directors must agree to a bylaw change.

If you were to review the bylaws of ten different organizations, you'd find variation in the order in which articles are presented. For example, you may find the board of directors specified in Article III or Article V. Bylaws also vary in how specifically they spell out what's required. Some bylaws specify the number and type of standing committees; others give the board president the responsibility of making those specifications. If you don't address a particular question in your bylaws — setting a quorum, for example — most states have a default position in their code that applies to the governing of nonprofit corporations.

Check out File0403 for a general guide to creating bylaws for your new nonprofit.

Holding Your First Board Meeting

Your organization's first board meeting is more or less a formality, but documenting it is important because it officially kicks off your new nonprofit corporation. If you've named directors in your articles of incorporation, each one should be present at the meeting. The first order of business is to elect the officers of the organization. For your second order of business, pass a resolution authorizing the board or its designate to open the necessary bank accounts. You need a copy of this resolution to open an account.

Prepare minutes of the meeting and keep them with your articles of incorporation. We say more about keeping records in Chapter 5, but now is a good time to start a *board book* — a binder containing a copy of your articles of incorporation, your bylaws, and the minutes of your first board meeting and every board meeting to follow. Also be sure to include a copy of the letter of determination that acknowledges your organization as tax-exempt when you receive it from the IRS. See the next section for how to make your application for tax exemption.

Applying for Tax Exemption

The final step in becoming a tax-exempt charitable organization is to apply for tax exemption from the IRS. Keep in mind that *tax-exempt* doesn't mean you're exempt from *all* taxes. You don't have to pay taxes on the organization's income, and donors who contribute to your 501(c)(3) organization can claim a tax deduction. But if your nonprofit employs staff, it does have to pay payroll taxes like any other employer. And your liability for sales and property taxes depends on your state and local laws. If your nonprofit has income that's unrelated to its charitable purpose, you're required to pay taxes on that revenue as well.

To apply for tax exemption, you need to request what's known as a *determination letter* or *ruling* — a letter from the IRS stating that it has determined that your organization qualifies as a tax-exempt organization under the applicable sections of the IRS code. You'll send copies of this letter to foundations, government agencies, and state tax authorities — in short, to anyone to whom you need to prove that your nonprofit organization is indeed tax-exempt.

Be sure to check with your state about what you need to do to register your nonprofit as a tax-exempt organization. Registration and reporting requirements vary from state to state. Chances are you received this information when you contacted your state office to begin your incorporation process; if you didn't, contact the appropriate state government office for more details. You can find contact information for all states on File0402 or on the IRS website at www.irs.gov.

Who doesn't need to apply for tax-exempt status

If your organization is a church, a church auxiliary, or an association of churches, you don't need to apply for tax-exempt status. Also, if your nonprofit had gross receipts of less than $5,000 in any previous year in which you operated, and if you don't expect your revenue to grow beyond this limit, you aren't required to submit an application.

Keep in mind that you still may apply for tax exemption even though you aren't required to do so. Having a determination letter from the

IRS acknowledging your tax-exempt status has some advantages. For example, you need to show proof of your exemption to get a bulk mail permit from the U.S. Postal Service. The determination letter also serves as a public acknowledgment that contributions to your organization are deductible to the donor. If you hope to receive foundation grants, your organization should be recognized as tax-exempt by the IRS as well.

You request tax-exempt status by submitting the Application for Recognition of Exemption or IRS Form 1023 to the IRS. You can download the form at www.irs.gov. Be sure to download the form's instructions at the same time and read the next section, "Tackling Form 1023."

Tackling Form 1023

Yes, Form 1023 is long, and yes, it's a little scary. If you can get help from your accountant or attorney (or both), we recommend that you do so. Don't discount getting help from your friends and associates, either. Two heads are usually better than one.

Read the instructions carefully. The application package includes line-by-line explanations as well as the various schedules that you may need to submit if you're applying as a church or school, for example. If a schedule isn't required for your type of nonprofit, don't submit a blank one. Toss it into the round file (also known as the trash can).

Understanding the difference between public charities and private foundations

Public charities and private foundations are both 501(c)(3) organizations (see Chapter 2 for more on these types of organizations), but you need to understand the important differences between them before you begin completing the application for tax exemption.

Private foundations have different reporting requirements from public charities and may be required to pay excise taxes on their income. Contributions to private foundations are deductible but not to the same extent as contributions to public charities.

One important determination that the IRS makes based on your application for tax-exempt status is whether your organization is classified as a public charity or a private foundation. Part X of Form 1023 addresses this question. We assume that you're striving for public charity status, so check the "No" box in line 1a and skip to line 5.

Establishing public charity status

The IRS applies several measures to determine whether an organization is a public charity. Generally, for a nonprofit to be considered a public charity, it must receive one-third of its revenues from public sources. It's complicated, and we can't cover all the nuances and technicalities here. But, fundamentally, it comes down to how much of your organizational income you get from the public.

A 501(c)(3) nonprofit organization wanting to be considered a public charity will undergo what's referred to as the *public support test*. To pass this test, the nonprofit needs to demonstrate, over a four-year average, that one-third of its revenue comes from contributions from the general public, support from government agencies, or grants from organizations that get their support from the public, such as United Way. So if your organization's average revenue is $60,000 per year and at least $20,000 a year comes from donations, state grants, and support from United Way, you're home free. Your nonprofit will be considered a public charity under code sections 509(a)(1) and 170(b)(1)(A)(vi).

But what if your organization doesn't get a third of its revenue from the public? Fortunately, it may be able to qualify under another test that gives more leeway on the percentage of public support. Under this test, only 10 percent of total revenue needs to come from those public categories. But your organization also must demonstrate that it has an ongoing fundraising program that's reaching out to the public for more donations. Other factors also are considered. If the nonprofit's contributions come in many small gifts rather than a few large ones, it's more likely to be given public charity status. It's even better if your organization's board of directors is broadly representative of the community. And if the organization makes its facility available to the general public, that's another feather in its cap.

A 501(c)(3) organization that expects to get a substantial portion of its revenues from fees related to its exempt purpose (but less than one-third of revenues from investment income) may qualify as a public charity under code section 501(a)(2).

When you get to Part X of Form 1023, you need to check a box indicating which public charity classification you seek. If you aren't sure — and, frankly, who would be? — you can let the IRS decide which category you fit by selecting the "i" box. Take schools as an example. To apply as a school, you have to submit Schedule B. Your school must provide regular instruction and have a student body and a faculty. In other words, you can't just start an organization and call it a school.

Every IRS rule has an exception or two, and qualifying as a public charity is, well, no exception. Churches, schools, hospitals, public safety testing organizations, and a few others are automatically considered public charities. If you have an intense interest in this rule, read Chapter 3 of IRS Publication 557, which is available at www.irs.gov. If you think your organization falls into one of these categories, check the appropriate box in Part X, line 5 (a through f) and answer the questions on the appropriate schedule included with Form 1023. But we don't recommend doing so unless you're absolutely certain that you know what you're doing. If you need further advice regarding these categories, we suggest you consult an attorney.

Until recently, a newly established nonprofit organization applying for a tax exemption usually requested an "advance ruling" on its public charity status. Typically, based on the sources of projected revenue given in the application, the IRS granted "temporary" public charity status for a period of five years. After this five-year period, the IRS reviewed the sources of the nonprofit's support over the previous years and, if the public support test was met, issued a "definitive" ruling of public charity status.

The advance ruling period has been eliminated. Organizations seeking to be classified as public charities will be considered as such if they can demonstrate in their Form 1023 application that the status is a reasonable expectation for the future. The public charity status is considered permanent unless and until substantial changes are seen in the organization's sources of support. This change in IRS procedure grants some leeway in an organization's sources of support for the first few years of its existence.

When you download Form 1023 and its instructions, be sure to include any change notices that describe new regulations and new instructions. Sometimes revisions to IRS forms lag behind changes in the regulations. Always be certain you're working with the most recent information.

Describing your activities

In Part IV of IRS Form 1023, you need to attach a narrative description of your charitable activities and how you plan to carry them out. You must provide more detail here than you have in your articles of incorporation or in your mission statement. The IRS wants you to list what you're going to do in order of importance, approximately what percentage of time you'll devote to each activity, and how each activity fulfills your charitable purpose.

When you fill out this form, chances are you haven't started operating yet, so you're simply listing *proposed* activities. If you've created an organizational plan (which we recommend), refer to the plan to make sure you cover all your activities. (Refer to Chapter 7 for help with planning.) If you've been operating your organization, explain what you've been doing and how it relates to your charitable purpose.

A nonprofit that provides family counseling and public education about strengthening families may say something like this in Part IV:

> *The charitable purpose of the Claremont Family Counseling Center is to promote the benefits of positive family interaction in the following ways:*
>
> *The primary activity will be to provide professional family counseling services, on a sliding scale fee basis, to families in Claremont County and surrounding counties. No family will be refused service due to the inability to pay for services, and services will be available to all members of the general public. (75 percent)*
>
> *The center will maintain a website that provides referral information, suggestions for strengthening family interactions, reference materials concerning families, and e-mail and bulletin board posting capabilities. (10 percent)*
>
> *Staff members will present information about families to local schools, service clubs, and churches through multimedia presentations. (10 percent)*
>
> *Brochures will be prepared and distributed on request. (5 percent)*

You're asked more questions about your specific activities in Part VIII of Form 1023, including, for example, how and where you intend to raise funds, whether you operate a bingo game or other gaming activities, and the extent of your involvement with foreign countries and organizations. Answering yes to these and other questions in Part VIII means that you must attach explanations.

In Part VIII, you're also asked whether your organization will attempt to influence legislation. If you answer yes, you're given an opportunity to elect section 501(h) of the IRS code by filing IRS Form 5768. If you do so, your organization's expenses for allowable lobbying activities are measured by a percentage of your revenue. Chapter 5 has more information about this subject.

Reporting salaries and conflicts of interest

The IRS revises its forms from time to time. In the past few years, Form 1023 has been revised to include more questions about staff salary levels, board member compensation, and business and family relationships of board members and staff. If you pay or plan to pay any staff member or consultant more than $50,000 per year, you need to report this fact. If you compensate or plan to compensate members of your board, you also have to share that information on Form 1023.

If you plan to compensate employees, directors, or consultants with *non-fixed payments,* that is, bonuses or revenue-based compensation, be prepared to describe these arrangements in detail.

You're also asked whether the organization has a conflict of interest policy and whether compensation has or will be set by comparing salaries of your staff to salaries of similar organizations. Although the IRS says these practices aren't required to get a tax exemption, they are recommended. The instructions for Form 1023 contain a sample conflict of interest policy statement. We suggest having your board adopt a conflict of interest policy based on the IRS model.

Part V of the application stretches over two pages and is clearly a reaction to increased public and legislative concern about financial abuse and self-dealing in both the nonprofit and business sectors. We say more about the increased scrutiny aimed at the nonprofit sector in Chapter 5. Keep in mind that nonprofits are, in a sense, "quasi-public" organizations because the government is granting them special status as tax-exempt organizations.

Dealing with financial information

The IRS wants to see financial information. (Surprise, surprise.) New organizations have to estimate their income and expenses for three years — the current year and two years following. Making financial projections sends shivers down the backs of many folks, but it's really not that difficult. Ideally, you've made plans for your nonprofit already, and you can take the figures from your organizational plan. If you haven't written a plan, now's a good time to do so. See Chapter 7 for planning information and Chapter 11 for help in creating a budget.

When you estimate your income, keep in mind the requirements for qualifying as a public charity (check out the earlier section "Establishing public charity status" for details). Diverse sources of income are important, both for qualifying as a public charity and for the stability of your nonprofit.

You also need to choose your annual accounting period. This period is usually referred to as your *fiscal year.* It can be any 12-month period you desire. Most organizations choose as their fiscal year either the calendar year (January 1 through December 31) or the period from July 1 to June 30. Most government agencies operate on a July 1–through–June 30 fiscal year, and nonprofits that get support from government grants and contracts often prefer to operate on the same schedule. Some organizations offering services to schools set the fiscal year to correspond with the academic year. But the choice is yours. You can set your fiscal year from November 1 through October 31, if you want.

Your first accounting period doesn't need to be a full 12 months; in fact, it probably won't be. If you form your organization in September and select a calendar year as your fiscal year, your first accounting period covers only four months, September through December.

If you have an accountant, seek advice about the best accounting period for your organization. Remember that your fiscal year determines when future reports are due to the IRS and also when you prepare year-end financial reports for your board of directors. The annual 990 report (see Chapter 5) is due, for example, four and a half months after the close of your fiscal year. So if your fiscal year is the same as the calendar year, the report is due on May 15. If you always spend early May traveling to the Caribbean, you may want to pick another accounting period.

Collecting the other materials

In addition to the completed tax-exemption application, you need to submit as attachments *conformed* (exact) copies of your articles of incorporation and the certificate of incorporation, if your state provides one. You also need to submit the bylaws of your organization, but remember that bylaws alone don't qualify as an *organizing document,* as do the articles of incorporation.

Every nonprofit applying for tax exemption must have an organizing document. Usually, this document is the articles of incorporation, because most nonprofit organizations are incorporated. However, in the United States, associations, trusts, and, in some states, limited liability companies, also may apply for tax-exempt status. An organizing document for an association may be the articles of association or a constitution; a trust is usually organized by a trust indenture or deed.

Put your organization's name, address, and EIN on each attachment and specify the section of the application that each attachment refers to. (The earlier section "Obtaining Your Employer Identification Number (EIN)" provides more details on obtaining your organization's number.) The application package you receive from the IRS has a checklist of the materials that must be included. Be sure to include this checklist with your completed application package.

Paying the fee

The fee for filing IRS Form 1023 is $850 for organizations that have had or anticipate having revenue of more than $10,000 per year. If your organization has been operating without a tax exemption and has income of less than $10,000 per year, or if you anticipate having revenues of less than $10,000 per year in the future, the fee is set at $400.

We don't recommend trying to save $450 on the application fee unless you're certain that revenues to your organization will remain under $10,000. We understand that the $450 difference in the fees can loom very large for a start-up nonprofit, but why play with fire? Although the penalties for misstating your income aren't clear, we wouldn't want you to find out the hard way.

Send the fee when you mail the form with all its appropriate attachments and schedules. Keep a copy of everything for your records. Then take a break! You deserve it.

Getting along until the exemption comes

After you file your tax-exemption application, your organization is in never-never land for a while. You don't have your exemption yet. Although making an accurate prediction is difficult, the IRS can take between two and six months to act on your application. The process may take longer if the application is returned for corrections.

During this period, your organization can operate and even solicit contributions. However, you must tell donors that you've applied for a tax exemption and are waiting to hear from the IRS. Assuming that your application is approved, if you submitted Form 1023 and the other required materials to the IRS within 27 months from the time you established the organization, your tax-exempt status is retroactive to the date of incorporation. Another option is to use a fiscal sponsor during this period. (See Chapter 2 for information about using and finding fiscal sponsors.)

If your organization had been operating for a longer period before you submitted Form 1023, the exemption may be retroactive only to the date on which you submitted the application. In this case, you also need to include Schedule E with your application.

Check with your state officials to find out what steps you need to take to have your tax exemption recognized by your state's government. If you didn't receive this information when you incorporated your organization, you can find contact information for the appropriate state office on File0402.

Chapter 5

Safeguarding Your Nonprofit Status

In This Chapter

▶ Making public disclosures

▶ Avoiding trouble over pay and politics

▶ Sending Form 990 to the IRS

▶ Filing state and local reports

*N*onprofit organizations are private organizations, but because they're granted special tax status and presumably are acting on behalf of the public, they're required to disclose more information than privately held for-profit companies are. Nonprofit status is a privilege.

A good way to think about it is to compare nonprofits to companies that sell shares of stock to the public. These companies must follow the rules and regulations set forth by the Securities and Exchange Commission about disclosing financial information. Nonprofits in the United States must follow the rules of the Internal Revenue Service (IRS) to make financial information available for public scrutiny. In some cases, state and local governments also have disclosure rules.

Your nonprofit organization can get into trouble with authorities in a few ways. However, keeping your nonprofit status isn't difficult if you follow the rules. This chapter lays out the reporting requirements that you need to follow and some pitfalls to avoid in order to maintain your 501(c)(3) public charity status. (See Chapter 2 for more on 501(c)(3) organizations.)

We don't aim to scare you! Just keep good financial records and stick to your mission, and you'll be fine.

Disclosing What You Need to Disclose

Disclose is a funny word, isn't it? It seems to imply that you're hiding something that must be pried from your clutches. Don't think of it that way. The IRS regulations that lay out the rules for disclosure refer to "the public inspection of information." That's much more genteel. In this section, we briefly cover what you are and aren't expected to disclose to the public.

What you do need to show

What information must be disclosed to the public? (Sorry, we can't help ourselves. We like the word.) It's simple, really. Your three most recent filings of IRS Form 990 and your IRS Form 1023 application for tax exemption and supporting documents — if you received your exemption after July 15, 1987 — must all be available to the public.

If you have a question that this chapter doesn't cover, refer to IRS Publication 557, which you can find at www.irs.gov.

Form 990 is the annual report that you must file with the IRS. We talk more about filing the 990 later in this chapter, but in a nutshell, it's a report of your annual finances and activities as a nonprofit organization. The IRS has three versions of the 990 form, and the version you file depends on your nonprofit's gross receipts and total assets held. Don't panic! We get into that later.

Current IRS regulations state that the three most recent 990 reports and attachments to the report must be available for public inspection at the organization's primary place of business during regular business hours. A staff member may be present during the inspection, and copies may be made for the person requesting them. If you make copies on your own copier, you may charge what the IRS charges: $0.10 per page for black and white or $0.20 per page for color.

The information provided in this chapter is about 501(c)(3) organizations that are considered public charities. If your organization is a private foundation, special disclosure rules apply. Check with the Council on Foundations (www.cof.org) about disclosure requirements.

If you work out of your home or really have no primary place of business, you can arrange to meet at a convenient place or mail copies to the person who requested them. You have two weeks to do so. The information also can be requested in writing, and if it is, you have 30 days to respond.

If you received your exemption after July 15, 1987, you must include your application for exemption and all the supporting materials submitted with it in the information you make available for inspection. Although the IRS doesn't say so, we assume that you include your articles of incorporation and your bylaws, if you attached them to your application.

You need to know the rules and regulations about public inspection of non-profit materials, but frankly, in the many years we've been working for non-profits, no one has ever asked to see our 990 forms. This doesn't mean that you won't be asked, however. Follow the Boy Scout motto and be prepared.

On your 990, you need to disclose compensation paid to board members. This information is available for public inspection, as are employee salaries and contractor payments of more than $100,000 per year.

Check your state and local government requirements to see whether your nonprofit must make other information available under local laws.

What you don't need to show

You don't need to reveal your donor list. Donors who contribute more than $5,000 must be named on Schedule B of your 990-EZ or 990 report, but 501(c)(3) public charities aren't required to make the information public.

Other items that may remain private include the following:

- ✔ Trade secrets and patents
- ✔ National defense material
- ✔ Communications from the IRS about previous unfavorable rulings or technical advice related to rulings
- ✔ Board minutes and contracts

IRS regulations go into more detail, but we think the preceding four items sum up the major points. If you have questions about a particular item, consult your attorney or tax advisor.

The public disclosure rules offer a nice tool for anyone who gets a bee in his bonnet and wants to harass your organization. So if you start getting request after request after request, check with the nearest IRS office. IRS officials have the authority to relieve you of the disclosure responsibilities if they agree that harassment is occurring.

Using the web to satisfy disclosure requirements

You can avoid the hassle of photocopying your Form 990 by placing the required information on the web. If you do so, be sure that you post an exact copy of the materials, not a summary or a retyped copy. You can scan documents and put them on your website as graphics, but the best way to do it is to put the documents in PDF format using Adobe Acrobat (www.adobe.com).

GuideStar (www.guidestar.org) keeps a database of basic information about U.S. nonprofit organizations as well as PDF files of 990 returns. You can add information about your nonprofit to the GuideStar database. Some states also maintain web databases of 990 forms of nonprofits incorporated in their jurisdictions. Remember that you need to make available your three most recent 990 returns and your application for exemption.

If someone arrives at your office and asks to inspect your 990 forms, you still need to allow them the privilege. Web access to the materials only relieves you of the responsibility of mailing out copies.

Avoiding Excessive Payments and Politicking

Paying excessive compensation and engaging in campaign politics can get a charitable nonprofit organization in trouble. It doesn't happen often, but you need to be aware of the rules.

Determining reasonable pay and benefits

In past years, if the IRS discovered wrongdoing in a nonprofit, it had little recourse but to take away the organization's tax-exempt status. However, when revised tax laws were passed in 1996, the IRS gained the authority to apply "intermediate sanctions" when nonprofits provide excess benefits to staff members or disqualified persons. Board members and their family members — really anyone who can influence the organization's activities — are disqualified persons.

Excess benefits can include excessive salaries for staff members or a business deal arranged to benefit a disqualified person in which the nonprofit overpays for a service. So, if you sit on a board of directors that decides to rent office space from your uncle at two or three times the going rate, you and your uncle may be in trouble. If you do decide to rent from your uncle, be sure you can document that you're paying a market-rate rent (if not less). Also, you shouldn't participate in the board vote about renting the space.

An excessive benefit for a nonprofit staff member is any sum that's above a "reasonable amount." You're probably thinking, "What's a *reasonable* amount?" and you're right to ask the question. In the case of executive compensation, it's up to the board of directors to find out what a fair salary is for nonprofit managers in your area and for an organization of your size and scope. (See Chapter 10 for tips on determining salaries.)

If the IRS finds that someone in your nonprofit has received an excessive benefit, the financial penalties are severe. The IRS levies a 25 percent tax on the excess amount, and the employee must pay the full excess amount (including interest and the 25 percent tax) back to the organization in less than a year. If payment isn't received by that time, the tax can go up to a whopping 200 percent. Board members also may be liable for penalties for approving excessive compensation.

These three tips can help you avoid excess benefits problems:

- ✔ Don't allow board members to participate in decisions that may benefit themselves or their family members. And, certainly, don't let the executive director participate in setting her own compensation.

- ✔ Rely on credible independent information about reasonable costs in business deals and compensation matters.

- ✔ Document the reasons that you make the decisions you make.

We don't want to frighten you with visions of huge tax bills. We're not saying that you can't pay nonprofit staff well or that you have to undertake a scientific study to determine fair compensation. Use your head, be reasonable, and exercise caution.

Document board decisions by keeping minutes of board meetings. You don't need to keep a verbatim record of board deliberations, but you want your minutes to reflect the discussions you have and the decisions you make. Maintain what's known as a *board book* — a binder that contains copies of your articles of incorporation, IRS letter of determination for tax exemption, bylaws, amendments to bylaws, notices sent to announce board and membership meetings, and a chronological record of your board-meeting minutes.

Using caution when getting involved in politics

We aren't saying that you shouldn't get involved in politics, because it's your right to do so. If you want to give your personal support and endorsement to a candidate, by all means do it. But be sure to separate yourself from your nonprofit organization when you do. Nonprofits in the 501(c)(3) category can't support or endorse candidates for political office.

If you want to talk to your legislator about the passage of a bill that benefits your clients, go ahead and make an appointment. But if you find yourself traveling to your state capital or to Washington, D.C., on a regular basis, step back and consider how much organizational time and money you're spending on the activity. Charitable nonprofits can spend an "insubstantial" amount on direct lobbying activities. If it's 5 percent or less of your organizational budget, you're probably within the limits allowed, according to the people who pay attention to these things.

Be more cautious with what's known as *grassroots lobbying,* or attempting to influence the general public to vote in a particular way. If lobbying is important to your overall mission as a 501(c)(3) public benefit nonprofit, you can elect the "h" designation, which requires more financial reporting to the IRS but allows you to spend more money on these activities. To do so, file IRS Form 5768 after you have a look at the regulations in IRS Publication 577.

Why all the fuss? Understanding the increased scrutiny

Nonprofit organizations face increasing regulation and public scrutiny in the years to come. Why? Three reasons come to mind:

- ✔ Concern about how nonprofit organizations use contributions that are made for disaster relief efforts

- ✔ A series of widely reported cases in which some nonprofits, both public charities and private foundations, have paid very high salaries to executives and trustees and otherwise pushed the limits of ethical behavior

- ✔ The number and degree of corporate-accounting and insider-trading scandals that have been revealed during the past few years in the for-profit sector

These factors have focused more public and legislative attention on how nonprofit organizations (and for-profit corporations) operate and how their affairs are regulated.

Greater accountability is being asked of nonprofit leaders, both managers and board members, in how money is raised, how conflicts of interest are avoided, and how funds are spent, especially for salaries and expenses. The National Council of Nonprofits has compiled good principles of nonprofit management from several states that provide overall guidance in this area. You can find them at `www.councilofnonprofits.org/resources/principles-and-practices`.

If you're involved with a start-up nonprofit that's operating on a shoestring, you may be asking yourself why you need to worry about getting paid too much. And you're right; you probably don't need to worry. But you should stay informed of changes in reporting requirements. You still need to have good, ethical operating policies in place; keep good financial records; and document your organizational decisions with board and committee meeting minutes.

If you're already involved with a medium or large nonprofit, be aware of the need for independent financial audits and board policies that address excessive compensation, self-dealing, whistle-blowers, and conflicts of interest.

Because the regulatory situation is always changing, and because it varies from state to state, we suggest visiting the websites of Independent Sector (www.independentsector.org) and BoardSource (www.boardsource.org) to keep abreast of the latest developments. If you have an accounting firm performing a review or audit, it should be able to keep you informed about current legislation and verify that you're in compliance.

Reporting to the IRS

The formal name of the report that nonprofit organizations must file annually is *Return of Organization Exempt from Income Tax,* and the IRS calls it the "annual information return." Everyone else refers to it as "the 990." It *is* IRS Form 990, after all. Depending on a nonprofit's gross receipts and total assets held, a version of this report must go to the IRS each year. The IRS made substantial revisions to its reporting requirements beginning with the 2008 tax year, and this section helps you sort through those changes.

The IRS uses gross receipts to determine which 990 Form your organization is required to file. *Gross receipts* refers to all funds that come into the nonprofit during the tax year before any expenses are subtracted. For example, if you have a special event that brings in $20,000, but you have expenses of $8,000 for a net income of $12,000, your gross receipts for that event are $20,000. This figure is added to grants, fees for services, contributions, and any other income to determine your gross receipts for the year.

No matter what report you file, it must be postmarked no later than the 15th day of the fifth month after the end of your annual accounting period: in other words, after the close of your fiscal year. When you filed your application for exemption, you selected your accounting period. If you use the calendar year as your fiscal year, your 990 has to be out the door on May 15. You can apply for an automatic three-month extension. If you need even more time, you can apply for an additional three-month extension — if you have a good reason.

The IRS has three versions of the 990: The 990-N, the 990-EZ, and the long Form 990. The report you file depends on the total gross receipts (and total assets) of your nonprofit organization. We focus on the 990-N and 990-EZ in the next couple of sections, but we do provide some advice for the long Form 990 as well. Most important, if your nonprofit organization is big enough to require filing the long Form 990, we advise that you seek professional help.

Using the 990-N

The 990-N is required for all 501(c)(3) nonprofit organizations (with the exception of churches and church-related organizations) that have annual gross receipts of $50,000 or less. This simple form must be filed electronically; in fact, the IRS refers to this form as an e-postcard, so you need a computer, Internet access, and an e-mail address.

The due date for filing this form is the same as for the 990-EZ or the long Form 990: the 15th day of the fifth month after the close of the tax year. However, at present there's no penalty for late filing. You can't file before the end of the tax year.

If your organization fails to file a 990-N for three consecutive years, its tax-exempt status will be rescinded.

The Urban Institute handles 990-N filings for the IRS. Go to epostcard. form990.org and follow the instructions. If your organization is new or if you haven't filed a 990-N before, you need to register to obtain a login ID.

The 990-N asks for the following information:

- The legal name of the organization and any other names under which it's doing business.
- A mailing address and a web address, if you have one.
- The Employer Identification Number, or EIN, of the organization. (See Chapter 4 for more on EINs.)
- The name and address of the principal officer, which is likely either the executive director or board president. Use the organization's address as the address for this individual.

You'll also be asked for the organization's tax year (the same as the fiscal year), whether the nonprofit normally has $50,000 or less in gross receipts, and whether the organization is still in business.

Taking it easy with the 990-EZ return

If your organization has gross receipts of less than $200,000 and assets of less than $500,000, you can file the 990-EZ form, which is a little more complex than the 990-N. The 990-EZ includes a lot of fine print, and the instructions are a good test of the importance of close reading. That said, the instructions are complete, and most terms are well defined. You can make your task easier by getting help from your accountant or attorney.

Keep in mind when reading the instructions that the 990-EZ report is used for categories of tax-exempt organizations other than 501(c)(3) public charities. This can be confusing unless you attend closely to the instructions. Because the 990-EZ is used for other types of nonprofits, be sure to check the 501(c) box.

Fill in the identifying information at the top of the form. Be sure to add your EIN. Also check the correct box to indicate whether you're using a cash or accrual accounting method. If you need help with that question, see Chapter 10.

Be sure to include a phone number where the IRS and members of the public can contact your organization. Don't forget that the 990 is a public document. So, if you've had an address or name change since you filed your last report, check that box in the "B" section. If these changes have required amendments to your articles of incorporation or if this is the first time your organization has filed the 990-EZ, check the corresponding boxes. If your tax-exempt application is still pending, indicate that as well.

If in the past year a single individual has given your 501(c)(3) organization a contribution of cash, a grant, or property that was valued at more than $5,000, *or* if a gift totaled more than 2 percent of your total grants and contributions, you must file Schedule B with your 990-EZ. If a single person gives you two gifts of $2,500 within the year, you must file the schedule. If you don't have grants or gifts in this range, check the box in the "H" section to let the IRS know you aren't required to file Schedule B.

The IRS doesn't require Schedule B to be disclosed to the public. If your organization must file its 990 report with its state to satisfy state reporting requirements, check about its disclosure requirements.

Parts 1 and 11

In Part I of 990-EZ, you report your financial activities over the past year. Chances are that the two lines that have the highest amount of revenue are line 1 (contributions, gifts, and grants) and line 2 (program service revenue, including government fees and contracts). You may have some income from membership fees for line 3 and income from investments or interest on a savings account for line 4.

Lines 5 through 8 deal with income from sales of materials or assets and income from special events. You're asked to report the costs and expenses associated with the materials sold and any direct expenses associated with special events. In other words, the IRS wants to see a net amount for sales and special events. The total you end up with on line 9 is your total revenue for the year.

If you earn more than $15,000 in gross receipts from special events (reported in line 6A), you need to complete Part II of Schedule G. If any part of these gross receipts came from gaming, such as bingo and pull tabs, you also need to complete Part III of this schedule.

Don't confuse your total revenue with your gross receipts. Gross receipts include all the income you receive from sales and special events *before* you subtract expenses.

Report your expenses on lines 10 through 16 in their appropriate categories and total the amount on line 17. Subtract line 9 from line 17, and you have your surplus (or deficit) for the year. This amount goes on line 18. We come back to line 19 in just a minute.

Part II includes lines 22 through 24, which is where you report your assets — cash, savings, or investments, as well as property and equipment. (Equipment goes on line 24, other assets. Attach Schedule O with the equipment list.) Total these figures for line 25.

Enter your total liabilities on line 26. They may include accounts payable, outstanding loans, and vacation time owed to employees, for example. Describe these liabilities on Schedule O. Subtract line 26 from line 25, and you have your net assets or fund balance. Put this amount on line 27. If you pay off all your bills and sell all your assets, this amount is what's left over — in theory.

Notice that you need to report assets and liabilities for the beginning of the year and the end of the year. (If this 990 report is your first, you provide only end-of-year totals.) Refer to the form you submitted last year for the beginning-of-year figures.

Now go back to line 19 in Part I. Enter your net assets from last year's form on this line. If an adjustment to your net assets was made during the year (usually done by an accountant), enter the figure for this adjustment on line 20 and explain on Schedule O. On line 21, enter the amount of your net assets at the end of the current year.

That's it for reporting your financial activities on the 990-EZ form. It *was* easy, wasn't it?

Parts III and IV

Part III of 990-EZ asks you to state your primary exempt purpose. This statement doesn't need to be long like the one you wrote for your Form 1023 application; a few words will do. You also need to describe your three largest programs, their objectives, program accomplishments, how many people you served, and a total cost for each program. The form has spaces for three separate programs, but if you have only one program, that's fine.

Part III includes a space to report grants in each program area. This space is for grants made *by* your organization, not grants *to* your organization. You probably didn't make any grants, but if you did, report them here.

Part IV requires a list of your directors, with the board officers identified, and key employees and their addresses. The only key employee you need to report here is the executive director, if you have one. You also need to state how much time is devoted to each position each week and record any compensation received, including salary, retirement benefits, and expense allowances. If you need more space than what's provided on the form, attach an additional sheet. You don't need to list addresses for any individuals in this section.

Parts V and VI

You're likely able to check no to the questions in Part V of 990-EZ or leave the items blank. But several things may need your attention.

- ✔ If you've amended your bylaws or articles of incorporation since you filed your last report, check that item and include a copy of the amended document when you send in the form.

- ✔ Line 35 refers to income that may have come to your organization through activities not related to your charitable purpose. This is called *unrelated business income,* and if it totals more than $1,000, you must report it on Form 990-T. You may be liable for taxes on this income. If you think your nonprofit has income in this category, you're wise to consult an accountant. (For more on unrelated income, check out the nearby sidebar "How the IRS decides whether income is unrelated.")

- ✔ If your organization loaned or borrowed money during the year from a director, trustee, or key employee — or if it has outstanding loans from the previous year — check yes on line 38a, fill in the amount on line 38b, and file Schedule L, Part II.

- ✔ In Part VI, lines 46 and 47 ask whether your organization engaged in political campaigns on behalf of a candidate or engaged in lobbying activities. If you can legitimately answer no to these questions, do so and move on. If you have questions about your nonprofit's engagement in these areas, seek advice from an attorney.

How the IRS decides whether income is unrelated

The IRS definition of *unrelated business income* is based on three questions: Does the income come from a trade or business? Is it regularly carried on? Is it not substantially related to the organization's exempt purpose?

To better understand what these questions mean, consider an extreme example. The Juniper Avenue Young People's Club, a 501(c)(3) nonprofit with the mission of providing recreational opportunities, mentoring, and job-skills training to adolescents, decides to open a shoe-repair business. It rents a storefront space, purchases equipment, hires employees, and begins soliciting business. The shoe-repair shop does very well. In fact, in the first year of operation, income exceeds expenses by $10,000. The club uses the money to pay some

costs incurred in working with young people in the neighborhood. The problem is that the shoe-repair shop has no relationship to the club's charitable purpose. In this case, the club is required to file Form 990-T and pay appropriate taxes on the $10,000. That's okay, however, because the club still realizes a profit that can be applied to some of its program costs.

However, what if the club opens the shoe-repair shop with the purpose of providing training in the shoe-repair trade to adolescents in the neighborhood? In that case, chances are good that any income from the business will be considered "substantially related to the organization's exempt purpose," and the unrelated business income tax (known as UBIT) won't be due on any proceeds.

Campaigning for a candidate under the banner of your nonprofit organization is a serious matter that could ultimately cause the loss of your tax exemption. An "insubstantial" amount of lobbying is allowed for 501(c)(3) public charities, but this is an area filled with shades of gray and shouldn't be taken lightly. Nonprofit organizations can engage in nonpartisan voter registration and public education activities, but to be on the safe side, you should seek professional counsel.

✔ List all employees and contractors who were paid more than $100,000 during the last year. Chances are, especially if yours is a start-up organization, you can put "NA" in these sections.

Be sure to have an officer of the organization sign and date the form. Often this officer is the board chair or board treasurer. If you used a paid tax preparer, she must sign, as well.

Schedule A

All 501(c)(3) public charities that submit the 990-EZ must complete and submit Schedule A so the IRS can apply the public support test to determine whether your organization qualifies as a public charity. (Refer to Chapter 4 for a discussion of the public support test.) Although it's a little more complicated and there are other ways to pass the test, in a nutshell, public charities must receive one-third of their support from the public.

During the first five years of a nonprofit's existence, data is collected but the test isn't applied. So even if you're sending in your first 990-EZ, you need to provide the information requested on Schedule A.

In Part I of Schedule A, you're asked to check one box from lines 1–11. Most 501(c)(3) organizations that are the subject of this book check either line 7 or line 9. Line 7 applies to organizations that qualify as public charities under section 170(b)(1)(A)(vi); in this case, you also need to complete Part II of Schedule A. Line 9 applies to organizations that qualify as public charities under section 509(a)(2). Organizations checking this box must complete Part III of Schedule A.

The IRS refers to the appropriate code section for your nonprofit in the letter of determination (tax-exemption letter) it sends you after you file your IRS Form 1023 application for exemption.

Parts II and III both ask for information about sources of financial support for the organization for the current tax year and the four previous years. If your organization has been in existence for less than this five-year period, you only have to provide information for the year or years in which your nonprofit has been active. Also, you don't need to compute the percentage of public support in Section C in either part until you've completed your sixth year of operations, although it's a good idea to complete a personal copy of the calculation for the first five years so you can keep track of how you're doing.

Using the long Form 990

If your organization has gross receipts of $200,000 or more or assets of $500,000 or greater, you're required to tackle the full 990 experience. The Form 990 emphasizes accountability and transparency in nonprofit organizations, which reflects growing public scrutiny of nonprofits. The first page of the form is a summary of the more-detailed information that follows. You have to describe your mission or "most significant activities" in the first question of Part I. In addition to questions about the number of board members, employees, and volunteers, you must present a summary of the detailed financial information requested in the final pages of the report.

Make no mistake, completing this report requires more time and effort than the 990-EZ. The long Form 990 spans 11 pages and is accompanied by 16 separate schedules. Although you won't be required to complete all the schedules, you may need to submit some of them, depending on the circumstances of your organization. One section of the 990 is a checklist with questions that must be answered "yes" or "no." Usually a "yes" answer triggers a requirement to complete one of the 16 schedules.

The IRS estimates that you need 16 hours to learn about Form 990 and nearly 24 hours to complete the form. We think this may be an underestimate. The instruction booklet contains 71 pages of dense reading. Answering the questions and providing the information required on this form should be a team effort. And, if at all possible, we recommend that a member of that team be a qualified accountant. It wouldn't hurt to have an attorney on board, either. If you decide to undertake the task of completing the long form without the assistance of professional help, start early and plan to spend lots of time with the instruction manual.

Providing financial information

When you use the long Form 990, you'll be asked for more-detailed financial information than is needed for the 990-EZ. The IRS wants to know more about where you get your money and where you spend it. Also, all your expenses must be allocated to one of three categories: program, management and general, and fundraising costs. You'll also need to provide a detailed balance sheet. (Chapter 10 includes more information about financial recordkeeping.)

The IRS wants to know what method of accounting you're using and whether you're following certain accounting standards. You'll also be asked whether your financial statements have been audited or reviewed by an independent accountant. If so, the IRS will ask whether your organization has a committee that provides oversight to the preparation of financial statements and audits.

If it looks like your organization will be required to file the full 990 report in the next year or two, start putting in place the accounting system you'll need to collect the appropriate information.

Describing your programs

In the long Form 990, you're asked to describe the program achievements of your three most expensive programs and whether any programs were added or eliminated in the year for which you're making the report. If you did make significant changes in your program offerings, you need to describe them on Schedule O.

The 990 report is a public document and is available for public review, so be sure to take the time to describe your activities and program achievements completely and clearly and without the use of excessive jargon.

Looking at management and governance

The sections relating to members of the board (the IRS refers to the board as the "governing body"), board policies, and highly compensated and key employees are detailed and require special attention.

For example, you're asked how many board members are independent. An *independent* board member can't be compensated as an officer or employee of the organization or receive more than $10,000 as an independent contractor of the organization. He or a member of his family also may not engage in a business transaction with the organization or a key employee that would trigger the requirement to submit Schedule L.

Also, although not required by the IRS code, the 990 asks whether the organization has established written policies for when it's appropriate to get rid of old documents. (Destroying old documents relates to protecting whistleblowers and guarding against conflicts of interest.) Finally, in the board sections, the organization must note whether a process exists for setting the compensation of the executive director and other key employees and whether the organization has a gift-acceptance policy. It's recommended that the board review the 990 before it's filed.

Getting your 990 to the IRS

Your 990 report (whether it's the 990-EZ, 990-N, or long Form 990) needs to be postmarked on the 15th day of the fifth month after the close of your financial year — unless, of course, you request an extension. Check the most recent version of the instructions to find the address to which the report should be sent. You can file the 990 reports electronically if you want, and some larger nonprofits are required to file electronically. Go to `www.irs.gov/efile` for instructions on electronic filing. The 990-N can *only* be filed electronically.

Large organizations that have assets worth more than $10 million and that submit more than 250 IRS reports in a year must file their 990 returns electronically.

Reporting to Your State and Local Governments

You'll almost certainly have reporting requirements for your state and possibly your local government, especially if you provide services under contract. Sometimes reporting to the state is as simple as completing a one-page form, attaching a copy of your 990, and paying a small fee.

More and more states (and some local governments) require registration for fundraising activities. Be sure to check local laws.

Some states require a separate financial form, although we think that most follow the federal form closely. You'll probably get all the needed reporting information when you ask for the incorporation packet, but if you didn't or you aren't sure, check with your state office that regulates nonprofit corporations. The contact list provided for Chapter 4 (File0402) is a good resource. Pop in the CD or click the link in the table of contents to view this file.

Part II
Managing a Nonprofit Organization

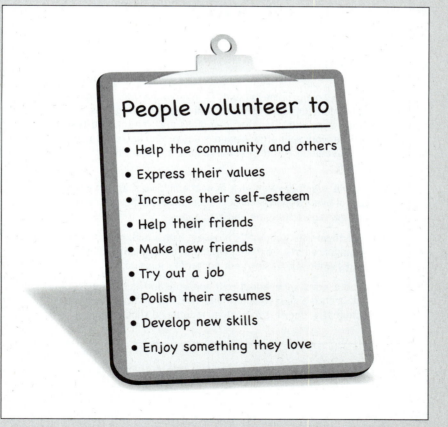

People volunteer to

- Help the community and others
- Express their values
- Increase their self-esteem
- Help their friends
- Make new friends
- Try out a job
- Polish their resumes
- Develop new skills
- Enjoy something they love

Illustration by Wiley, Composition Services Graphics

If you want to provide a bit of structure during your board meetings, consider using Robert's Rules of Order. Go to www.dummies.com/extras/nonprofitkit for an article that outlines the basic rules.

In this part . . .

- ✔ Looking for people to sit on the board of directors can be a daunting task. Get the inside scoop on appointing people to the board and holding effective meetings.

- ✔ See how plans come in handy for everything from laying the foundation for your organization to setting up programs. The best way to know whether your plans are on track is to evaluate the work your organization is doing. Find out how to conduct evaluations, interpret the results, and apply the findings.

- ✔ People, whether volunteers or paid employees, are an essential part of every nonprofit organization. Discover how to recruit and manage volunteers and employees.

- ✔ Nail down your nonprofit's numbers with a budget and other financial reports. Good management requires balancing your books while addressing your nonprofit's mission.

- ✔ Let the world know about your nonprofit and its good works with a strong marketing strategy. Find tips on everything from contacting reporters to posting updates on social media.

Chapter 6

Building Your Board of Directors

In This Chapter

▶ Recognizing the roles of a board of directors

▶ Recruiting the right board members

▶ Understanding why having staff members on your board can be tricky

▶ Getting the most out of your board

Some boards of directors do miraculous things. Others just muddle through. But no nonprofit organization has an ideal board of directors all the time. You may get the impression that your board is so disorganized that you may as well close up shop and go fishing. Don't despair. Boards can always get better, and many nonprofits do excellent work with boards of directors that would send shivers down the backs of most nonprofit consultants. The purpose of this chapter is to help you understand how nonprofit boards work in a perfect world. (We don't live in a perfect world, though. So please keep that in mind while reading.)

We're the first to agree that working with a board can drive you a little batty sometimes. Doing all the work yourself may seem easier, but the strength and success of a nonprofit organization grows from its board of directors. It's surprising what a group of people working together can accomplish. So take the time to build a good board and work with its members to achieve your mission — trust us, you'll be glad you did.

Understanding the Functions of a Nonprofit Board of Directors

A *board of directors* (which we refer to simply as *a board* from here on) is a group of people who agree to accept responsibility for a nonprofit organization. A board is responsible for ensuring that the nonprofit organization is fulfilling its mission. It makes decisions about the organization, sets policy for the staff or volunteers to implement, and oversees the nonprofit's activities. Raising money for the nonprofit is another important responsibility that many, but not all, boards assume. Board members almost always serve without compensation; they're volunteers who have no financial interest in the nonprofit's business. However, they do have responsibility for financial oversight and are held accountable for the accounting and financial reporting of the organization.

Paid staff members may serve as board members and often do in start-up and small nonprofit organizations. However, they're being compensated as employees, not as board members. Skip to the section "Putting Staff Members on Your Board" for details on why we don't recommend having staff serve on your board.

A nonprofit organization doesn't have owners like a for-profit business does, but a board of directors guides and oversees the organization like an owner might. No one owns city, state, and federal governments either, so citizens hand over the responsibility of running the government to elected officials. In turn, they expect those officials to govern the affairs of their city, state, and nation. The job of a nonprofit board is similar; in fact, it's referred to as *nonprofit governance*. If you need more information on this type of governance than you find here, grab a copy of *Nonprofit Law and Governance For Dummies,* by Jill Gilbert Welytok and Daniel S. Welytok (Wiley).

Primary role: Preserving public trust

A board's primary governance responsibility is *fiduciary* — to uphold the public trust. Laws in the United States give special rights and privileges to nonprofits recognized by the Internal Revenue Service (IRS) as public charities. Primarily, these nonprofits earn the right to exemption from corporate income tax and the right to receive contributions that are tax-deductible for the donor. The government gives nonprofits this special status because they provide a public benefit. A board's leadership and oversight keep the organization's focus on that public benefit and make sure it doesn't abuse these rights and privileges.

Suppose that a nonprofit begins with a mission to rescue stray cats. People who support this idea make contributions to the nonprofit with the belief that their money is being spent on programs to help the plight of stray cats. But unknown to the donors, the nonprofit begins to spend its money on programs to support preschool education. Supporting preschool education is a worthy goal, but it's a long way from the original purpose of helping stray cats. So in this example, even though the nonprofit is using its contributions for a good cause, it isn't using them as the donors intended or to fulfill the organization's original purpose.

A nonprofit that collected funds for helping stray cats but instead used the funds for the personal benefit of the board members and staff would be even worse. This dishonest act is serious and possibly a crime. Aside from potential felony fraud charges, such an activity violates IRS rules and can result in the revocation of the nonprofit's tax-exempt status.

In a for-profit business, the higher-ups can share the net earnings (in other words, profit) at the end of the year among the company's owners or stockholders. If nonprofit board members decide to divide surplus funds among themselves, it's called *inurement,* a big word that basically means personal enrichment, which isn't allowed in the nonprofit world. Board members and staff — or anyone, for that matter — can't personally benefit from nonprofit funds except for compensation for services provided or for reimbursement of expenses. A board must not only ensure that the nonprofit is doing what it set out to do but also make sure that it spends its funds properly. If a board does nothing else, it must make sure the organization adheres to these standards.

Keep in mind that a board's responsibilities are legal responsibilities. The three main duties that every board must uphold are care, loyalty, and obedience. Although they sound like vows one may take when entering a monastery, they actually describe established legal principles. Here's what these duties entail:

- ✔ The duty of care refers to the responsibility to be a prudent board member. In other words, board members must pay attention to what's going on and make decisions based on good information.

- ✔ The duty of loyalty means that a board member must put the organization's welfare above other interests when making decisions.

- ✔ The duty of obedience requires that board members act in accordance with the nonprofit's mission, goals, and bylaws.

Basic information about board governance is available from BoardSource (www.boardsource.org) without charge. You can access more in-depth material by paying a membership fee.

Secondary role: Dealing with planning, hiring, and other board tasks

In addition to the legal and fiduciary responsibilities, a nonprofit board performs other roles, too, including those described in the following sections.

Providing a guiding strategy

Every nonprofit should have an organizational plan, and every board should play a part in creating and maintaining that plan. Thus, an important role of any board is to guide the overall planning and strategy of its organization. At the most basic level, this job means reviewing the organization's mission statement and goals on a regular basis. Turn to Chapter 7 for more information on planning.

Hiring and working with the executive director

A nonprofit board is expected to hire the organization's executive director. Of course, many nonprofit organizations operate without paid staff, but if your nonprofit does have employees, finding the right executive director is one of the board's most important tasks. See Chapter 10 for information about hiring paid employees.

A board works with its executive director to set goals and objectives for the year. Board members shouldn't look over the director's shoulder every day, but they should have a good idea of the director's work plan and should ensure that her efforts are in line with the agency's purpose.

Overseeing the organization's finances

A board must make sure the organization has the resources to carry out its goals. As part of this duty, many boards are active in fundraising. But a board also is responsible for reviewing the organization's budget and staying informed of the organization's financial situation. Nothing is more dismal than finding out, for example, that an organization hasn't been sending in its payroll taxes. A word to the wise — insist on good financial reporting. At a minimum, have the board treasurer (or perhaps the executive director or bookkeeper, if you have one) prepare quarterly financial reports and distribute them to your board for review.

Many people join boards because they care about and understand the nature of the service that the organization provides, but they may not be trained in bookkeeping and accounting. These board members must try not to let their eyes glaze over when the financial report gets passed around at the board meeting, because part of a board member's job is to understand finances. If members don't understand the financial fine points, they need to ask questions of staff and other board members until they do understand them. Of course, they also can study Chapter 11 on nonprofit budgets and financial statements.

Establishing an advisory board

Some organizations form *advisory boards,* which don't have governance responsibilities. Advisory boards are optional, and how they operate and relate to the governing board of directors varies widely among different nonprofit organizations. Generally, their role falls into one of the following two categories:

✔ Advisory boards that have members who provide advice and guidance because of their professional expertise

✔ Advisory boards that are formed so prominent names can be listed on the organization's letterhead

We favor advisory boards that actually give advice (which generally means you have to ask for it) — even if they do so only once a year. Some organizations also use advisory board appointments as a way of getting to know potential board members.

Sometimes the problem is more than a lack of comprehension. For instance, the financial information may need to be presented more clearly. If one board member doesn't understand the financial reports, chances are good that other board members don't understand them, either. If your organization uses an outside accountant or bookkeeper to keep track of finances, ask for a brief meeting with him to explain how he has presented the information. Many nonprofit service organizations offer affordable workshops on nonprofit finances and recordkeeping to assist board and staff members; others have programs that place volunteers from businesses into nonprofits. (Check out the article on nonprofit resources at www.dummies.com/extras/nonprofitkit for more on these service organizations.)

Sharing responsibilities among the board, staff, and volunteers

Defining roles causes problems for a number of nonprofit organizations. Should the board of directors be involved in day-to-day management decisions? No, probably not. An executive director and her staff don't need board members to approve every management decision that comes along. The board must trust the staff to run the organization. To put it simply, the board sets the overall goals and policies, and the staff implements them. But (and this is a big but) many nonprofits have limited staff or even no staff at all. What happens when the organization's work is done by the board and other volunteers?

In the case of volunteer-run organizations, board members must wear two hats. Most importantly, they must exercise their fiduciary responsibilities. When they meet as a board of directors, they must see the larger picture and make group decisions that benefit the organization and its programs and clients. But, at the same time, when they have to do the hands-on work needed to provide the services and perform the day-to-day tasks of running a nonprofit, board members must act as if they were employees. They may even hold regular, unpaid volunteer jobs with job descriptions and scheduled hours. Confusing, isn't it? Still, anyone who serves as both a board member and a volunteer or staff member needs to keep this distinction in mind.

In any organization, building practices that create financial checks and balances is a good idea. These practices are particularly important when board members also act as staff. For example, an organization has better financial oversight and control when one person approves bills for payment, a different person signs the checks, and yet another person reviews the canceled checks and monthly bank statements. You don't *have* to use this system — it's just one way to make sure that everything is used and accounted for properly. (For more on having staff members serve as board members, check out the later section "Putting Staff Members on Your Board.")

Finding the Right People for Your Board

You don't want just anybody to serve on your board. You want to choose the most generous members of your community who believe in what you're doing, will come to all your meetings, will be advocates for your programs, will provide honest and ethical oversight to the organization, and will sweep the floor on weekends.

Perhaps not surprisingly, you won't find many board members who fit this description. Even so, the following three traits are critical to the success of the organization:

- Believing in your mission
- Being a strong advocate on behalf of your programs
- Serving the organization as a careful and honest board member

Sure, having wealthy members who do the dirty work when needed is nice, but, most importantly, you must find board members who understand and believe deeply in what you're doing. Showing up for board meetings is a nice habit, too.

You also need to think seriously about the skills that board members bring to your organization. Do you need an accountant to set up financial systems? A public relations specialist to help with media campaigns? An attorney to help with legal matters? Yes, you probably do. But don't expect the accountant to do your audit or the attorney to represent you in court. You need a disinterested professional to do that work.

Your board should reflect your organization's character and mission. A community-organizing group dedicated to collective decision making may want board members who work well together. A neighborhood development organization clearly wants board members from its neighborhood. A youth leadership organization may want to invest in future leadership by creating positions for youth members on its board. (***Note:*** Before adding young people to your board, check whether your state laws allow minors to serve on nonprofit boards. If your state prohibits minors from serving, consider inviting them to serve on advisory committees instead.)

Although having a friend or two on the board is fine, be careful about overloading the board with golfing buddies and carpool partners. Boards need diverse opinions and honest feedback from members.

Persuading someone to join your board

Many people think a board member's primary role is to raise money. In fact, a popular slogan addressed to board members who aren't raising funds is "Give, get, or get off." Harsh, isn't it? But nonprofits can't fulfill their purposes effectively without money, and board members who take an active interest in the organization's financial vitality are important. But a board member's role is broader than fundraising. Other roles include staying well informed about the organization's work, selecting leadership, setting policies, planning, overseeing, and serving as an ambassador for the organization. Many highly skilled volunteers think they shouldn't serve on boards because they aren't wealthy, and this misconception represents a real loss to nonprofit organizations.

Some people are reluctant to serve on boards for other reasons, including personal and financial liability. However, unpaid volunteers who aren't grossly negligent and act in good faith have some protection under the Volunteer

Protection Act of 1997. If you need more information about the possible liabilities of board members and other volunteers, we suggest that you get in touch with BoardSource (www. boardsource.org) or your state's association of nonprofit organizations through the National Council of Nonprofits (www.ncna. org).

Organizations can protect their boards by purchasing directors' and officers' insurance (see Chapter 21). Generally, the organization's creditors can't come after its board members' personal wealth for payment. An exception is that the IRS can hold board members financially accountable when organizations fail to pay payroll taxes. But even the IRS will work with an organization to develop a payment plan and schedule to catch up on taxes. People are right to take the responsibility of board service seriously, but nonprofit board work also can be fun and satisfying.

Keeping the board fresh

Building a board should be a continuing process. Therefore, we highly recommend that your organizational bylaws specify terms of service. Two three-year terms or three two-year terms are the most common terms for board service. In most cases, bylaws allow reelection to the board after one year's absence. Limiting terms of service helps you maintain a fresh supply of new ideas, which are more likely to come from people who are new to your organization. Plus, terms of service can help you recruit new board members because your potential recruits know their time commitment is of limited duration.

To avoid having all your board members leave in the same year, stagger the years when terms expire. You can allow someone to serve an extra year or ask others to serve shorter terms.

If you're thinking about recruiting new members, draw a grid to help you visualize the skills you need to seek out when you're looking for new members. Along the top of the grid, list the skills you think you need on your board. Along the side, list your current board members and place check marks under the skills they bring to the board. Check out File0601 for a sample grid for planning board recruitment.

So where do you find new board members? Start with your organization's address book. Whom do you know who may make a good member and be willing to serve? Who benefits from your agency's work? Who are your agency's neighbors? Who is actively involved as a volunteer for your agency? Some cities have nonprofit support organizations that can help in this regard. Check out the article on nonprofit resources at www.dummies. com/extras/nonprofitkit for a list of these organizations. Also consider asking your funders for suggestions and look at former board members of other high-functioning nonprofit organizations with similar missions.

Even if you don't specify board terms, continuously recruiting new board members is important. As time passes, board members' lives may change in ways that draw them away from your organization. Many nonprofit organizations lose vitality when their boards don't refresh themselves with new members.

Big boards versus little boards

Opinions differ about the ideal number of board members. One school of thought holds that big boards are better because the members can divide work among more people, consider more diverse viewpoints, and reach into the community more extensively. Other people say that smaller boards are better because maintaining a working relationship with a smaller group is easier and decision making is better because the board has to consider fewer opinions. Those who support small boards also say that board members can easily become invisible in a large group, meaning that no one will notice if they don't do their share of the work.

In our opinion, there really isn't one right answer to the board-size question. Nonprofits vary widely in size, function, and type, so what works for one nonprofit may not work for another. Nonprofit board size is truly a case where the phrase "one size fits all" doesn't apply.

Following are some points to consider when setting your board's size:

- ✓ **Start-up nonprofits tend to have smaller boards than more mature organizations.** Start-up budgets tend to be smaller, and building a board of directors takes time.

- ✓ **Boards that are actively engaged in fundraising for major gifts and special events tend to be larger because both fundraising techniques are fueled by personal contacts and friendships.** The more board members you have, the more personalized invitations you can send to your next event. Some large cultural and arts institutions have 50 board members or more.

- ✓ **Boards that govern nonprofits funded mostly by grants and contracts tend to have fewer members, perhaps an average of 10 to 12 members.** Board members in these nonprofits usually have fewer fundraising responsibilities for the organization and frequently are representatives of the communities or clients served. They also may have professional experience in the types of service provided by the nonprofit.

The founder or founders of start-up nonprofit organizations often seed their boards with personal friends. Within reason, this isn't a problem initially. However, as your nonprofit grows and matures, you need to move beyond your own address book to find board members who have wider contacts in your community and who can bring an objective eye to the organization's activities and plans.

Selecting board officers and committees

Typical officer positions of most nonprofit boards include president, vice-president, secretary, and treasurer. Sometimes the positions of secretary and treasurer are combined into one office. Your state laws may specify which officers are required. Seniority on the board, professional expertise, and skills at negotiating with and listening to others are common traits sought in a board's leaders. Ultimately, however, the board of directors chooses the officers. They're usually elected to two-year terms. The following list outlines the responsibilities of board officers.

- ✔ **President (or chairperson):** Presides at board meetings, appoints committee chairpersons, works closely with the executive director to guide the organization, and acts as public spokesperson for the organization (but also may assign this responsibility to the executive director)

- ✔ **Vice-president (or vice-chairperson):** Presides at board meetings in the president's absence and serves as a committee chairperson as appointed by the president

- ✔ **Secretary:** Maintains the organization's records, takes minutes at board meetings, and distributes minutes and announcements of upcoming meetings to board members

- ✔ **Treasurer:** Oversees the organization's financial aspects, makes regular financial reports to the board, and serves as chairperson of the board finance committee

Check out File0602 for more detailed job descriptions you can use. Pop in the CD or click the link in the table of contents to view this file.

If the board has *standing,* or permanent, committees, the board president appoints committee chairpersons. Typical standing committees include finance, development or fundraising, program, and nominating committees. Other possible committees that may be either standing or *ad hoc* — a temporary committee organized to deal with time-limited projects — include planning, executive search, investment, special events, and facilities. The following list outlines the responsibilities of common standing committees.

- ✔ **Development:** Sets fundraising goals and plans fundraising activities for the organization

- ✔ **Finance:** Assists the treasurer in overseeing financial reports and official tax filings, making budgets, and maintains relationship with professional accounting firm, if applicable

- ✔ **Nominating:** Recruits new board members and nominates board officers for election to their positions

- ✔ **Program:** Oversees the program activities of the organization

Board committees make regular reports to the full board about the organization's activities in their particular areas. Board officer terms and the number and type of standing committees are written into the organization's bylaws.

If your organization is large enough to conduct an annual financial audit, your board may be legally required to appoint an audit committee. Be sure to check the laws in your state.

Executive committees are standard groups on some larger boards of directors. Usually the members of the executive committee are the officers of the board, but the committee sometimes also includes the chairs of the standing committees. The executive committee may hold regular meetings to set the agenda for the meetings of the full board and to advise the board president, or it may come together on an as-needed basis. Sometimes an organization's bylaws empower the executive committee to make decisions on behalf of the full board in an emergency or in other special circumstances.

Introducing new and prospective board members to the organization

Boards of directors exhibit all the characteristics of small groups, maybe even families: Friendships develop, alliances form, and disagreements occur. Over time, the group develops routines and habits that help make members feel comfortable with one another and help guide the board's work. When a new member joins the group or when a prospective new member visits, the existing members need to make that person feel comfortable and share with her the collective wisdom they have accumulated.

Invite a prospective board member to observe at least one board meeting before electing her to membership. That way, the new member gets a chance to see how the board operates, and the current members have an opportunity to size up the new person. Encourage the prospective member to ask questions. Also, if your nonprofit provides programs, such as childcare, a health clinic, or a music school, give your prospective board members a tour of the facilities before they join.

When asking someone to serve on your board, don't shy away from sharing a clear picture of the work to be done. You may be afraid that your prospect will say "no" if it seems like too much work. However, keep in mind that being asked is an honor, and contributing good work to a good cause is satisfying. Besides, if the person does decide you're asking too much of her, isn't it better to know now rather than later?

A packet of background materials about the organization and board procedures can help new members get up to speed quickly. The following information is useful for orienting new members:

- Board job descriptions
- Board minutes for the last two or three meetings
- Bylaws
- Calendar of the organization's events and scheduled board meetings

 ✔ Description of board member responsibilities and expectations

 ✔ Description of programs

 ✔ Financial audit or financial statement

 ✔ Mission statement

 ✔ Names, addresses, and phone numbers of other board members

 ✔ News clippings about the organization

 ✔ Organizational plan (if one is available)

This information may seem like a lot of reading — and it is. But even if a new board member doesn't read everything from cover to cover, she at least has the reference material when she needs it.

We also suggest that the board president or the executive director meet with a new board member soon after she begins serving on the board, both to welcome her and to answer any questions.

Putting Staff Members on Your Board

As a general rule, paid staff shouldn't be board members. The situation can get too complicated. For example, *conflict of interest* is always a potential problem, especially when board and staff have different priorities, such as when employees want raises but the board says no.

Some exceptions to the rule do exist, though. In fact, many nonprofits have at least one staff member on their boards. In start-up nonprofits, for example, founders frequently serve as both board members and staff members. This situation isn't surprising. Who's better suited to bring the vision and passion needed to create a new organization than the person who formed it in the first place? In many new nonprofits, of course, paying the staff isn't even possible; resources are so limited that all work is done on a volunteer basis.

If a founder or other staff member serves on the board, we recommend that he not be elected board president because doing so tends to put all responsibility for vision and leadership in a single person's hands. Sharing that leadership can be an important first step toward broadening an organization's base of support.

Laws vary by state, but in many cases, having a paid staff member on your board is permitted. For example, under California nonprofit corporation law, up to 49 percent of the members of a nonprofit board are allowed to receive compensation from the nonprofit. But the standards of philanthropy set forth by the Better Business Bureau Wise Giving Alliance say that a board should include no more than one paid staff member. Check out the state contacts list from Chapter 4 (File0402) for a list of state offices where you can get information about nonprofit corporation law in your state.

Using Your Board to Full Capacity

If you spend any time around nonprofit staff, you'll probably hear a few complaints about the board of directors. They may say, "I can't get my board to do anything" or "I can't get them to face hard decisions or raise money." Worst of all, you may hear, "I can't get them to show up to meetings."

Motivating the board is an important part of any nonprofit leader's job. Keeping members well informed so they can make thoughtful, appropriate recommendations is essential. Sometimes your most important task is gently steering the board's attention back to the organization's mission and immediate needs. Whether or not your nonprofit has paid staff, you can take steps to help the board do its work well.

The working relationship between the executive director (if you have one) and the board president is a key factor to having an effective board and organization. Ideally, the relationship between these two leaders is one of respect and trust.

Encouraging commitment from board members

Getting members of a board to pull their weight sometimes seems like a problem that you can't solve. Not every board member will contribute equally to the work involved in governing a nonprofit organization. If everyone on your board shows up at every meeting, reads all the materials, studies the financial statements, and contributes to fundraising activities, consider yourself fortunate.

Here are some techniques you can use to encourage full board member participation:

✔ **Board contracts:** Some nonprofits ask new board members to sign an agreement that outlines expectations for board service. The contract may include a commitment to contribute financially to the organization, attend all board meetings, and serve on one or more committees. Although board contracts aren't legally binding, they provide a clear understanding of responsibilities for each board member. With a board contract, no one can say he didn't understand what he was getting into when he joined the board. Check out File0603 for a sample board contract.

- ✔ **Bylaws:** Organizational bylaws can state the requirements for board participation. For example, a board member may face dismissal from the board if he misses three consecutive board meetings.

- ✔ **Job descriptions:** Just like employees, board members often do better when they know exactly what they're supposed to do. Creating job descriptions for officers, committee chairpersons, and individual board members may clarify responsibilities and make them easier to fulfill. If a member isn't pulling his weight, a committee chairperson should speak with him and remind him of his responsibilities.

- ✔ **Reliance on board members:** Solicit opinions from members between board meetings. Use their expertise and recognize their contributions.

- ✔ **Self-evaluation:** Sometimes encouraging a board to look at itself motivates board members or encourages those who aren't pulling their weight to resign.

Board members fail to contribute equally to the work of the board due to time constraints, business travel, and just plain laziness. Give each member some slack. But if a board member's lack of participation impacts the full board, the decision is up to the board president (often in partnership with the executive director) to ask the member to reconsider his commitment to the organization.

To a great degree, each board member's work reflects his commitment to the organization's mission. Board members who truly believe in what you're doing do everything they can to help you succeed.

Holding effective board meetings

Most board work is done in meetings, either with the full board or in committees. The board president is responsible for ensuring that meetings are well organized and begin and end at a scheduled hour. We can't think of anything that damages board effectiveness more than poorly organized meetings that don't stay on topic and that continue late into the night. Nonprofit board members are volunteers; they aren't being paid by the hour.

If the organization has an executive director, the president may delegate some responsibilities for setting up meetings. Ultimately, however, part of the president's job is to see that board members have the information they need to make good decisions and that they do so in a reasonable amount of time.

Getting the members to show up

Saying how often a board of directors should meet is impossible. The only real answer is as often as it needs to. A meeting schedule depends on the organization's needs and the amount of business conducted at board meetings. Some nonprofit boards meet only once a year, the legal minimum. These tend to be small but stable organizations with one or two employees. Most nonprofit boards meet more frequently than once a year; some meet quarterly, some meet every other month, and others schedule monthly meetings. Of course, the board president may call a board meeting at any time if the board needs to handle special business.

The advantage of having more frequent board meetings is that board members are more engaged in the governance of the organization. The disadvantage — especially if the agenda doesn't include much business — is that board members may be more tempted to skip meetings.

Some boards schedule meetings at the beginning of the year for the entire year. By entering these dates in their appointment calendars months in advance, board members are less likely to schedule other events on the same days and are more likely to attend the meetings. For example, if you meet monthly, you may schedule your meetings for the second Tuesday of each month. If you aren't this organized, always schedule the next meeting before the end of the present meeting. Doing so is much easier than trying to schedule a meeting by telephone or e-mail.

Some boards use a listserv, Google Groups, or other online resource to communicate between board meetings and to compile documents in an easily accessible place.

Conducting efficient meetings

If you're looking for some tips to ensure effective board meetings, check out the following ideas:

- ✓ **Schedule a meeting between the executive director and board president prior to the meeting.** This can be done in person or via phone, but it's an important step in determining the agenda and the focus for the upcoming meeting. The meeting also allows the executive director to update the president on staff issues, funding opportunities, and any areas where the board needs to offer additional guidance and support.

- ✓ **Ten days to two weeks before a board meeting, send an announcement of the meeting to all board members.** Include the minutes from the last meeting and an agenda for the upcoming meeting. Also include any committee reports, financial statements, or background research that the board will discuss at the meeting.

If the meeting minutes include a list of tasks for board members to complete before the next meeting, try to send members a rough draft of the minutes as soon after the meeting as possible so they can get started. (File0604 contains an outline of meeting minutes that the board secretary can fill in during the meeting.)

✔ **Limit the length of meetings to two hours or less, if possible.** After two hours, especially if you're holding the meeting in the evening, attention begins to wane. If you must go longer than two hours, take a break. Offering refreshments is always a good idea.

✔ **Try to find a conference room for the meeting.** Holding a discussion around a conference table is much easier than holding one in someone's living room. The table offers a place to set papers, and people won't argue over who gets the recliner. It also sets the stage and implies that work is to be done.

Avoid holding meetings in restaurants and cafes, if possible. The noise levels are too high to make good discussion possible, and all the activity is a constant distraction. You also have no privacy. Believe us — we've tried it!

✔ **Stick to the agenda.** Don't allow people to wander off topic. Some agendas set the time allowed for discussion after each item. You don't have to do this, but if your meetings have been veering off course, setting time limits may help control them. File0605 and File0606 are samples of common agenda types you can use as models.

✔ **Follow *Robert's Rules of Order*.** You don't need to be overly formal in your meetings (many board meetings are very casual), but having a basic knowledge of when to make a motion and when to call the question is helpful. Having a copy of accepted parliamentary rules can come in handy. For more details on keeping order in meetings, check out the article at www.dummies.com/extras/nonprofit.

✔ **Thank your board.** Board members are volunteers who give time and money to your organization. Take every opportunity during meetings to make sure they're appreciated. Mention their names when appropriate in newsletters and media releases. Small gifts are sometimes useful, but don't be extravagant. You don't want to be accused of wasting the organization's money.

Chapter 7

Planning: Why and How Nonprofits Make Plans

*T*he word *planning* can be intimidating. It brings up images of daylong meetings in stuffy conference rooms with consultants wielding marker pens. Of course, not all planning takes that sort of effort. People make plans all the time, from organizing a vacation to deciding how to get all the errands done on a Saturday afternoon.

Organization planning, however, requires more effort. It's a group project that calls for research, brainstorming, discussion, and, in the end, agreement on a goal and the strategies and tactics needed to reach that goal. Simply put, organizational planning is deciding where to go and how to get there. The planning process helps ensure that everyone is headed in the same direction.

In this chapter, we cover planning for nonprofits in all its forms, from organizational planning to work planning to program planning to facility planning. Plan to join us!

Understanding the Importance of Planning

No organization has unlimited funds. Even the largest, wealthiest nonprofit needs to decide how to allocate its resources effectively. Planning helps you make decisions about how to spend your organization's resources by answering questions such as "Is now the best time to invest in a new program?" or "Is our tutoring program still filling a community need?" or "Is our office convenient to the people we're trying to serve?"

A nonprofit organization undertakes planning for the following reasons:

- ✔ To build a structure that guides its activities in pursuit of its mission
- ✔ To allocate organizational resources in the most effective ways
- ✔ To create a framework against which the organization's performance can be evaluated
- ✔ To adapt to changes in the external environment
- ✔ To reach agreement among board, staff, and supporters on desirable goals for the organization and well-considered ways to meet those goals

Think of a plan as a blueprint or scheme describing what needs to be done to accomplish an end. In an ideal world, if your organization completes every step of its plan, you achieve your goals. However, not all plans are written as recipes that — if followed closely — will serve up a perfect meal. Scenario plans, for example, help an organization think through alternatives it may choose among; other planning approaches invite organizations to assess and revisit their strategies frequently.

The *act* of planning has value apart from the written document that's ultimately created. That's because, in theory, the planning group comes to a shared understanding of the organization's mission, and the decision-making process ensures that everyone understands what needs to be done and agrees that it's worth doing.

Making Your Organizational Plan

Organizational planning is what people usually think about when they consider planning. An *organizational plan,* usually covering a three- to five-year period, sets goals for the organization and describes the objectives that must be accomplished to achieve those goals.

The steps for successful organizational planning are as follows:

1. **Decide whether it's the right time to plan.**

2. **Look at your mission.**

3. **Assess the external and internal situation.**

4. **Hear from stakeholders.**

5. **Make decisions about goals and strategies to meet them.**

6. **Write the plan.**

7. **Act on the plan.**

Planning is an ongoing activity. A formal effort to develop an organizational plan may occur only once every three to five years, but planning for the purposes of refining objectives, creating a budget, and developing fundraising programs goes on all the time.

Getting ready

Make no mistake: An all-out organizational planning effort requires considerable time, energy, and commitment from everyone involved. Some nonprofits spend a year or more developing an organizational plan.

Don't jump into the planning process without understanding that it will add to your workload and complicate your life for a period of time. Also, keep in mind that you can't plan by yourself. If you're the executive director of a nonprofit organization who thinks that a full-bore planning effort is needed, but the board of directors doesn't agree, don't try to start the process on your own. Take a couple of steps backward and begin the work of persuading board members that planning is worth the effort.

Don't start the planning process if your nonprofit is in crisis mode. It's tempting, for example, to launch an organizational planning effort if you just lost a major source of funding. But you have more immediate concerns to deal with in that situation. Delay organizational planning until you see a period of smooth sailing.

If you have the support, and foreclosure isn't hanging over your agency's head, the best way to get started is to form a *planning committee.* This small group of board members, staff, and one or two outside people can take on the role of guiding the planning process and, in the beginning, pull together the questions, facts, and observations that you need to make your planning decisions.

Is it long-range planning or strategic planning?

People often use the terms *long-range planning* and *strategic planning* as if they describe the same thing, but many planning experts make a distinction between the two. *Long-range planning* is setting a path to accomplish goals several years in the future. *Strategic planning,* on the other hand, is making decisions based on the current state of affairs in your nonprofit and the outside environment.

We think both planning approaches are necessary. A nonprofit should have long-term goals that lead to accomplishing its mission, but nonprofit staff and board members also should always be thinking of the current situation and making choices that serve the organization and its clients today.

Working from your organization's mission

Reviewing the organization's mission statement is one of the first tasks facing an organization that's developing a plan. (Chapter 3 covers mission statements.) Ask yourself these questions:

✔ Is the problem we set out to solve still a problem?

✔ Do the organization's current programs and activities address the mission in a meaningful way?

✔ Is the mission statement flexible enough to allow the organization to grow and adapt?

Keep your mission statement in mind throughout the planning process. At every turn, ask yourself: "If we do this, will we be true to our mission?"

Surveying the external situation

Early in the planning process, you need to collect information about external factors that influence your nonprofit's operation. Someone, or a subcommittee of the planning committee, should find the answers to the following questions and distribute them to everyone on the committee before the formal planning meetings begin:

✔ Are other nonprofits providing similar services in the community? If so, how are our services different? Should we be working together?

✔ What are the demographic trends in our area? Will these trends have an impact on the number of people who may need or use our services?

✔ What are the trends in the professional arena in which our nonprofit operates? Are new methods being developed? Does the future show a shortage of professionally trained staff? Is technology changing the way people acquire knowledge or services?

✔ How stable are the funding sources on which we depend? What about changes in government funding? Can we find new potential sources of funding?

The decisions you make are only as good as the information on which you base them. Therefore, it's important to find the best and most up-to-date data available that may have an impact on your organization and its programs, and it's important not to overlook unfavorable trends.

You may want to collect information from the general public or a particular constituency of your nonprofit — perhaps its clients, major donors, foundation representatives, and other nonprofits that work closely with you. Surveys, interviews, and focus groups are ways to gather input from the public. Before you undertake any of these techniques, however, spend some time thinking about what you want to learn. Write a list of questions for which you want answers.

If possible, consult with someone experienced in preparing surveys or interview protocols, because the phrasing of questions and the way you distribute your surveys affect the answers you get. Look for expertise in this area from consulting firms that work with nonprofits, at local colleges and universities, or from marketing or market-research firms.

Planning for uncertainty

No matter how well you plan, circumstances can, and probably will, change. So, of course, creating an organizational plan requires that you make assumptions about the future; sometimes these assumptions turn out to be wrong. Maybe, for example, a dependable funding source drops out of the picture; maybe a major industry in your city closes its doors; or maybe new government regulations affect your programs. Unexpected events within your nonprofit or in your community can dump cold water on your carefully designed plans.

But this doesn't mean that your nonprofit should abandon planning. Fundamentally, planning is about making decisions that are based on the best available information and the most careful thought you can muster. If conditions change or a new opportunity arises, the analytical muscles that your organization has developed through that thoughtful decision making should prepare it to respond quickly and appropriately to apply new strategies. Remember that all plans are living, breathing documents and can be adjusted as conditions change. It's wise to include wording in the plan that addresses this; then, if you do make adjustments, it's not a reflection of poor planning but of thoughtful response to environmental changes.

Bad information leads to bad decisions. Or, put another way, garbage in, garbage out. So when gathering background information to guide planning decisions, take the time to get the most accurate, up-to-date facts available.

Looking at the internal situation

In addition to surveying the environment in which the organization operates, you need to expend some effort assessing the organization itself. Consider the following factors when doing an internal analysis:

✔ What are the organization's major accomplishments? What are its milestones?

✔ Is the board of directors fully engaged with the organization? Should any weaknesses on the board be filled? Is the board engaged in fundraising?

✔ What are the staff's capabilities? Does the organization have enough staff to implement changes in how it operates? Is staff training needed?

✔ Has the organization operated within its budget? Is financial reporting adequate? Are appropriate financial controls in place?

✔ Is the organization's office and program space in the right location and of the right size?

✔ Does the organization have adequate technology? Do employees need additional training in using technological tools? What are its future equipment needs?

✔ Does the organization have a variety of funding sources? Are funding sources stable?

Hearing from all your stakeholders

Unless you have a very small organization, you probably can't include every single person in the planning process. You do need to include all stakeholder groups, however. A *stakeholder* is someone who has a reason for wanting the organization to succeed. Paid employees and, presumably, members of the board certainly qualify. But these two groups, who are the most closely connected to the nonprofit, are by no means the only people who have a stake in the organization's success.

Scenarios for the future

Scenario planning is an approach that involves imagining several futures in which your organization may find itself and then using those imagined futures to determine the strategies that your nonprofit needs to thrive in the years to come. The practitioners of scenario planning don't pretend that they're prophets or seers, but this planning method provides a framework for deep strategic conversations among the leaders of the nonprofits, corporations, and government agencies that engage in it.

Scenario planning pushes you to define the most pressing issue facing your organization. For example, if your organization works to provide equal access to information technology for everyone, you may want to ask what limits some people's access now — be it equipment, service costs, training, or available Internet access — and what conditions are changing that might solve or exacerbate the problem.

After you've figured out the question you want to address — often the most difficult thing to do — you need to collect as much information as possible about trends that may impact access to technology. You may want to find out about future cost projections for computers; projected family income figures; trends affecting libraries, adult education, and after-school programs that have provided free access to technology; business trends in the technology industry; and efforts by local governments to provide wireless access to their communities, to name only a few.

Then you can begin thinking about how the future may play out by creating several descriptions — some would say stories — of possible future conditions. After you arrive at this point, you begin to talk about the roles your organization could play in each of those stories that would enable it to fulfill its mission.

In our view, you should include a representative from the following groups in planning:

- ✔ Board of directors
- ✔ Community leaders
- ✔ Donors
- ✔ Staff
- ✔ Users of services
- ✔ Volunteers

Check out the sample planning-retreat agenda in File0701 for some guidance in organizing your own planning retreat. Pop in the CD or click the link in the table of contents to view this file.

One purpose of organizational planning is to bring stakeholders together in pursuit of a common goal. People work harder to achieve the goals when they're asked to help set the goals.

Guard against bias. Sometimes people get so close to the situation they're evaluating that they can't see the true picture with an objective eye. Include outside people who gain no personal benefit from the outcome.

Also, don't assume that all your stakeholders know what they're talking about in every instance. For example, if someone says that getting a grant to pay the costs of a program start-up is a piece of cake, check with potential funders before you agree that it's an easy task.

Yes, honesty can create conflict. Be prepared for it. Set some rules when going into planning meetings. Make sure that all the participants have a chance to state their cases. Arguments can be productive if they exchange ideas about what is best for the organization and don't disintegrate into shouting matches.

Calling in the SWOT team

One common way to analyze the information you've collected is to perform a SWOT analysis. *SWOT* is an acronym for strengths, weaknesses, opportunities, and threats. SWOT analysis is usually done in a facilitated meeting in which the participants have agreed-upon ground rules. If you prefer, however, stakeholders can complete their version of the analysis individually and then come together to discuss the results as a group.

We recommend using a professional meeting facilitator. A facilitator brings experience and a neutral viewpoint to the proceedings and can be effective in helping a group arrive at a consensus about organizational goals — even goals that may be unpopular with some staff or board members.

Be honest when looking at your organization's strengths and weaknesses. It's tempting, for example, to put the best face on the activities of the board of directors. They're volunteers, after all. How much time do they really have to give to the organization? But if you avoid identifying important deficiencies because you don't want to hurt someone's feelings, your planning efforts will be handicapped by bad information.

For example, the results of a SWOT analysis for an organization providing counseling services to unemployed adults may look something like the following:

Strengths

✔ The program staff is highly qualified and committed.

✔ Clients give program services a high-quality rating.

✔ The organization has an accumulated budget surplus equal to approximately five months of operating expenses.

✔ Program costs are funded largely by government grants.

Weaknesses

- ✔ The cost per client is higher than in similar programs.
- ✔ Contributed income from individuals is low.
- ✔ The programs aren't well known in the general public.

Opportunities

- ✔ Closure and shrinking of nearby industries indicate that the client base will increase over the next ten years.
- ✔ The organization has a new website that has attracted additional visitors.
- ✔ The organization has modest cash reserves to invest in growth.

Threats

- ✔ Local government (the primary funding source) projects a budget deficit during the next three fiscal years.
- ✔ Over the past five years, program costs have increased at a rate of 3 percent per year.

As this example shows, one or more items often can be listed as both strengths and weaknesses. Here, the fact that the organization is largely funded by the government is a strength, but it's also a weakness because it creates a situation in which the organization relies on a single source of funding.

A review of this SWOT analysis reveals an organization that has been successful in providing quality services and getting those services funded by government contracts. It has been financially prudent and developed modest cash reserves. However, the program's future may be in jeopardy if organizational change doesn't take place. Depending on one source of income for most revenue is a problem, especially because the primary funding entity apparently needs to make budget cuts in the next few years.

This organization has limited time and resources to begin to diversify revenues. If its government funding is cut completely, it will likely have to close, spending its cash reserve on connecting its clients to other services, meeting with its donors to thank them, telling stories of its clients' successes on its website, providing modest severance packages to loyal employees, and taking necessary accounting and legal steps to close.

If its government funding declines but doesn't cease, it has opportunities to develop an individual donor campaign led by the board of directors; meet with other nonprofits, local colleges, and business leaders about sharing job counseling and training services; and seeking coverage of its programs in the local media.

Mapping the matrix

One approach to planning that may work well as a tool to guide your organization is the creation of a *matrix map*. The matrix map encourages nonprofits to take a hard look at their "dual bottom line" — both how well the goods and services they provide address their mission and each of those services' costs and earning potential. To create a matrix map, you and your planning committee follow four steps:

✔ Identify each of your "lines of business" or activities.

✔ Assess how well each of those activities addresses your mission.

✔ Analyze how well each of those activities covers its costs either through fees and admissions or by attracting grants and contributions.

✔ Create a chart or matrix that illustrates how programs compare to one another according to value in addressing your mission and contribution to the organization's financial stability.

The result of this process — easily understood illustrations comparing an organization's programs — can help a planning committee choose among options. We include a sample matrix map in File0703.

Yet another approach is to develop new products and services that may appeal to foundations or garner the support of local businesses. Such services may help the organization further its mission and better serve its clients while also diversifying its donor base — a win-win-win situation.

A SWOT analysis can be a powerful guide to developing a plan because it looks at both your organization's inner workings and external environment. As your committee moves on to the next planning step, where you decide together on goals and strategies for coming years, it can refer to the SWOT analysis as a reminder to celebrate and further develop strengths, tackle weaknesses, and prepare for change.

File0702 contains an example of how you can map your organization's strengths, weaknesses, opportunities, and threats to determine your overall SWOT.

Putting the plan in writing

After the research, analysis, and discussion, it's time to determine future directions and put the results into a final plan. Ideally, the plans of the organization become apparent after sifting through and discussing the material assembled. If the planning group can't reach a consensus, it may want to test its ideas on the board of directors or a few trusted peers to help it come to an agreement.

It can be easy to come up with a long "laundry list" of goals and then skim lightly over the strategies you'll use to achieve them. We recommend limiting your goals to a half dozen or fewer and paying full attention to the related strategies.

Ensuring your goals make sense

Organizational goals need to be specific, measurable, and attainable within a set period of time. Don't set a goal like "In five years, the XYZ Tutoring Project will be the best tutoring program west of the Mississippi." You have no way to evaluate whether the organization is the best tutoring program west of the Mississippi, and even if you can determine the "best" program, the goal is so general and vague that you can't set objectives to achieve it.

Instead, an organizational goal for this program might be, "In five years, the XYZ Tutoring Project will provide tutoring services that are recognized by classroom teachers as effective in improving student performance." This goal can be measured. It's also attainable through implementing a series of strategies that may include better training for tutors, improved communication with classroom teachers to determine student needs, acquisition of computers to aid in tutoring sessions, and so on.

Itemizing the parts that form your plan

When you reach a consensus about your organization's goals, assemble a written plan. The components of the plan should include the following items, in the order shown:

- ✔ An executive summary
- ✔ A statement of the organizational mission
- ✔ A description of the planning process
- ✔ Organizational goals
- ✔ Strategies to achieve those goals
- ✔ Appendixes that contain summaries of the background material used to determine the plan, including a list of the people who participated in creating the plan

Assign the task of drafting the document to your best writer. When he finishes the draft, the planning committee should review it to ensure that the plan is stated clearly. Submit the final draft to the full board for discussion and adoption.

A common failing of planning documents (and grant proposals, for that matter) is the use of jargon and vague language. An organizational plan that uses such wording and lacks clarity is a poor guide and does nothing to increase your credibility with your constituents or your funders. You don't want readers to finish reading it and ask, "What is it that they're going to do?"

Check out File0704 to see an example of how an organizational plan may be presented.

Adjusting your plan as needed

Although having a plan is important, flexibility in its implementation is just as important. Things change. Reviewing your plan is an ongoing activity; at least once or twice a year, your board should revisit it to check on the progress you've made and identify whether assumptions and predictions were correct. You may find that you need to employ new strategies to achieve your carefully developed goals.

Putting Plans into Action

Unfortunately, too many well-crafted plans end up in a drawer or on a bookshelf. Participants may have expended great effort to create the document, and board and staff may have formed close bonds during the planning process. But if the decisions made during that wonderful board/staff retreat at the charming lakeside inn aren't translated into tasks, what's the point besides camaraderie?

No matter what sort of plan you create — organizational, fundraising, marketing, program, or facility-related — you need to break the larger, all-encompassing strategies into a sequence of steps that enables you to chart your progress over time. The following sections help you do that.

Defining and setting goals, strategies, objectives, and outcomes

Getting lost in all the terminology of planning is easy. Here are brief definitions of four common terms — goals, strategies, objectives, and outcomes — using a simple example of traveling from Chicago to New York to attend a professional conference:

✔ *Goals* are your organization's aspirations. Goals can be set at the organizational level, the program or department level, or the individual employee level. Using a road trip as an analogy, a goal is traveling from Chicago to New York.

✔ *Strategies* are approaches or ways to achieve goals. Usually, more than one option exists. You can travel to New York by several methods: plane, train, automobile, bicycle, or on foot. After considering the costs, your schedule, and your hiking ability, you decide to travel by car.

✔ *Objectives* are smaller steps that one must accomplish to reach a goal, and they're always stated in a way that can be measured. So on a trip from Chicago to New York, an objective may be to drive 325 miles on the first day. When you pull into the motel parking lot, you can check your odometer to see whether you've achieved your objective.

✔ *Outcomes* describe the results of reaching a goal. In this example, you reach the goal — New York — and learn useful information at your conference.

To see how all four terms come into play, look at the example of a development plan in Table 7-1. Reading from top to bottom, you have the whole plan, from organizational goal to outcome.

Table 7-1	Organizational Goal to Outcome
What We Call It	*Example*
Organizational goal	Diversify income
Strategy	Increase individual contributed income
Strategic goal	Develop a reliable annual campaign
Objective 1	Compile prospect list with your board's help
Objective 2	Create appeal letter
Objective 3	Mail appeal letters containing personal notes from board members
Outcome	Organization is less dependent on a single funder

Don't get bogged down in terms. How you label the different steps in your plan is less important than clarifying what you need to accomplish and the steps you'll take to succeed.

Creating a work plan

You can see in Table 7-1 that the objectives are general. Add a way of measuring them by stating how many prospects you want to acquire, how much the appeal costs to produce, and how many appeal letters you plan to mail, and the time frame for completing the appeal and generating income. But each objective in the table requires several steps. Here's where *work plans* come into play. Work plans break tasks into small steps so they can be easily managed.

Work plans are the nuts and bolts of planning. They're also called *action plans*. They contain strategies for achieving specific objectives, identify deadlines for completion, and note who's responsible for completing the task. A work plan answers the following questions for each objective:

- ✔ What is the end result? (If possible, quantify the results. For example, 3,000 letters will be mailed.)
- ✔ How long will it take to do the job?
- ✔ Who will be responsible for doing the job?
- ✔ What resources are needed?

A typical work plan may look like Table 7-2.

Table 7-2	Sample Work Plan: Create an Appeal Letter			
Objective	By When	By Whom	Resources Needed	Date Completed
Attend workshop on fundraising letters	February 28	Allen	Find workshop through the Foundation Center	February 26
Draft letter and seek feedback	March 15	Allen and board com-mittee	Committee meeting for feedback	March 15
Revise and copyedit letter	March 20	Ashley and Gina	Experienced editor	March 25

Work plans require that a job be broken down into smaller tasks. In Table 7-2, for example, the three objectives can be split into even smaller tasks.

Be aware that you can take the creation of a work plan to the point of absurdity. Don't make work plans so detailed and specific that writing the plan takes more time than doing the work that the plan specifies.

Planning for Programs

Program planning is such an important part of nonprofit work that we think it needs its own section. Nearly all nonprofit organizations provide a service of one sort or another. The organization provides services through programs. A small nonprofit may have only one. Larger nonprofits may have dozens. No matter how many programs you have, you may be thinking of adding a new one or changing the ones you have. We walk you through the process in the following sections.

Assessing needs

A *needs assessment* is an important part of program planning. If you're thinking of starting a new program, for example, a needs assessment to determine whether the program is necessary should be the first step you take.

A needs assessment is more or less a research project. You don't necessarily need to hold to the strict requirements of scientific inquiry, but just as you do when collecting information to help guide organizational planning, you should do everything possible to ensure that the information is accurate and free of bias.

Determining the questions to be answered

Your needs assessment should evaluate the answers to the following questions:

- ✔ **Are other organizations providing the same service?** Obviously, you don't want to duplicate services if another organization is already doing the job. If you believe that your competition isn't doing a good job, that's another question. Jump to the second point.

- ✔ **How many people might use the service?** Getting a good estimate of the number of people the new program will serve is important. Doing so helps you justify establishing the program and helps you plan for staff needs.

- ✔ **Can and will people pay for the service?** If so, how much? How many of the people you hope to serve will need discounted tuition or scholarships, for example?

- ✔ **Do we need to meet any special requirements for providing the program?** Does the program need to be near good public transportation? Is parking important? Will people come to the neighborhood where you're providing the services?

✔ **What are the trends?** Will the number of people using the service increase or decrease in the future? Is the population in your community increasing, decreasing, or staying the same? If you begin with 25 clients, how many clients do you expect to have in three years?

Finding the best data

Just as when you collect information for organizational planning, your goal in program planning is to get the most accurate, unbiased data available. Don't depend on only one source. Here are some ways to get the information you need:

✔ **Talk to colleagues in your community.** Ideally, you have relationships with the people and organizations that provide similar services. Ask their opinions about your ideas for new programming.

✔ **Look at census data.** The best sources for population information are the numbers collected through a census (www.census.gov). Some municipal and regional planning groups also publish population-growth projections. These projections are estimates, but census data doesn't represent an absolutely accurate count of the people in your community, either. Gather all the numbers you can get.

✔ **Visit a Foundation Center library.** By looking at funding trends, you can piece together a picture of what services are available and who is supporting them. You can find a Foundation Center library near you at www.foundationcenter.org or subscribe to its services online.

✔ **Get information from potential users of the service by distributing questionnaires and holding focus groups.** The questions you ask in large part determine the answers you get. If possible, find someone who has experience in preparing survey questions to give you a hand.

✔ **Look at similar programs in other communities.** Although you can't always depend on the experience of others fitting exactly with your particular situation, examining what others have done is always wise.

We've put together a needs assessment questionnaire (File0705) as an example of a simple survey.

Some people say they don't want to share an idea with others because they're afraid someone may steal it. Although you can't rule out the chances of this happening, we believe that it's a rare occurrence. In almost all cases, being open about your plans is a good idea.

Going beyond the needs assessment

Just because a new program is needed doesn't necessarily mean that your organization should be the one to start it. You need to take other factors into account. Consider the factors in the following sections when assessing your ability to start a new program.

Paying attention to the budget

A new program is almost always going to add expenses to your organizational budget. If we thought about it long enough, we could think of an example in which increased program costs aren't a factor, but we don't have all year.

To be sure that you don't get yourself into a financial hole, carefully project the extra costs you'll have from additional staff, increased space, equipment, and insurance. After you have solid expense projections, you have to project where you're going to find the added revenue needed to pay these costs.

Evaluating organizational and staff capability

Does your organization have the knowledge and expertise to provide the program services? This question may not be a concern if the proposed program is merely an extension of what you've been doing. If your organization is branching out into new areas, however, be sure that you or someone else in the organization has the credentials to provide a quality program.

Also pay attention to hidden staff costs. For example, consider whether your current program director will have sufficient time to provide adequate supervision for the new program. Will you need to hire a new staff person or consultant to implement the program? Is this a one-time cost or recurring cost to continue the program? Will this person require a computer, cellphone, insurance, or office space?

Remembering special requirements

Check whether you need additional licensing or accreditation to provide the program. This issue is especially important for human-services programs. For example, if you've been working with teenagers and want to expand to elementary and preschool children, find out whether your program space must meet additional building-code requirements in order to serve a younger client group.

Fitting it into the mission

From time to time, we're all tempted by the idea of doing something new. Gee, wouldn't it be nice if we could sell goldfish in the front lobby? But you have to ask yourself what selling goldfish has to do with your organization's mission. If you go too far afield, you can detract from the hard work of addressing your organizational purpose.

To explain your program, take a tip from the business sector

If you were starting a new business and looking for investors, one of the first things you'd do is create a business plan. Nonprofits are wise to follow this model when developing a new program. A business model is useful in explaining the program and can form the basics of grant proposals when you seek funding.

Business plans should include the following information:

✔ An executive summary that covers the main points of the plan.

✔ An explanation of the need for the program and who will use it. (This information is comparable to the market analysis in a for-profit business plan.)

✔ A description of the program and your strategies for implementing it.

✔ Why your organization is best poised to implement the program.

✔ Resumes and background information about the people who will provide and manage the program services.

✔ Three-year projections of income and expenses for the project, including an organizational budget for the current year.

Thinking long term

An idea that looks good today may not look good next year or the year after. Don't forget that costs rise year after year. Your staff appreciates occasional raises. Try to imagine where the program will be five and ten years into the future.

Funding sources may be available to launch a new program or expand services. But it's wise to have a plan for sustaining the program after it is launched by identifying funding sources for its ongoing support after the initial funding source is gone.

Doing program planning as a team

As with organizational planning, program planning should be done as a group exercise. It doesn't have to be as extensive as the organizational planning process, but you gain more acceptance of the new program and guard against omitting important details when you work with others to develop new programs.

Facility Planning: Finding a Place to Do Your Work

If your organization is grappling with a move to a new (or its first) office building, you're facing important decisions. And guess what? You need to write a plan!

This effort is likely to have three phases:

- ✔ Planning for your needs
- ✔ Identifying possible locations
- ✔ Analyzing the feasibility of the locations you find

How much space and of what kind?

Before you go out to seek a location, make a list of your organization's specific needs. If you've ever shopped for an apartment or house, you know that some features are critically important and some are desired but not essential. Breaking down your space needs by function and then including a list of general requirements helps. Consider current programs as well as programs you're planning to introduce in the near future.

To help you anticipate and specify all your organization's facility needs, we provide a link in File0709 to planning guides and a glossary of terms on the Nonprofit Finance Fund website, as well as its sample list of required spaces (File0706).

Location, location, location

Many nonprofit organizations have learned the hard way that having a beautiful new facility doesn't necessarily mean that their students, patients, or audiences will go there. We suggest that an organization conduct a simple marketing test of a location they're considering. This "test" may take the form of a written survey, interviews, or an open house/walk-through at the proposed site followed by a discussion with current constituents. Also, talk to nearby residents, merchants, and the local police, and spend time observing the site at different times of day.

Organizations often move to larger facilities when they want their programs to grow, and they discover the hard way that offering more seats, classes, or therapy sessions doesn't necessarily mean that they'll be used. Do you have clear evidence of growing demand for your services and that your organization's current physical space is inhibiting its growth? When you conduct your marketing test, you need to know whether more people will go to your new location: Reach out to both potential clients and your current followers.

Your ideal location may change over time as the neighborhood changes. Even if your organization has been based in one place for a long time, before signing a new lease, explore whether its location is still meeting its needs.

Owning, leasing, or taking a free ride

Stability, convenience, and cost — in addition to location — are key factors to consider when selecting your organization's home. In this section, we discuss the implications of ownership and leasing, or of accepting donated space.

In considering your real-estate choices, also consider your context. Is the real estate market changing? Are interest rates rising or falling? How well are tenants' rights protected by law? Is the building that you want to lease likely to be sold?

The pros and cons of owning

Because of the tax benefits of private homeownership, many people assume that owning a building is best for a nonprofit organization. Although a nonprofit's building can be a valuable asset, remember that a nonprofit is already exempt from paying most business taxes, so any interest it may pay on a mortgage or building loan isn't a deductible expense — it's just an expense.

Two possible advantages of building ownership include:

- ✔ **Ownership stabilizes costs.** If your organization is based in a real estate market where prices are rising, purchasing a building may help to prevent steep rent increases or an untimely eviction.

- ✔ **Ownership improves the public image of your organization.** Organizations owning their own buildings appear in the public eye to be stable institutions. This perception may help them raise money.

Major disadvantages of building ownership for nonprofits can be that it increases the staff's workload and requires a continuing investment. If the organization buys a building that's larger than its needs, it may become a landlord to others and must be prepared to advertise the property, negotiate leases, and manage maintenance and repairs. Whether or not it has tenants, it becomes fully responsible for the building's care. Rental income can be an unrelated business income. Check with a tax attorney for advice before entering into this type of arrangement.

If your nonprofit organization buys its own building, be sure to set aside a cash reserve for building maintenance. Otherwise, if a boiler explodes or the roof leaks, you may have to suspend operations for an extended period of time to fix the problem.

Considering renting

When you rent a home for your nonprofit organization, you're taking on costs that you need to cover month after month. Often these costs increase from year to year. Rent may not be the only such expense. Here are a few things you want to understand fully before signing a lease:

- ✔ What costs are covered? Is your nonprofit responsible for all or some of the utilities?
- ✔ How long is the lease and does it include options for you to renew it at a similar rate?
- ✔ If property or other taxes increase while you're a tenant, do you pay for the increase or does the landlord?
- ✔ Which repairs are the landlord's responsibilities and which ones are yours?
- ✔ Who's responsible for routine building maintenance?
- ✔ What will the landlord permit you to change about the building?

We recommend budgeting for your monthly building costs and your one-time move-in costs and creating a facility contingency fund to cover minor repairs or occasional expenses (from tree trimming to clogged plumbing).

Deciding whether to take a freebie if it's offered

Taking a free ride through the donation of space sounds wonderful, doesn't it? Indeed, it lowers your operating costs and enables you to use more of your resources for programs. But you must be willing to look a gift horse in the mouth.

A free building is worthwhile only if it's in the right location and is the right size. Doing effective work is very difficult in an inappropriate space. Ask yourself this: If the building weren't free, would you have chosen it for your nonprofit?

Making a move

Organizations with what seem to be straightforward plans for moving into new facilities often overlook the true costs of making such a move. Some spaces may need to be altered to suit your organization's needs. Even when you fit right into your new offices, you encounter one-time charges such as signs, cleaning deposits, phone and Internet hookups, and fees or deposits for starting up your utilities.

The most important *things* for you to move are your constituents. You want to make a thoughtful, sustained effort to invite them into your new facility.

Taking on a capital project

What if no existing building suits your organization's needs? You may just need to move some walls and expand the bathrooms, or you may be in for a major effort to substantially renovate a space or construct a new building. If you're one of these brave and hardy types, you want to read this part of the chapter along with Chapter 18, which addresses planning and raising money for building projects in greater detail.

Even a small organization with the right board and campaign leadership can manage a successful capital campaign if its expectations are reasonable. So can organizations whose projects are happening at the right place and at the right time — such as those organizations qualifying for redevelopment agency funds or low-interest bank loans for community development.

To determine whether your organization can manage a capital campaign, you need to plan (no surprise, right?). Your facility plan should ask hard questions, including the following:

✔ What will the project cost?

✔ Are your board members in a position to contribute to a capital campaign above and beyond their usual annual gifts to your organization?

✔ Do public or foundation resources in your region support capital projects? Are they likely contributors?

✔ Do you have staff knowledge and time to contribute to this effort?

We include several items on the CD and through the link in the table of contents that help you carefully think through a possible capital project, in particular Planned Change and Facilities (File0707) and links to online resources of the Nonprofit Finance Fund (included in File0709).

Having examined these preliminary questions, organizations that are considering capital campaigns often go through a planning step called a *feasibility study* — research most often led by a consultant who interviews people who support the organization and other generous donors in their communities whose grants and gifts are essential to its success. As with other types of planning, you're gathering information from key stakeholders, but you're focusing your attention on those who may become contributors. Through these interviews, the consultant estimates how much the organization is likely to raise with a capital campaign. Find out more about this practice in Chapter 18.

Chapter 8

Evaluating Your Work: Are You Meeting Your Goals?

In This Chapter

▶ Recognizing the need for evaluation

▶ Knowing what the evaluation process involves

▶ Looking at the results and implementing them

*H*ow do you know if your nonprofit organization is meeting its goals? How do you know if your approach is valid, your staff is qualified, and your clients benefit from what you do? When your nonprofit's resources are scarce, you may want to put all of them into providing direct benefits to the people you serve. But, wait. When resources are scarce, it's especially important that they be used in the best possible way. That's why you want to set aside some of the organization's time, money, and attention for evaluation.

Most organizations gather information during the normal course of doing their work. A good evaluation can be one in which you collect information in a consistent, systematic way and ask the right questions so you learn from its patterns and particulars. This chapter outlines what goes into a meaningful evaluation and explains how to interpret the results and implement any necessary changes.

We use the word "evaluation" as a general term in this chapter to mean any act of reflecting upon the quality and success of your nonprofit's work. Some professionals differentiate between "assessment" and "evaluation." From their perspective, "assessment" means the ongoing use of measures or tools (such as exams or surveys) to indicate progress being made, and "evaluation" means a systematic, rigorous comparison of one's results to defined expectations, standards, or another program.

Realizing the Importance of Evaluation

Unlike for-profit businesses, nonprofits can't evaluate their performance solely by showing a profit at the end of the year or increasing the value of their stock. Indeed, they may generate a budget surplus to invest in their future work, but that isn't their primary purpose. Some people say that nonprofits have to achieve a "double bottom line," one in which their finances are healthy and their activities are meeting their goals. That's where evaluation comes in: It can measure how successful you've been at focusing on your purpose and achieving those challenging goals.

Indeed, continually evaluating your work is so important that it goes hand in hand with every aspect of leading and managing your organization. An evaluation can:

- ✔ Tell you if your planning strategies are working and whether you need to adjust them
- ✔ Guide you in hiring the right staff for the work to be done and in making good use of volunteers' time and energies
- ✔ Help you draft your annual budget by pointing out where resources are most needed
- ✔ Convey the information you need to market your work to the constituents you wish to serve
- ✔ Strengthen your fundraising by arming you with information for reports on your work to foundations and donors

In short, to know where you're going, you need to know where you've been. Evaluation can tell you whether you're on the right road or need to recalibrate your route.

Not every organization or project requires the same level of evaluation. If you're trying something brand new, you may take a "light touch" approach to track what has been done, measure whether activities were finished in a timely way, compute whether your cost projections were accurate, and count how many people took advantage of your programs.

Working through the Evaluation Process

You've probably been part of evaluation processes before, whether a personal performance evaluation or a program evaluation, but maybe you've never been in charge of the entire process. Not to fear. This section provides an outline of the process, gives you some pointers about what to evaluate, and helps you select who will perform the evaluation.

Evaluations have three main components:

- ✔ **Setting up an evaluation:** This step involves determining what type of evaluation you need to perform, asking the right questions, assigning someone the responsibility to gather and analyze the information you need to answer those questions, and deciding where and how you'll find that information.

- ✔ **Conducting the evaluation:** During this step, you gather the information you need in a consistent manner and measure what you're learning in an honest (perhaps self-critical) way. You may find that you need to devise tools to gather that information — such as surveys of constituents, focus groups, formal observations, or one-on-one interviews.

- ✔ **Interpreting the data:** In almost all cases, your understanding will be deeper (and your findings more valid) if you compare the information you compile to something else. That "something else" may be results for the people you serve before they participated in your program. It may be results for people who didn't take part in any comparable program (a placebo). Or it may be results for people who participated in a different kind of program. We address this stage in the "Analyzing Results and Putting Them to Work" section at the end of the chapter.

Selecting the right kind of evaluation

Evaluations come in many varieties. The type you choose will depend on whether a program is brand new or has been refined, how much is known about what works in the field in which you're operating, whether you want to prove that your approach is a model that can influence others, and how much money you have to invest in evaluation.

Your organization may consider these two basic types of evaluation:

- ✔ **Formative evaluation,** in which you analyze the progress of your non-profit's work while it's in process.

- ✔ **Summative evaluation,** in which you come to the end of a phase or a project and look back on its accomplishments.

Now that you can drop these terms easily into conversations, let us introduce three other kinds of evaluation you want to know:

- ✔ **Process evaluation:** Did the project do what it was supposed to do and on schedule? Did you acquire an office, hire three key staff, promote programs, or sign up participants? Very good. In your process evaluation, tell your readers about the steps you took — the story of your program activities.

✔ **Goal-based evaluation:** In a goal-based evaluation, you measure what took place and compare it to the original intentions. Did the project reach its goals? For example, your goal may be to "establish a tuberculosis awareness program in the southeastern quadrant of the city that reaches 500 individuals during its first year." Determining whether a program was established is simple; figuring out how many people the program actually reached is a little more difficult. This answer depends, of course, on what method the project is using to reach people. In other words, you must define what you mean by "reach" before you start measuring the program's results.

✔ **Outcomes (or impact) evaluation:** In an outcomes evaluation, you ask whether you met your objectives and outcomes. Did the project have the desired outcome and make a meaningful difference? Although it requires time and attention, this type of evaluation is relatively straightforward. For example, if you oversee a tuberculosis awareness program, a desired outcome may be increased numbers of people being tested for TB and, if they have contracted it, taking their medication consistently to improve their health and reduce the likelihood they will infect others. Evaluating such an outcome requires an in-depth study of the population in that section of the city to determine whether they acted on the knowledge they gained and — if they were infected — continued to follow a strict regimen for taking their medication. Public health department data about rates of tuberculosis infections can be tracked yearly for the neighborhoods served.

One of the hardest and most important things to ascertain in an outcomes evaluation is whether your organization has set the most meaningful objectives and outcomes.

Planning for evaluation

Before you jump into launching a new organization or program, we strongly recommend that you decide how you're going to evaluate it. That way, from the beginning you can set up methods for collecting information, identify who will be responsible, and budget for the costs. By establishing an evaluation plan at a program's inception, you can collect initial information about the people or places you plan to serve so you have data to which you can compare your results.

You want to gather baseline information about the people you serve. Trying to backtrack later to re-create such information is profoundly difficult.

Shaping an outcomes evaluation

As an example of shaping an outcomes evaluation, let's say your organization provides shelter to people who don't have homes. You may have identified the following aspirations:

Objective 1: Provide temporary housing to an average of 40 people per night over the course of a year.

Objective 2: Twenty people per month complete counseling to identify barriers to their finding and maintaining secure housing.

Objective 3: Fifteen people per month enroll with local and federal subsidized housing programs.

Outcome 1: Over the course of one year, 25 percent of the people who took advantage of nightly shelter beds, counseling, and connections to subsidy programs secure long-term, affordable housing.

If this were your organization and your evaluation to devise, you could measure whether you met the first three objectives by keeping intake records for people staying at your organization and taking advantage of its counseling and referral services. It would be harder to measure the outcome, but possible if you had good working relationships with the local and federal housing program staffs or if part of your organization's work involved sending out case workers to check on former clients to see how they're doing.

If you want to consider whether you've established the right objectives and outcomes or whether there may be a better way to serve your constituents, you can do the following:

✔ Survey your constituents to find out how they lost their housing and ask what they think they most need to maintain a stable place to live.

✔ Talk to colleagues (perhaps partners at the local and federal programs with which you're working) about gaps in services available to people who lack stable housing.

✔ Invest in research into your region's job and housing markets, and investigate the types of mortgages that were common to people who lost their homes. You may find that your best goal is to address some of the root causes of your constituents' situation.

As you set up your evaluation, first identify the purpose and audience. Are you trying a risky new approach to offering a program? Do you need to fulfill requirements of a government contract? Are you expected by a foundation to share your results with peer organizations doing similar work? Are there standard practices or protocols in your field that your evaluation should follow? Are you hoping to publish your results to be read by a general audience? Or, do you just want to share what you learn with your board and staff to make program adjustments and strengthen your work?

Before you design elaborate surveys and interview plans, ask yourself what information your nonprofit already has at hand. It may include attendance records, referrals from other nonprofits, unique visitors to your website, instructors' progress reports, numbers of trees planted, and many other data points that can illustrate your program's progress and reputation.

Even if you're evaluating your work because you need to fulfill contract or grant requirements, be sure to share and discuss what you discover with your board and staff. Strong nonprofit organizations remain self-critical, learn from their work, and press themselves to do better.

Does your evaluation need to be completed on a particular timeline? Whether that timeline is short or long can affect whether you undertake a simpler or more elaborate evaluation plan.

Also critical are the resources you have at hand to invest in your evaluation. "Resources" may include money to pay for consultants, invest in focus groups, or purchase data sets. The term also includes staff and volunteer time. We've heard estimates that an organization's taking on a rigorous evaluation will require 15 percent of the executive director's time. We can't swear that is an accurate estimate, but it's a valuable reminder that staff oversight and leadership are needed even if you hire experts to manage the work.

The Regional Nonprofit Alliance, based at Ohio University, offers an excellent primer on evaluation that includes a list of best practices, and the W.K. Kellogg Foundation offers a primer on evaluation for its grantees. We provide links to both resources in File0801.

Crafting valuable questions

The most important (and often the hardest) step to take in evaluating your nonprofit organization's work is to ask the right questions. What do you need to know to understand whether you've been successful?

If your organization has written a long-range plan, an obvious place to begin is by looking at the measurable objectives defined in that plan and asking whether you've met them. You may want to push yourself harder and ask whether you met your outcomes, which describe longer-term change you intend to achieve.

Some other topics nonprofits often ask about when evaluating their work are:

- ✔ **Cost-benefit:** What does it cost per person to provide the service? Is that more or less than an industry standard? If you have multiple programs, does the one that is being studied cost more or less per person than others?

- ✔ **Sustainability:** Have you been able to raise the funds needed to continue the program? Have you been able to retain qualified staff?

- ✔ **Staff and board reflection:** What are you learning from your work? What have you done well, and what has surprised you?

- ✔ **Participation:** Are you attracting the people you intended to serve?

✔ **Client satisfaction:** What do your constituents say about the program? Do they refer others to it? Do they believe their suggestions and criticisms are taken seriously?

✔ **Volunteer engagement:** Are you attracting and retaining volunteers? How do they rate their satisfaction with their participation? Do they refer others to your volunteer opportunities?

✔ **Best practices:** If you work in a field in which studies have identified the traits of effective programs, does your program have those traits?

✔ **Context:** Has the context in which you offer your services changed? How has that affected the people you serve? Have their needs changed?

✔ **Critical feedback:** What do experts (theater critics, researchers, and so on) have to say about your work and how it compares to the work of others?

✔ **Model program:** Are you recognized by others for the quality of the program? Are you called upon to share your approach and advise others?

Don't be afraid to ask yourself, "What needs to happen for our nonprofit to no longer be needed?" Maybe it's that streams and creeks are running free, a healthy marsh system is in place, and your town's low-lying areas are no longer flooding. This answer may seem far away from what you can achieve in three or five years, but it's valuable to ask the question and remind yourself that your nonprofit wasn't created to operate forever, but rather to work toward achieving a meaningful outcome.

Choosing evaluators: inside or outside?

One key decision you must make about your program evaluation is who will be responsible for conducting it. The work may involve gathering information from a number of staff members and clients and, after that information is compiled, analyzing what it means. You need one or more people to:

✔ Design the evaluation plan and clarify the questions to be asked

✔ Create the evaluation tools (surveys, interview protocols, and so on) if needed

✔ Collect the information to be analyzed (or train others to collect it)

✔ Organize and analyze the findings and write a report

If you're undertaking a simple process evaluation, a well-organized and fair-minded staff member can be put in charge. Who else can better understand the purpose of the organization and the nuances of what it's trying to do than someone who is directly involved in the work? To institute some checks and balances in the process, one person may be responsible for compiling the information, and then a team of staff or board members may discuss its interpretation before a report is written.

"Inside" evaluation offers several advantages. It's usually less costly than hiring an outsider, and the insider doesn't need to be briefed on the work of the nonprofit. On the other hand, the selected person may not be trained in evaluation, and some staff members may resent having their work judged by a fellow staff member. It may also be difficult for those who are steeped in the day-to-day work of a nonprofit to step back and cast a critical eye over it. Their closeness to the work may bias the findings.

A person who works inside of your organization may do a good job of reporting on whether programs are meeting their goals. It can be harder for that person to recommend other approaches that may be more effective.

If you're undertaking a more complex evaluation, you may want to hire a professional evaluator who knows your field and who writes well. In hiring such a person, you gain the advantages of his or her expertise in research methods, knowledge of the work of comparable organizations, and lack of bias in interpreting the information collected. An assessment made by an independent evaluator may be taken more seriously by your funders and peers. We can't claim that anyone who is paid a fee by your nonprofit to work for you is 100 percent unbiased: He or she may hope to be hired again in the future.

What if you have a modest budget and still want good consulting practices to be worked into your evaluation? Three approaches we've used in the past have been to:

- Contact local colleges and universities to see if a graduate student or faculty member is interested in evaluating your work for academic credit, a dissertation, or a publication.

- Hire an evaluation firm to design your tools and protocols, train your staff to implement them, and then write an independent analysis of your findings after your staff has compiled them.

- Compile information to be evaluated internally, share it with an evaluator, and hire him or her to analyze and write about the findings.

Conducting Your Evaluation

After you have thought through the planning steps, refined the questions to be asked, chosen your tools for measuring results, and put the right person in charge of your evaluation, doing the work to study your program or nonprofit is relatively easy. You'll want to decide on a time frame (either one discrete period or a defined number of days or hours per month) for conducting your study and stick to it. If someone on your staff is responsible for the evaluation, be careful that the individual isn't pulled away by other tasks.

If you are using a survey, exam, or checklist for making observations, you'll want to make sure it's designed by someone who knows how to word and structure such a tool. (We write more about surveys in Chapter 12.) How that tool is used is just as important as its design: If several staff members or volunteers are helping to collect data, be sure to brief them as a group before they begin so everyone is recording the information consistently. Of course, you'll want to check for and insist on accuracy and thoroughness. Data is meaningless if it's gathered inconsistently.

Analyzing Results and Putting Them to Work

Imagine that you've collected and organized the information that will tell you what you want to know about your organization. It's at hand in lists and charts and graphs. Now you know whether your programs are outstanding and whether your clients' lives are enhanced by your work.

Wait! Not so fast. Just as you must decide on the right questions to investigate as you set out on your evaluation, you need to ask questions of the data you've compiled. Having data and descriptive information isn't the same thing as having knowledge and understanding. Now you must interpret the information and decide how to apply it.

Evaluation software can help you organize and review your findings. Idealware's "Understanding Software for Program Evaluation" can help you choose among good options. We provide a link in File0801.

Interpreting results

Although it may seem unscientific, we suggest that before you look closely at the information compiled, you ask yourself what your hunches are. What do you think it will show you? Be honest with yourself: What do you think the findings are going to show, and what do you wish they would show?

Often a moment of insight comes when the pattern revealed in the data isn't what you expected to find. After identifying any such surprises, you can probe more deeply to ask why and how those results didn't meet expectations.

After you've read the data against your assumptions, it's time to look at it anew as if you had no expectations. What general picture does it present? What stands out? Is the information consistent over the course of the year, or does it vary — perhaps according to the season, age of participants, or changes in your staff?

Asking more of the data

Any finding, be it positive or negative, is worth probing more deeply. Let's take the case of an education policy and advocacy group as an example. The group invested in a communications manager and an improved website and data systems to expand its reach. When it wanted parents and other community members to know about legislation under review in the state senate or assembly, it sent alerts by e-mail and through social media posts.

Because the group was using the web and social media as its programmatic tools, it made sense for the group to look at its online analytics, many of which looked good:

✔ Its e-mail list was growing steadily, and the click-through rate to its website was higher than the industry average.

✔ The number of unique visitors to its website grew from month to month, and, on average, visitors read three pages when they went there.

✔ The number of people who "liked" the group on Facebook grew steadily, and many of them shared its posts with others.

✔ A small but gradually expanding number of people followed its tweets.

These are good signs of a growing online presence, but it's still worth asking whether the people who like the group on Facebook also take action and contact their representatives or talk to their school boards about the subjects raised. Social media friends and followers are a good thing, but do they include people with influence in local or state government or education policy?

As is true in many cases, the depth and quality of involvement of people in this organization can be more important to its success than the total numbers of passive fans.

We recommend that you include others in this exercise — ask a few key staff and board members and maybe even a few of your constituents. What do they see? What is surprising to them? Of course, if you hired an evaluation consultant, let his or her experience guide you at this phase.

Although you don't want to confuse people with ambivalent or "anything goes" interpretations, having more than one point of view can be valuable. Bring a balanced perspective to the findings: Don't embrace all the praise and discount all the criticism (or vice versa). You can learn from both.

Using your evaluation to strengthen your work

You've looked at your evaluation findings with trusted colleagues; you've turned them inside out and upside down to see them from every angle. Now it's time to interpret them, to tell their story. Likely what you've discovered is not all positive and not all negative. Likely you've noticed that some services are rated more highly than others and some short-term objectives have been met, but others remain elusive. It's time to step back from your organization and programs, and acknowledge any disappointing results and set short-term and long-term goals to improve upon them.

A program may be flawed in its design, in how it's executed, or in who is leading it; and its effectiveness can be smothered by external circumstances that are beyond its control — a shift in the economy or demographics, a change in public policy, or even a natural disaster can derail it.

Some changes will be obvious and easy to do. Maybe a different program schedule would be more convenient for working parents, or better training for volunteers would make them feel more involved and successful. When your findings don't suggest easy responses, turn to ideas from others — best practices in your field, model programs, or scholarly research. Don't forget to ask the clients you serve.

Evaluation findings also should be shared with your board, which is ultimately responsible for your nonprofit's fulfilling its mission and purpose. It may decide that some programs aren't a good investment of the nonprofit's hard-won resources and recommend cutting them.

Telling the truth

If your evaluation results are disappointing, face them honestly and share what you've discovered. You may share them discreetly with your board or with the funders who know you well, but doctoring your data or analyzing the findings in a disingenuous way can hurt the reputation of your organization and of your evaluation consultant, if you hired one. And all that time and effort you put into your evaluation is lost if you allow it to sit on a shelf collecting dust.

These days the public deeply values transparency. Unless your report contains confidential information, we recommend that you create an executive summary of your findings and publish them as a brochure or PDF available through your website or shared with donors.

You may find that a poor evaluation lowers staff morale, but if those staff members are invited to participate in creative problem solving, improving customer service, and other goal-setting activities, working with the evaluation can contribute to building their teamwork and resolve.

Ultimately, it's important that you yourself embrace and attempt to understand the evaluation findings. Many of us start nonprofits based on our ideals, and many of us work long hours with limited resources to achieve very ambitious results. Achieving those results depends on collecting good information to guide you and interpreting that information with integrity and resolve.

At the end of the day, the purpose of your evaluation is to benefit your nonprofit organization.

Chapter 9

Getting the Work Done with Volunteers

*V*olunteers are the lifeblood of the nonprofit sector. The Bureau of Labor Statistics reports that more than 26 percent of the U.S. population over age 16 performed some kind of volunteer work during the 12-month period ending in September 2012. That's a lot of people — 64.5 million!

Just about every nonprofit charitable organization uses volunteers in some capacity. For example, in most cases, board members serve without compensation. And for many nonprofit organizations in the United States, volunteers do all the work, from planting the trees to paying the bills. Even if your organization employs paid staff, volunteers still provide valuable service. Organizations depend on volunteers to staff telephone hotlines, lead scout troops, provide tutoring, coach youth sports teams, serve hot meals, organize fundraising events, and stuff envelopes. So if you're going to manage a nonprofit organization, you need to know how to work with volunteers.

Of course, you may be sitting in your office asking, "Where are these millions of volunteers?" This chapter offers suggestions to help you decide what kind of volunteers you need, figure out how to find them, and keep them happy after they arrive.

Understanding Why People Volunteer

The classic stereotype of a volunteer is someone who has lots of time to spare and is looking for something to do. Although this perception may have been true in the past, when many women stayed out of the workforce and gave their free time to charity, that stereotype no longer fits. It's true that more women volunteer than men, but people between the ages of 35 and 44 are the likeliest to volunteer. This is the age range when both men and women are probably balancing careers with raising families, not to mention taking care of aging parents, going to the gym, and keeping up with e-mail and social media accounts.

Why is it that people, even very busy ones, volunteer their time? We think it's because they've recognized the benefits of volunteering time to a favorite organization and because nonprofit organizations have become smarter about asking them.

Understanding why people volunteer makes it easier for you to find volunteers, organize their work, and recognize their contributions. However, not everyone is motivated by the same factors. People volunteer for a variety of reasons, including their desire to

- ✔ **Help the community and others.** Helping others usually comes to mind first when people think of the reasons that people volunteer. But as you see when you read deeper into this list, volunteers' motives aren't always this simple.

- ✔ **Express their values.** Believing in an organization's mission is an important motivator for volunteers. If a person believes it's important for all children to have access to a quality education, she will be more likely to volunteer at her local school or tutoring program.

- ✔ **Increase self-esteem.** Volunteering makes people feel better about themselves. Giving a few hours a week, or even a month, to an organization creates good feelings.

- ✔ **Help out their friends.** Friends are often the first people we turn to when we need help. Volunteering is also a great way to get together with friends on a regular basis.

- ✔ **Make new friends.** Volunteering is usually a social activity. People use this opportunity to meet interesting people who share their interests and values.

- ✔ **Try out a job.** People considering a job in the nonprofit sector often discover that volunteering is a good way to get a peek at what happens on the inside.

- ✔ **Polish their résumés.** Adding volunteer experience to a résumé shows a commitment to helping others or to working in a particular field.

- ✔ **Develop new skills.** A volunteer job often gives people an opportunity to learn how to do something they didn't already know how to do.

- ✔ **Enjoy something they love.** Many volunteer jobs come with intrinsic benefits for their participants. Ushers at the symphony get to hear the music. Gardeners removing invasive plants from a native plant preserve get to spend a day in a beautiful natural setting.

Keep this list in mind, and you'll realize that you don't have to focus your recruitment efforts exclusively on retired people or others who have a lot of leisure time. If you provide an environment in which volunteers can bring their friends, meet others who share their interests, and learn new skills, you can lure even the busiest people into helping. Remember that you have no reason to be apologetic about asking for help: Volunteering benefits those people who step forward to assist you.

Designing a Volunteer Program

Most start-up organizations depend on volunteers because money to pay staff is unavailable. But a lack of resources isn't the only thing that drives a nonprofit to operate with an all-volunteer staff. Some nonprofits make a deliberate decision to operate solely with volunteers to contain their costs and to achieve results with a collective effort among people who care deeply enough to contribute their time and effort.

Considering a volunteer coordinator

Although volunteers don't expect to be paid every two weeks, that doesn't mean they come without costs. Recruiting, training, managing, retaining, and thanking volunteers require effort from someone in the organization. We recommend assigning someone the job of *volunteer coordinator,* a person responsible for overseeing or performing the following duties:

- ✔ **Recruiting:** Volunteers don't grow on trees. Depending on how many volunteers you need and the turnover rate of current volunteers, recruiting may be a continuous process.

- ✔ **Training:** Volunteers don't come to work knowing everything they need to know. They can do any job for which they're qualified, but don't expect them to know the ropes until they're told what to do and how to do it.

✓ **Scheduling:** Volunteers need a schedule. Scheduling is even more important if your organization uses volunteers to staff an office or manage other tasks that require regular hours.

✓ **Appreciating:** Volunteers need to know that their work is valuable to the organization. This item is the last on our list, but it may be the most important. You don't have to pass out plaques, but we do recommend heartfelt acknowledgment. Saying thank you and acknowledging the impact made by volunteers on a regular basis is essential to retaining your volunteers.

If your organization depends heavily on or is staffed exclusively by volunteers, consider recruiting your volunteer coordinator from among board members or more-experienced volunteers. You can create committees to take responsibility for many jobs, but some detail-oriented tasks — such as scheduling or bill paying — are better managed by a single responsible person.

Determining your need for volunteers

Look around your nonprofit organization and decide how many volunteers you need and what functions they can perform. We recommend creating (or helping your volunteer coordinator create) a schedule of tasks to be completed — planning what needs to be done and how many people it will take to do the work. Table 9-1 lists the kinds of volunteer assignments you may jot down. By having such a list and prioritizing the tasks, you know what to do when an unexpected volunteer walks in the door.

Table 9-1	Sample Volunteer Task List	
Task	*Number of People*	*Time*
Data entry — donor list	1 person	3 hours per week
Newsletter mailing	4 people	5 hours per month
Lawn cleanup	1 person	2 hours per week
Childcare	2 people	3 hours on Saturdays
Filing	1 person	2 hours per week

It's possible to have too many volunteers. Almost nothing is worse than asking people to help and then finding you have nothing for them to do. You may want to have both your chart of immediate tasks (such as Table 9-1) and a few back-burner projects — such as sorting team uniforms by size or taking inventory in the supply cabinet — in case you end up with more people than you need on a given day.

In the beginning, you may have to experiment before you know exactly how many volunteers you need for a particular job. For example, you may eventually discover that a 2,000-piece mailing takes about five hours for four people to complete. You also may find that preparing the soil and planting 700 seedlings takes two volunteers a full day.

Writing volunteer job descriptions

Volunteers perform better if they know what they're supposed to do. Preparing job descriptions for volunteer positions also helps you supervise better and know what skills you're looking for in volunteers. (Take a look at Chapter 10 for detailed information on writing a job description.)

Volunteer job descriptions should be even more complete than paid-employee job descriptions. And if you can break jobs into small tasks, all the better, because volunteers often share the same job. For example, a different person may answer the office telephone each day of the week. In that case, to bring consistency to the job, you can keep by the telephone a job description that includes a list of telephone procedures, staff extensions, frequently used telephone numbers, and other important information.

See File0901 and File0902 for some sample volunteer job descriptions. Pop in the CD or click the link in the table of contents to view these files.

Organizing volunteers

Many nonprofits invite their volunteers to participate in committees. These committees enable volunteers to step forward, offer their best skills, and learn how to do new things. An advantage of forming committees is that it reinforces the social benefits of volunteering. As committee members get to know one another and figure out how to manage their tasks successfully, you or your volunteer coordinator can step back and let them take full responsibility.

Here's a fictitious example that gives you an idea of how to organize committees: A small nonprofit called the Sunshine and Health Project provides telephone referral and information sources for people seeking help with weight loss. It was started by three people who had lost weight and decided to help others do the same. A ten-member board of directors provides governance for Sunshine and Health Project and undertakes key volunteer roles in the organization. The board forms the following committees, which are each chaired by a board member but made up of individuals who provide volunteer services:

✔ **Telephone committee:** Sunshine and Health Project provides most of its services via telephone. The office receives about 60 calls each day from people seeking information about weight loss and referrals to health clinics and counselors. The telephones are answered 12 hours a day, from 9 a.m. to 9 p.m., Monday through Friday. Two volunteers share responsibility for the phones in three-hour shifts. The nonprofit needs 40 volunteers each week to answer phones and provide information. Sunshine and Health Project also needs backup volunteers in case someone is ill or can't make his shift for some other reason.

✔ **Program committee:** This committee researches programs to which callers can be referred, maintains the database containing referral information, and provides training to telephone volunteers. Committee members include one physician and two registered nurses, all of whom provide professional oversight.

✔ **Publicity committee:** Sunshine and Health Project uses several methods to tell the public that its services are available. The publicity committee prepares and sends news releases and creates and distributes public service announcements to radio stations. In addition, the committee operates a speakers' bureau of people who have benefited from Sunshine and Health Project's services. The committee has also developed a website, a Twitter feed connected to any news that is posted on the website, and a Facebook page; each of these outlets offers basic information about weight loss and invites readers to sign up for a monthly e-mail newsletter. The website maintains links to recommended programs in cities across the United States and Canada.

✔ **Fundraising committee:** Sunshine and Health Project raises funds in several different ways, including annual family-oriented walk-a-thons, e-mail appeal letters sent to people who have joined its contact list through its website, and gifts from businesses promoting a healthy lifestyle. Committee members plan and coordinate the fundraising events, write and transmit the appeal letters, and make personal calls on the business sponsors. They also call upon all volunteers to make personal gifts, identify possible donors, and provide lists of contacts.

✔ **Administration committee:** Sunshine and Health Project receives individual donations from people who use its services, grants from foundations, and limited support from the health department in the city in which it's based. The administration committee is responsible for maintaining the organization's financial books, writing thank-you letters to donors, and maintaining a database of past donors.

You may discover other tasks that can be assigned to additional volunteer committees. The kinds of jobs that need to be done vary, depending on the type of service your organization provides. The point to remember is that volunteer work needs to be organized (and supervised) in much the same way that paid work is organized.

In an all-volunteer organization, the responsibility for ensuring that the work is finished appropriately resides with the board of directors. The board must be committed to finding new volunteers and supervising their work. And board members must be ready to step in to do a job if no volunteers can be found.

Board members who also serve as program volunteers must remember to keep their roles as board members (governance and fiduciary) separate from their roles as program volunteers. In the latter case, the volunteers are operating like staff, not board members. Yes, there is a difference. See Chapter 6 for information about understanding and defining board members' roles.

Hunting for Volunteers

Most organizations are always on the lookout for volunteers. After all, volunteers move away, get tired, lose interest, or take new jobs with new hours. If your organization depends on volunteers, you probably need to maintain an ongoing recruitment process. This section shows you how.

Using the tried-and-true methods

To cast a wide net, you want to use more than one method to find volunteers, and you don't want to spend much money on those methods. After all, you're looking for free help. Persistence matters: Good volunteer recruitment is like a healthy habit that you want to repeat. Here are a few of the most common and most successful methods for recruiting volunteers:

- **Placing announcements in the media:** Newspapers and radio and television stations sometimes publish or air short public service announcements for nonprofit organizations. (Head to Chapter 12 for more information about writing and distributing news releases.)

- **Posting fliers:** Grocery stores, churches, coffee shops, college campuses, laundromats, schools, and civic buildings often have bulletin boards where you can post announcements. For best results, place them thoughtfully. For instance, put your call for foster homes for kittens at the pet food store and your community garden poster at the plant nursery.

- **Taking advantage of word of mouth:** Encourage your current volunteers to recruit others. Have a "bring a friend" day with time for socializing. Ask your volunteers to post your posters in their places of business, and don't forget to invite your own friends and associates.

- **Contacting schools and churches:** Both of these institutions look for ways for students and members to get involved in community service. *Service learning* — through which students learn about a topic by volunteering in their communities — is a growing practice. In fact, many high schools and colleges maintain centers for community relations and student volunteering.

Don't forget to reach out to the young people in your area. By doing so, you benefit from their skills and ideas, and you also contribute to training the next generation of volunteers!

- **Relying on clubs and fraternal groups:** Many professional and social clubs include serving the community in their missions. From Kiwanis International and local Elks lodges to the Junior League, chamber of commerce, and campus-based sororities and fraternities, clubs and membership groups can be excellent volunteer resources.

- **Approaching corporations and businesses:** In some communities, businesses look for community involvement opportunities for their employees. If a company has a community relations, community affairs, or corporate giving department, it's likely to be a good place to begin asking about employee volunteers.

Using the web

Finding volunteers may be as easy as booting up your computer. Besides posting volunteer listings on your organization's website, you also can post on other sites. Several organizations maintain web databases where your organization can list its volunteer needs. Prospective volunteers can search the databases by ZIP code and the type of volunteer work available. Check out the following sites:

- **VolunteerMatch** (www.volunteermatch.org) invites nonprofits to set up accounts identifying the kinds of volunteers they need.

- **Points of Light** (www.pointsoflight.org) manages several projects linking volunteer centers to one another. Its HandsOn Network links volunteers at 250 centers in 16 countries to meaningful projects. It also operates networks for youth volunteers, alums of AmeriCorps who want to continue volunteering, and corporate volunteers.

- **Idealist** (www.idealist.org) and **Craigslist** (www.craigslist.org) are other widely used tools for finding volunteers.

- **Service Leader** (www.serviceleader.org/vv) maintains the Virtual Volunteering Project, which can connect your organization with volunteers who aren't physically located near your office. Maybe you can use online volunteers to tutor students, answer questions via e-mail, help write grants or news releases, or consult on designing your website.

- ✔ **United Way** (www.unitedway.org) may have a volunteer tutoring or mentoring program in your area.

- ✔ **Youth Service America** (www.ysa.org) helps you involve young volunteers in your work. It organizes an annual Global Youth Service Day and other opportunities for volunteers between the ages of 5 and 25.

Nonprofit organizations also recruit volunteers through their pages on social networking sites, such as Facebook (www.facebook.com), Twitter (www.twitter.com), and LinkedIn (www.linkedin.com). To get your name out there, create a page for your organization. These platforms work particularly well when you describe specific activities that your contacts can do to assist your nonprofit, and when people who know your organization well post photographs and news for their friends to read. Their networks extend your nonprofit's reach. Remember, opportunities to do things with friends motivate many people to volunteer. Chapter 12 provides more information about using social media to make friends and influence people.

Looking for volunteers at other organizations

No, we don't suggest that you steal volunteers from other nonprofits, but some organizations do exist to provide volunteer help. Many communities have volunteer centers that participate in a national network of organizations that recruit and place volunteers in nonprofits.

Similarly, the Corporation for National and Community Service (www.nationalservice.gov) was established by Congress in 1993 to operate AmeriCorps, Senior Corps, the Social Innovation Fund, and the Volunteer Generation Fund. This agency is charged with encouraging national service through volunteering and helping nonprofits and public agencies make the best use of this resource. The corporation awards grants that help organizations strengthen their community through the use of volunteers.

If your organization wants to take advantage of a program offered by the Corporation for National and Community Service, you may need to apply for a federal or state grant, which usually requires sound accounting procedures and extensive reporting of program activities. Turn to Chapters 16 and 17 for information about government grants.

> ## Using the web to recruit volunteers
>
> Take tips from other nonprofits about ways to reach out to and invite volunteers through your website. Remember, you can do much more than describe your nonprofit on your website or social media pages: You can even put people to work for you who don't step inside your nonprofit's doors. Among many fine examples, four sites that inspire involvement are:
>
> ✔ **DoSomething.org** (`www.dosomething.org`): This social networking site invites people to identify causes they care about and then volunteer. Its use of strong visual imagery, surveys, and clearly described activities is a good model for a social media site that succeeds at engaging volunteers.
>
> ✔ **The Humane Society of the United States** (`www.humanesociety.org`): The home page offers clear, prominent instructions on actions you can take to advance the well-being of animals.
>
> ✔ **The Surfrider Foundation** (`www.surfrider.org`): This site prominently features a "Take Action" menu on its home page, which invites visitors to advocate for legislation and activities that protect shores and the ocean.
>
> ✔ **Water.org** (`www.water.org`): This site makes excellent use of photographs, graphs that illustrate the effectiveness of its work, and a "Get Involved" menu.

Finding volunteers with special skills

If you're looking for volunteers with special training or experience, spend some time thinking about where you can find them. Limit your recruitment efforts to places where you're most likely to identify the people with the talents you need.

Suppose that your organization is seeking someone with accounting experience to help maintain your books. Local accounting firms, corporate offices, and professional accounting societies may be good recruiting grounds for someone who can assist with bookkeeping. If your organization needs help with a legal matter, some bar associations link nonprofits to attorneys who are willing to volunteer.

Sometimes your nonprofit competition won't mind sharing contacts who are loyal to a particular kind of volunteer activity. In our city, for example, several organizations put on film festivals once each year, and volunteers who love to see the films volunteer to sell tickets, greet the media, and manage other tasks, migrating from one festival to the next. Rather than detracting from their contributions to one organization, their "migrant volunteering" makes these volunteers more knowledgeable and strengthens their skills. When recruiting for short-term volunteer assignments, don't be afraid to ask your "competition" if you can invite some of their great bird-watchers, marathon runners, brownie bakers, or scarecrow makers.

Hiring interns

Interns are specialized volunteers who come to you as part of an education or training program. In most cases, a student intern's goal is to develop practical, hands-on work experience.

Sometimes internship programs require your organization to pay a fee or provide the intern with a modest stipend. You also want to consider including interns on your liability insurance policy. (Refer to the later section "Insuring your volunteers" for more details.)

As with employees and volunteers, you should provide the intern with clear expectations about job duties, attendance, and so on. If you decide to go this route, be ready to spend time supervising and evaluating the intern's job performance. Don't forget that the intern's experience is part of his grade.

Interviewing and Screening Volunteers

Require potential volunteers to fill out job applications just as if they were applying for paid work. Ask for references and check them. Review résumés and conduct formal interviews. (See Chapter 10 for information about job interviews.) Avoid paranoia, but don't discount your gut feelings, either.

If you're using volunteers in professional roles, such as accounting, check their qualifications just as you would check the qualifications of an applicant for a paid position. It's possible that this process may offend potential volunteers, but it's far better to make sure that the person can do the job, even if she's doing it for free.

If you're placing volunteers in sensitive jobs, such as working with children or providing peer counseling, screen your applicants carefully. Criminal background screening, including a fingerprint check, is sometimes required by law, by licensing requirements, or by your insurance carrier. Some states and counties also require a test for tuberculosis. Check with local authorities about the requirements in your area.

See File0903 for a volunteer intake form.

We realize that screening can be a delicate issue. You're walking a tightrope between the right to privacy and the right of the organization to be sure that no harm befalls its clients. Some potential volunteers may be offended by background checks. Explain that the procedures aren't directed at them personally but are in place to ensure that clients are protected. Also, treat all volunteer applicants the same. In other words, don't pass up screening someone just because she's a personal friend.

A cheat sheet for the FAQs

Be prepared to answer questions when people call to volunteer. If you're already using volunteers to answer the telephone, prepare a list of common questions and answers and place that list near the telephone. Here are some sample FAQs that the Sunshine and Health Project, a fictional nonprofit discussed in the section "Organizing volunteers," may need:

What are the hours I would be needed? We answer the phones five days a week from 9 in the morning until 9 at night. We ask people to work a three-hour shift once a week.

How will I know what to say? All volunteers receive one day of training. Training is offered once a month, almost always on Saturdays.

What kind of advice can I give? Our volunteers can't give medical advice or advice on specific diets. Volunteers refer callers to existing services and professionals. We ask volunteers to be positive and to offer general support to all callers.

How do I know where to refer people? We have a complete database of weight loss-related counseling services. It's a simple matter of looking through a loose-leaf notebook or our computer database to find the appropriate phone numbers.

What if I get sick and can't cover my shift? We have volunteers on standby to cover unexpected absences. If you aren't able to volunteer on a regular, weekly basis, you may consider being a backup volunteer.

Are we asked to do any other work? Sometimes we ask volunteers to help with mailings between phone calls.

Will you pay my auto (or public transportation) expenses? We're sorry, but our budget doesn't cover reimbursing volunteers for expenses. Some expenses may be deductible on your income tax, however. You should check with your tax specialist.

Can I deduct the value of my time from my income taxes? No, the IRS doesn't allow tax deductions for volunteer time.

These questions and answers also can be printed in a brochure and mailed to potential volunteers who request more information. Be sure to include background information about your organization in the mailing.

Managing Your Volunteers

Just like managing paid employees, working with volunteers requires attention to management tasks. Volunteers need training and orientation as well as clear, written lists of responsibilities and expectations. Basic expectations for volunteers are easily outlined in a *volunteer agreement form*. You also want to maintain records of the time and tasks volunteers contribute to your organization and consider whether to include volunteers in your insurance coverage.

See File0904 for a sample volunteer agreement form.

Providing adequate training

The degree and extent of volunteer training depends on the type of job you're asking them to do. Volunteers who answer telephones, for example, may need more training than those who stuff envelopes for the publicity committee. To successfully answer phones, these volunteers need to know background information about the program or service, information about the types of services available, proper telephone etiquette, and emergency procedures, among other details.

If you need to provide a full day's training or training over a longer period, we suggest consulting with a professional trainer to either provide the training or help you design the curriculum. Although you may be concerned about investing too much of volunteers' valuable time in training, remember that key motivations for volunteering include meeting people and enjoying time with friends. Trainings can be great opportunities to introduce volunteers to one another and build camaraderie among them. It's a good idea to schedule refresher training sessions for ongoing volunteers, too.

In addition to offering on-site training, give volunteers written materials that restate the information covered in the training. Include with these materials attendance requirements, details about whom to contact in case of illness, and other necessary information that volunteers may need to know when carrying out their tasks.

Larger organizations that use many volunteers sometimes publish a *volunteer handbook*. Such a handbook doesn't need to be an elaborately printed document; it can be several typed pages stapled together, a simple loose-leaf notebook, or a PDF posted on the organization's website. The more information you provide, the better your volunteers can perform.

Keeping good records

Keep records of your volunteers and how much time they spend doing work for your organization. You may be asked to provide a reference for a volunteer who's working to develop job skills or providing a service through an organized volunteer program. You also may need to dismiss a volunteer who's unreliable, and having clear, written records of hours and tasks can justify that difficult act.

If you use professional volunteers to perform tasks that you'd otherwise have to pay for, you can include the value of the volunteer time as an in-kind contribution on your financial statement. Chapter 11 explains more about financial statements.

Insuring your volunteers

Typically, nonprofit organizations carry liability and property insurance. Almost all states require that workers' compensation insurance be in place to cover on-the-job injuries to employees (but not necessarily to volunteers). Beyond this basic insurance, coverage depends on the type of services provided and the degree of risk involved.

Keep in mind that volunteers usually aren't liable for their actions as long as they work within the scope of the volunteer activity to which they've been assigned, perform as any reasonable person would perform, and avoid engaging in criminal activity. Unfortunately, people these days have become more eager to file lawsuits. If someone sues you or one of your volunteers, you have to legally defend the case even if it's without merit. One advantage of having liability insurance is that your insurance carrier takes on the responsibility of defending the suit.

Workers' compensation may or may not be available to volunteers in your state. If you can include volunteers under your state law, consider doing so, because a workers' comp claim usually precludes the volunteer from filing a suit for damages against your organization. Plus, you want your volunteer to be covered if he suffers an injury.

Insuring volunteers is a subject of debate in the nonprofit sector. Some people take the position that insurance agents and brokers try to persuade you to insure anything and everything. Others believe that liability insurance and, in some cases, workers' compensation insurance should be provided. As is the case with all insurance questions, evaluate your risks and decide whether the cost of insuring against risks is a good investment. This process is called *risk management.* To find information about risk management for nonprofit organizations, contact the Nonprofit Risk Management Center (www.nonprofitrisk.org).

Eliminating bad volunteers

If you work with lots of volunteers, especially volunteers who perform complex and sensitive jobs, you may discover one or more volunteers who don't have the skills or personalities to perform at an acceptable level. We hope you never face this situation, but if you do — for example, maybe someone is giving out inaccurate information or acting rudely — you shouldn't ignore the situation.

Discussing the problem behavior with the volunteer is the first step. Treat this meeting as if you were counseling a paid employee whose job performance was below par. Written job descriptions, written standards for performance, and records of volunteer time and contributed tasks are important when discussing problem behavior.

Exercise caution when meeting with a volunteer about her unacceptable behavior, especially if you don't have clearly written performance guidelines. Volunteers who are released have been known to sue nonprofit agencies. If you have concerns about this possibility, consult an attorney before you do anything.

Talking to someone, volunteer or not, about poor work is never pleasant. However, if someone working for your organization is being disruptive, giving out inaccurate information, or otherwise causing potential harm to your program or the people you serve, you have a responsibility to correct the problem.

Saying Thank You to Volunteers

Volunteers give their time and, in many cases, expertise to help your organization succeed. It's only right that you thank them and thank them often. Thank them in the hallway after they've completed their work for the day, and also formally recognize their contributions. Here are some standard ways of recognizing volunteers:

- ✔ **Annual recognition event:** This kind of event is the most formal (and probably the most expensive) way of thanking volunteers. Some organizations have a sit-down dinner or wine-and-cheese reception once a year to say thanks and give awards to volunteers who've made extraordinary contributions.

- ✔ **Gifts:** Although tokens of appreciation may be much deserved, we recommend caution when giving gifts to volunteers. Don't spend lots of money buying presents, because you can bet that some volunteers will ask why you're spending scarce nonprofit money on something that isn't necessary. Getting a local business to donate gift certificates or other items is a better way to go.

- ✔ **Admission to performances or events:** If your organization presents plays, musical performances, lectures, or readings, consider offering free admission to some events.

✔ **Public acknowledgment:** You can identify your volunteers in your newsletter or on your website. An alternative is an annual newspaper ad that lists the names of your volunteers.

✔ **Thank-you letters:** Don't underestimate the power of a simple thank-you note. Unless you have hundreds of volunteers, make sure you write your notes by hand. Most people appreciate a handwritten note more than a form letter or e-mail. Try to let volunteers know how their work has made a difference.

In addition to thank-you letters and recognition events, you can increase volunteer satisfaction (and retention) by treating volunteers well on a day-to-day basis. Here are some easy tips to keep volunteer satisfaction high:

✔ **Don't make volunteers work in isolation if you can avoid it.** Many volunteers give their time because they enjoy socializing with others.

✔ **Vary the job to avoid boredom.** You may need help cleaning the storeroom or hand-addressing 1,000 envelopes, but try to assign jobs that offer more mental stimulation, as well.

✔ **Pay attention to the work done by your volunteers.** Your interest in what they're doing adds value to their work and recognizes that many of them are volunteering to develop new skills.

✔ **Help volunteers understand your nonprofit's work.** If they've been answering the telephones in the front office, give them a behind-the-scenes tour or a chance to observe or participate in other activities of the organization.

✔ **Bring in pizza or doughnuts once in a while as an impromptu thank you.** Food can provide a great break from a monotonous job or a celebration of a major task's completion.

✔ **Talk to your volunteers.** Get to know them as friends of your organization who are committed to its work.

Chapter 10

Getting the Work Done with Paid Staff

Some nonprofits have paid staff from the very beginning. For example, nonprofits that start out with grant funding to operate a program may have paid staff. Other nonprofits may start more slowly, with the board of directors and other volunteers initially doing all the work and hiring paid employees later. And many nonprofits never have any paid staff. These organizations may use consultants or rely on volunteers.

No rules exist about when a nonprofit organization should start employing paid staff. The organization must determine whether it has enough work to justify a paid staff and whether it has the resources to pay salaries and associated expenses. Hiring your first staff member should be cause for celebration. It means that your nonprofit has reached a milestone in its development. But it also means that the organization (and the board of directors) will have more responsibilities to raise funds and ensure that proper personnel policies are put in place and followed. This chapter covers the details.

Deciding That You Need Help

Knowing when to take the leap from being an all-volunteer group to being a boss or paid employee isn't easy, and it's not a leap to take without looking at where you're about to land. Hiring employees creates responsibilities for the board, not the least of which is paying a salary every two weeks. You also need to pay payroll taxes and provide a workplace, equipment, and — don't forget — guidance and supervision. Expect to have more bookkeeping duties and more complex financial reports because you need to keep track of payroll records, vacation time, and sick days and decide which holidays your organization will observe. (The last one should be a snap, right?)

To ease into the transition, a nonprofit may begin by hiring an independent contractor to handle a specific task, such as bookkeeping or grantwriting, and then go from there. (We discuss working with independent contractors and consultants later in this chapter.)

A variety of situations, such as the following, may signal that it's time to hire your first employee:

✔ Volunteers are growing tired, and the work isn't getting done as well or as quickly as it should.

✔ The demand for your organization's services has increased to the point that someone needs to focus consistently on administrative details.

✔ Resources have increased to the point that you can now pay a regular salary.

✔ The organization is starting a new activity that requires someone with a specific professional license or degree, and no volunteer is appropriately qualified.

✔ The nonprofit receives a major grant that both provides more resources and requires significant recordkeeping and program management.

Hiring salaried employees should be a long-term commitment. For this reason, you need to have sufficient cash flow to ensure regular payment of salaries, benefits, and payroll taxes.

A crisis can sometimes take place when a volunteer-run organization hires its first staff member. Knowing that they're now paying someone to be responsible, board members may decide to sit on their hands and let others do the work. Bringing on a first staff member is a good time to honor board and volunteer contributions to the organization (to keep motivation high) and to invest in a board retreat or training that reminds everyone of the work ahead and the board's important role in it.

When you add paid employees to your organization, you assume legal responsibilities that begin with the recruitment process. We recommend that you consult *Human Resources Kit For Dummies,* 3rd Edition, by Max Messmer (Wiley), to be sure you cover all the bases.

Readying Your Nonprofit for Paid Employees

Before you write a job description or place an ad on Craigslist, you need to invest time in some upfront prep work, readying your organization to take on paid employees. This preparation, which we cover in the following sections, includes writing personnel policies, setting up payroll systems, and deciding on benefits.

Developing your personnel policies

Personnel policies and procedures outline how an organization relates to its employees. They're essential for both supervisors and employees because they provide guidelines about what's expected in the workplace and on the job. They lay out expectations for employees, ensure that all employees receive equal treatment, and provide the steps necessary for disciplinary action if it's needed.

Many start-up and small organizations that have only one or two full-time employees give personnel policies a low priority. We suggest, however, that you begin early to formalize your rules with an employee handbook. Doing so really doesn't take much time, and it can save you headaches down the road.

You must follow federal and state labor laws when establishing personnel policies. The U.S. Department of Labor website (www.dol.gov) contains the latest information. If you're uncertain about whether you can require certain behavior or work hours from your employees, consult an attorney.

When forming policies, begin with the easy stuff: Decide on your organization's office hours, holidays, vacation policy, and other basic necessities.

Determining work and off time

Most organizations follow the lead of others when setting holiday and vacation policies: Although you find a lot of variation, many nonprofits in the United States grant two weeks' vacation per year to new employees. Employees typically receive more vacation time after a longer period of service, such as three weeks after three years, and four weeks after five to eight years. The most common sick-leave policy is ten days per year. While you're at it, you want to give some thought to bereavement and maternity/paternity-leave policies.

Paid vacation time is a benefit to both employees and employers. Employees return from vacation rested and ready to give their best efforts to the organization. For this reason, you should encourage people to take vacations during the year in which they earn the vacation. Most organizations and businesses don't allow employees to accrue vacation time beyond a certain amount. This policy ensures that employees use vacations for the purpose for which they're intended. Such a policy also limits the need to make large cash payments for unused vacation time when employees resign or are terminated.

Consider reviewing the personnel policies of other nonprofit organizations in your area. A few telephone calls to other executive directors may help answer questions that arise as you refine your policies. Community Resource Exchange has sample personnel policies in its Tools for Nonprofits section at www.crenyc.org/resources_tools.

Covering other important items

In addition to vacations and holidays, which are discussed in the preceding section, you should cover these other basics in your personnel policies:

- ✔ A statement that the board of directors may change the policies.

- ✔ A statement of nondiscrimination in employment, usually presented as a policy established by the board of directors — especially important if your organization is seeking government grants or contracts — and other policies established by the board.

- ✔ A statement of procedures to encourage and protect employees and volunteers if they report wrongdoing — a whistle-blower policy. The National Council of Nonprofits provides guidance in this area at www.councilofnonprofits.org.

- ✔ A statement about parental leave and long-term disability policies.

- ✔ A statement of hiring procedures and the probationary period (see "Evaluating your new hire's progress" later in this chapter).

- ✔ A statement of the employment termination policy, including a grievance procedure.

Many organizations also include a statement of the organization's mission and values and a brief outline of its history.

Setting up a payroll system

When an organization begins employing workers, it first must establish a payroll system. The organization needs to decide how often to distribute paychecks, for example. You can disburse paychecks on any schedule you choose — weekly, biweekly, semimonthly, or monthly. (*Biweekly* means every two weeks and results in 26 paychecks per year; *semimonthly* means twice a month and results in 24 paychecks per year.) In our experience, semimonthly is the most common schedule for payment, but the decision is up to the organization.

Although in-house staff can handle payroll, contracting with a payroll service is a better option. Most banks either provide payroll services or can recommend a service. Payroll services are inexpensive — they're almost always cheaper than assigning a staff person the job of handling payroll. They make the proper withholding deductions based on income level, number of dependents, and state laws; make tax deposits; and maintain a record of vacation and sick leave. Usually when you contract with such a service, it requires that you keep enough funds on deposit with the company to cover two or three months of salaries and benefits.

If you decide to handle your own payroll, be sure to make tax deposits on time. Failure to pay federal and state payroll taxes can get your organization in serious trouble. Check the Internal Revenue Service (IRS) website (www.irs.gov) for the latest information.

Typical deductions include the following, although state tax laws vary:

- ✔ Federal income tax withholding
- ✔ Social Security and Medicare (must be matched by the organization)
- ✔ State income tax withholding
- ✔ State unemployment and disability insurance

Providing benefits and perquisites

Health insurance is a benefit that your organization may or may not be able to provide to your paid employees. The cost of health insurance decreases based on the size of the group to which you belong. If your organization has only one employee, purchasing health insurance may be costly unless you can join a larger group. Check with state associations for nonprofit organizations or your local United Way office to see whether they have a health insurance program that will cover your employees. Larger organizations (50 or more full-time employees) should be aware of insurance requirements under the Affordable Care Act.

Once your nonprofit organization is thriving, you may want to consider offering more benefits, such as retirement plans and long-term disability insurance.

Preparing to Hire

After you write your personnel policies, put your payroll system in place, and decide on your benefits, you're finished with the groundwork needed to hire one or one hundred employees. You're probably just hiring one person for now. To set off on that path, you want to clearly describe what the job entails, set salary levels, and announce the position. This section walks you through those important steps.

First things first: Writing a job description

One of the first things you should do when looking to hire a paid employee is to write a job description for the position you want to fill. Going through this exercise helps you clarify the skills needed for the job and guides you in selecting among applicants. The final description serves as a job blueprint for the new employee.

A job description usually includes the following information:

- ✔ A short paragraph describing the job and the work environment
- ✔ A list of duties and responsibilities
- ✔ A list of skills and abilities needed for the job
- ✔ Experience and education required
- ✔ Special qualifications required or desired

We include several standard job descriptions on the CD and through the link in the table of contents. See File1001 for an executive director job description, File1002 for a development director job description, and File1003 for an office administrator job description.

When writing your job description, keep in mind that work in nonprofit organizations can be split into three broad areas:

- ✔ **Services:** Services are the reason the organization exists in the first place. They may include developing protected open space on a coastal bluff, providing home visits and hot meals to seniors, or organizing after-school activities for children. This list is almost unlimited.

- ✔ **Administrative functions:** These functions include bookkeeping and accounting, office management, property or building management, marketing, website design, clerical services, benefits administration, and contract management. You can add to this list as needed.

- ✔ **Fundraising:** This area falls under various names, including *resource development* and *advancement*. Depending on the size of your organization, one person may be in charge of all aspects of raising money, or different people may specialize in writing grants to foundations and government agencies, creating sponsorships with corporations, or raising money from individual donors.

The larger these areas (or departments) are, the greater the specialization within them. But when you're looking to hire your first staff member, that one person may have job responsibilities in more than one area, perhaps even in all three areas. It may seem like too much to describe in a single document, but that complexity and the high level of responsibility this person will have make it particularly important to create a job description that's crystal clear.

Considering necessary qualifications

Some nonprofit jobs require various levels of formal education and special training. If you're hiring someone to provide counseling services, for example, that employee probably needs to meet certain education and licensing requirements to provide the services legally. If you're hiring someone to work with children, the applicant may need to pass various background checks, depending on the laws of your state.

Professional and business associations can provide helpful information about job qualifications. In addition to any degrees and certifications, you may want to specify that applicants have a certain amount of experience doing the work you're going to ask them to do. However, if you do so, be prepared to pay a higher salary to fill the position.

You can't, of course, require that an applicant be of a particular ethnic background, race, age, creed, gender, or sexual orientation. You can't deny employment to a woman because she's expecting a child. You also can't refuse employment to a person with a disability as long as he can perform the job with reasonable accommodations.

Establishing salary levels

Deciding on a fair salary for your employees isn't easy. Compensation levels in nonprofits range from hardly anything to six-figure salaries at large-budget organizations. (Keep in mind, however, that large nonprofits represent only a small percentage of active nonprofits.) We guide you through the process in the following sections.

Considering factors that affect salary

Although exceptions always exist, the following factors may determine salary levels:

- **Geographic location:** Salary levels differ from place to place because of the cost of living. If your nonprofit is in a major metropolitan area, expect to pay more to attract qualified staff than if you're located in a rural area.

- **Experience and education:** Someone with ten years of experience can command higher compensation than someone just beginning his career. Education levels also affect salary, as does having specialized knowledge or skills.

- **Job duties and responsibilities:** Employees who direct programs and supervise others typically earn more than employees who have fewer responsibilities.

✔ **Nonprofit type:** Compensation levels vary from one nonprofit to the next. Organizations providing health services, for example, typically have higher salary levels than arts organizations.

✔ **Union membership:** Labor unions set standards for salaries and benefits in many fields, from classical musicians to nurses and educators.

✔ **Organizational culture:** This category, which is more difficult to define, is connected to the organization's traditions and values. For instance, nonprofits with boards of directors filled with business and corporate members often offer higher salary levels than organizations with boards that don't have the corporate perspective.

Finding out salaries of comparable positions

A salary survey, which you can conduct by phone or mail, is a good way to assess the current salary levels in your area and for your nonprofit type. Telephone surveys probably should be done from board president to board president because most people are reluctant to reveal their own salaries. Mail surveys can be constructed so respondents remain anonymous.

The simplest method of finding salaries of comparable positions is to look at other job listings. Not all ads give a salary level, but those ads that do can give you a general idea of what others are paying for similar work.

Some nonprofit management organizations conduct annual or biannual surveys of salary levels in the areas in which they work. More often than not, access to the surveys requires payment, but it's probably a good investment because these surveys tend to be the most complete and up to date. A good place to inquire about salary surveys is through your state association of nonprofits (see the National Council of Nonprofits website at www.ncna.org) or Opportunity Knocks (www.opportunityknocks.org). Local community foundations also may be a good resource for salary data in your geographic area and budget size organization.

Using a search firm can be helpful, especially if the position requires a national search. Be prepared to pay a hefty fee, however. Fees are often based on a percentage of the first year's salary.

Announcing the position

After you decide on the qualifications and skills needed for the job you want to fill, advertise its availability. Here's a list of places to publicize your job opening:

✔ **Professional journals:** If you're hiring for a professional position, professional journals are the place to advertise the job. Search the web to track down the addresses of appropriate trade-specific journals.

- ✔ **Bulletin boards:** Posting job announcements on bulletin boards at colleges, universities, other agencies, and job centers is an inexpensive approach. You can put as many details as you want on a small poster. Many of these organizations also have online resources for job postings.

- ✔ **Websites:** The web has become a valuable marketplace for job seekers. Many websites charge a fee for posting a job opening. Opportunity Knocks (`www.opportunityknocks.org`) and Idealist (`www.idealist.org`) are popular sites. Also consider Craigslist (`www.craigslist.org/about/sites#US`), Monster (`www.monster.com`), CareerBuilder (`www.careerbuilder.com`), and LinkedIn (`www.linkedin.com`).

- ✔ **Word of mouth:** Spread the word to other nonprofits — especially those in your field — places of worship, and anywhere else people congregate. Place a job description on your website and announce it on your Facebook page and Twitter feed. Don't forget to e-mail the announcement to colleagues and appropriate listservs.

Making the Hire

When it comes time to make the big decision, sifting through resumes, conducting interviews, and deciding on an employee can be a daunting task. Sometimes the right choice jumps out at you; other times, you have to choose between 2 or 3 (or 20!) candidates who have equal qualifications. That's when making up your mind becomes difficult.

Looking at resumes

Resumes and cover letters give you the first opportunity to evaluate candidates for a position. Respond quickly with a postcard or e-mail to tell applicants that you have received their materials. If possible, give a date by which they can expect to hear from you again. Doing so reduces the number of phone calls you get asking whether you've received the resume and when you plan to make a decision. It's also the polite thing to do.

Resumes come in various formats, and we don't really have an opinion as to which one is best. Regardless of how the resume is organized and whether it's on paper or online, here are the questions we ask ourselves when reviewing a resume:

- ✔ **Is it free of typographical errors and misspellings?** A typo may be excused if everything else appears to be in order, but more than one or two errors implies that the candidate is likely to be careless in her job.

✓ **Is the information laid out in a logical, easy-to-follow manner?** The relative clarity of the resume can give you insight into the applicant's communication skills.

✓ **Does the applicant have the proper job experience, education, and licenses, if needed?** We like to give a little slack on experience because sometimes highly motivated and effective employees are people who have to "grow into" the job. Also, nonprofit organizations often receive resumes from people who are changing careers. They may not have the exact experience you're looking for, but maybe what they learned in their previous jobs easily transfers to the position you're trying to fill.

✓ **How often has the applicant changed jobs?** You can never be guaranteed that an employee will stay as long as you want him to, but you have to ask yourself, "If I hire this person, will he pack up and move on even before he finishes job training?" At the same time, don't automatically let higher-than-average job switching turn you off to an excellent candidate. Maybe he has an explanation. Ask.

Cover letters can also be good clues to an individual's future job performance. For one thing, you get an idea of the applicant's writing abilities, and you may even get some insight into her personality. Some job announcements state that a cover letter should accompany the resume, and some even go so far as to ask the applicant to respond to questions such as "Why are you well suited to this job?" or "What do you think are the major issues facing so-and-so?" It's up to you to decide whether asking a list of questions enables you to more easily compare applicants to one another.

If good writing skills are required for a job you're posting, ask applicants to include writing samples with their cover letters and resumes.

You'll probably reject at least half the resumes out of hand. We never cease to be amazed by how many people apply for jobs for which they don't have even the minimal qualifications. We understand that searching for a job is difficult and frustrating, but we also wonder whether applicants read our "position available" ads as closely as they should.

Separate your resumes into two piles — one for rejected applications and one for applications that need closer scrutiny. Send the rejected candidates a letter thanking them for their interest. From the other pile, decide how many candidates you want to interview. Reviewing the resumes with one or two board members to bring several perspectives to the choice is often helpful. One technique is to select the top three applicants for interviews. Reserve the other applicants for backup interviews if the first three aren't suitable or if they've already accepted other jobs.

Interviewing candidates

After you've chosen the top three to eight resumes, invite the applicants in for an interview. Interviewing job candidates is a formidable task. Big companies have human resources departments with trained interviewers who spend their days asking questions of prospective employees. We're neither human-resources specialists nor trained interviewers, but here are some tricks we've learned over the years:

- **Prepared lists of three or four standard questions that you ask all applicants enable you to compare answers across applicants.** The interview shouldn't be so formal that it makes both the candidate and you uncomfortable, but standardizing it to some degree is beneficial. Here's a short list of typical questions:

  - Why are you interested in this position?

  - What do you see as your strengths? As your weaknesses?

  - How would you use your previous work experience in this job?

  - What are your long-term goals?

- **Group interviews with three or more people can give interviewers good insight into how the applicant will perform in board and community meetings.** Also, different people notice different things about each applicant. Avoid making the candidate face a large group, which can make her unnecessarily nervous.

- **If an employee isn't your first hire and the job to be filled is for a director or supervisor position, have each finalist meet at least some of the staff he'll be supervising.** Giving staff members a chance to meet their potential new boss is courteous, and their impressions are helpful in making the final selection.

You can't ask an applicant personal questions about his age, religious practice, medical history, marital status, sexual orientation, or racial background. You can't ask whether he has been arrested or convicted of a felony without proof of necessity for asking. You also can't ask whether he has children. Nor can you ask about any physical or mental conditions that are unrelated to performing the job. HR World has a useful list of 30 questions you can't ask in a job interview at `www.hrworld.com/features/30-interview-questions-111507`.

Taking notes during the interview is acceptable, and you may also find that preparing a checklist on which you can rate the applicant in different areas is a helpful exercise. If you do, try to rate applicants discreetly. Job interviews are stressful enough without letting the applicant know that you rated him a three on a scale of one to ten.

Digging deeper with references

Letters of recommendation can be helpful starting points in evaluating candidates, but we assume that no one would include a negative recommendation in her application packet. Therefore, we do think it's necessary to check references by telephone or even in a personal meeting, if possible.

But sometimes even talking to references doesn't provide much useful information. A job applicant wants to put her best face forward, so naturally she chooses people with favorable opinions as references. Also, employment laws are such that speaking to a former employer often yields little more than a confirmation that your applicant was employed between certain dates.

If you do have the opportunity to have a good conversation with the candidate's former employer, pay close attention to what she's not saying as well as attending to her description of the candidate's abilities. For example, if you need someone who pays careful attention to financial details, but the former employer only talks about the applicant's friendliness and phone manner, you may not have found the right person for your position. Some typical questions ask what duties the applicant handled in her previous jobs, what her strengths and weaknesses were on the job, whether the candidate had a positive attitude toward work, and whether the reference would rehire the candidate.

If the applicant is working for another organization, don't contact the current employer. You don't want to breach her confidentiality.

You can conduct formal background checks of education credentials, criminal history, and other information as long as you get the applicant's permission. If you feel that this type of research is necessary, we suggest hiring a reputable company that specializes in this sort of work.

The lengths to which you go to collect information about an applicant depend on the magnitude of the position. If you're hiring someone to lead a large and complex organization, you likely want to dig deeper into a candidate's background than if you're hiring a data entry clerk. But for any position, you want to know as much as possible about an individual's previous job performance before hiring her.

We've included a sample reference-checking form in File1004.

Making your decision

We can't tell you how to make the final decision about whom to hire. You have to weigh qualifications, experience, poise, and desire. These decisions can be difficult, and, frankly, you may not be certain that you've made the right choice until the new employee performs on the job. If possible, get more than one opinion.

If qualifications and experience are equal, intangible factors come more into play. Will the candidate fit well into the organizational culture? Will the candidate's style of work fit with the organization's management style? Do the applicant's professional goals fit with the organization's goals? If this employee is going to be your first, is the candidate a self-starter type or does he need active supervision to do a good job?

Make sure you document your reasons for making a personnel decision: They should be based primarily on the candidate's performance in previous jobs and experience that's relevant to your position. Be cautious when making a personnel decision based on intangible factors. A candidate who's charming may be a treat to have around the office, but that doesn't always mean that he'll do the job well.

Bringing a New Hire Onboard

Much hard work is behind you after you've made a hiring decision. But keep in mind that any employee's first days and months are challenging, and you want to give careful attention to helping your new staff member make a good start.

Confirming employment terms in writing

After a new employee accepts a position orally, we recommend that you send a letter to put the details in writing. Enclose a copy of the personnel policies (see the section "Developing your personnel policies" earlier in this chapter) and place a signature line near the lower-right corner of the letter so the new hire can acknowledge receipt of the letter and the personnel policies. Ask the employee to return a copy of the signed letter to you, and keep the letter in the employee's personnel file.

The letter should include the employee's starting date, job title, and salary as well as other information that you agreed to in the pre-hire discussions held between the organization and the employee. For example, you may include a brief statement about the employee's responsibilities and agreed-upon work schedule.

We put a sample hire letter in File1005 so you can get a better idea of what we're talking about.

Getting your new hire started on the job

In the United States, one of the first things a new employee must do is complete a W-4 form (for income tax withholding) and an I-9 form (to show proof of the employee's legal right to work in the country). These forms are required by law and are available on the IRS website (www.irs.gov).

After all the necessary paperwork is out of the way, you need to spend some time getting your new hire acclimated to the working environment. New employees don't begin producing at top form on the first day of work. Absorbing the details of the organization and discovering the ins and outs of new job duties take time. This fact is particularly true when the person hired is the organization's first employee and has no model to follow.

Whether you're a board member for an organization that's hired its first employee, or the director of an organization bringing someone new onto the staff, here are some ways to ease an employee's transition to a new job:

- **Provide good working conditions.** You may think that a reminder to purchase the basic furniture and tools someone needs to perform his work is too basic, but we've heard about new employees who didn't even have a desk on their first day.

- **Show the new person around.** Provide a tour of the office and programs and introduce him to volunteers and board members. Review office emergency procedures on day one. Oh yeah, and don't forget to show the new employee where the restroom is!

- **Give the employee information about the organization.** Make available the organization's files and records. Reading board minutes, newsletters, solicitation letters, donor records, and grant proposals will steep him in the organization's work.

- **Answer questions.** Encourage new employees to ask questions, and provide the answers as soon as possible. Particularly if he's the organization's one and only employee, board members should check in regularly, making themselves available as resources. Being a one-person staff can be lonely and overwhelming.

- **Offer special training.** A new employee may need special training — for example, about a software program or laws and regulations specific to your nonprofit —to perform his job. Sometimes you may have to send the employee to a workshop; other times, he can be trained by a board member, a volunteer, or another staff member.

Evaluating your new hire's progress

Most organizations establish a period, usually three to six months, when new employees are "on probation." During this time, new employees learn their jobs, and managers can observe them at their work. Although we don't especially like the term *probationary* because it conjures an image of misbehavior, this period is important for both the new staff person and her manager. Be honest with yourself and the employee. If it becomes apparent that the person can't do the job, making a personnel change during this period is easier than after she becomes a permanent employee.

Be sure you've included an explanation of your probationary period in your personnel policies and that the new employee is aware of the policy. Consider adding an option in your personnel policies to extend the probationary period in case job performance is below expectations.

Conduct a performance evaluation at the end of the probationary period. The evaluation should be written (and added to the employee's personnel file) and discussed in a meeting with the employee. Rating employees on a number scale on various aspects of the job was once the common format. Today, a narrative evaluation that addresses performance in achieving previously agreed-upon goals and objectives is much more helpful.

Many employees are happier in their jobs if they have ongoing opportunities to learn new things and develop new skills. An annual employee review is an excellent opportunity to review professional development goals with the employee. It's also a good time to review ways — through workshops, training, or trying on new roles — that she may continue to grow in the job.

Managing Employees

Much of this chapter focuses on small organizations that are hiring their first staff members. In these organizations, the board oversees the staff member, and someone taking on the coordinator role — either board or staff — oversees the volunteers.

What if your organization has grown more complex? Everyone needs a boss. In nonprofit organizations, the board assumes that role for the executive director, who in turn provides supervision to other employees, either directly or through a management team. The common way to visualize these relationships is through an *organizational chart,* a schematic drawing showing the hierarchical management relationships in an organization.

A chart such as the one in Figure 10-1 may be overkill for your nonprofit, especially if you're the only employee, but for larger organizations, charts help delineate management responsibilities and clarify who reports to whom.

Sample Organizational Chart

Figure 10-1: Organizational chart of a typical larger nonprofit agency.

Illustration by Wiley, Composition Services Graphics

Understanding what a manager does

The responsibility of managing employees includes the following aspects:

- **Planning:** Planning occurs at all levels, beginning with the board of directors, which carries out organization planning, and ending with the custodian, who plans how best to complete cleaning and maintenance tasks. It's best if managers work closely with the employees they're supervising to develop department and individual goals.

- **Leading and motivating:** You may want to add "inspiring" to this category. Good management grows out of respect and cooperation. Be sure that staff members are familiar with the organization's goals and that they know how their work helps foster those goals.

- **Gathering tools and resources:** Don't ask someone to dig a hole without giving him a spade. In other words, you can't expect employees to do a good job if they don't have the means to do it. Time, equipment, proper training, and access to information are necessary.

- **Problem solving:** This is one of the most important aspects of good management. You can bet that problems will arise as you manage your organization and employees. Be understanding and creative in solving these problems. Ask for help in the form of ideas and suggestions from the employees you supervise.

✔ **Evaluating:** Employees should receive formal evaluations once each year. Effective evaluation begins with goal setting, and you want to help subordinates set clear goals and objectives.

Communicating with your staff

We can't say enough about the importance of good communication. If your nonprofit has only 1 or 2 staff members, your job is easier than if you need to communicate with 50 or more employees. Either way, good communication is essential.

Of course, confidentiality is important in some matters. For example, if the organization is contemplating a major change, such as a merger with another organization, some information needs to be withheld from the staff. On the other hand, letting rumors circulate about changes that may affect staff can create worse problems than being forthcoming about the details of a potential change. Give people as much information as you can and be sure they have a chance to tell you how they feel.

Communication is a two-way street. A good manager keeps an open ear and devises ways to ensure that his employees have a way to voice complaints, offer suggestions, and participate in setting goals and objectives.

Holding regular staff meetings

Too many meetings can be a waste of time, but having regularly scheduled staff meetings is a good way to transmit information to employees, give them an opportunity to offer input and feedback, and keep everyone working toward the same goal. Keep these points in mind when arranging staff meetings:

✔ **Try to schedule the meetings at a specific time on a regular basis.** Hold meetings no more often than once a week and no less often than once a month, depending on the needs of the organization.

✔ **All meetings should have an agenda.** Nothing is worse than going to a meeting that has no point and no direction.

✔ **Keep to a schedule.** Unless you have big issues to talk about, one hour is usually long enough to cover everything you need to discuss.

✔ **Provide time on the agenda for feedback.** Be sure that everyone has a chance to speak.

Writing memos to staff

Use memos to introduce new policies and other important information so you don't have any misunderstandings. By putting the information in writing, you can clearly explain the situation. If the policy is controversial, distribute the memo shortly before a scheduled staff meeting so employees have an opportunity to respond.

Some larger organizations create staff newsletters that cover organizational programs and achievements. People work better if they receive recognition for their work. Stories about client successes, gains made by the organization, and announcements about staff comings and goings help instill feelings of accomplishment and organizational loyalty.

For very large organizations, a dedicated website or intranet that's accessible only to employees can transmit information and offer staff the opportunity to provide feedback and communicate with one another.

Talking around the water cooler

Although formal written communication is important, nonprofit leaders also need to communicate informally by being accessible to staff in the hallways and around the water cooler. Some people communicate concerns better in an informal setting than in a staff meeting. Managers who sit behind closed doors all the time often have a difficult time relating with their staff. However, don't force the camaraderie. Let it develop naturally.

Letting a staff member go

Some people enjoy barking, "You're fired!" We don't. We've spent sleepless nights before and after terminating an employee who wasn't right for a job. Although you may not lose sleep over letting an employee go, it's obviously not something to take lightly.

When do you need to consider cutting ties with an employee? Sometimes the employee isn't producing the quality of work required by the job or isn't producing work in a timely manner. Other times the employee may be fired for inappropriate behavior, such as not following your organization's guidelines for appropriate interaction with clients.

If you're a boss and facing the need to terminate an employee, we recommend that you

✓ **Review the written personnel policies that you provide to all employees.** Document in writing the employee's poor performance or inappropriate behavior and make clear the connection between your complaints and those policies.

Many people deserve an opportunity to improve. Sit down with the employee and speak candidly and firmly about the level of improvement or change in behavior that you expect. Set written goals for an improved performance and a date for a follow-up consultation.

✔ **Respect the employee's privacy.** Don't share your complaints with others except, if necessary, your board chair.

✔ **Encourage the employee to leave as soon as she's terminated, watch as she collects her personal items, and walk her to the door.** Disgruntled former employees can damage your organization's records and documents in a few days, hours, or even minutes.

Wrongful discharge lawsuits are common and can be very expensive. If you need to terminate an employee and aren't sure how to proceed, consult with a human-resources expert or an attorney. The upfront investment may save you much time, expense, and trouble later. If your personnel policies specify the steps for ending employment (and they should), be sure to follow them to the letter.

Sometimes organizations have to let employees go because they no longer have sufficient money to pay the employees' salaries. If you're a boss in this situation, try to do the following:

✔ **Give the employee as much warning as possible about the date of her termination.** Don't keep it quiet while pulling out all the stops to raise money to save her position. Surprising employees with the bad news is inconsiderate.

✔ **Try to plan ahead and provide some severance pay to help her while she seeks a new job.** Although you may want to keep her on the job until the last possible minute, good employees deserve good treatment. If she leaves your agency with good feelings, you're in a better position to hire her back in the future.

✔ **Offer to serve as a reference or write letters of recommendation.** If the money isn't coming in, and you can't find a way to keep the employee on, this gesture is one of the best things you can do.

Using Independent Contractors

Maybe your organization isn't quite ready to take the leap into the employment waters. However, if you have work that needs to be done that volunteers can't do, working with an *independent contractor* may be a way to accomplish some organizational goals.

According to employment and tax laws in the United States, you can hire people in two ways: as salaried employees or as independent contractors. Rarely do you say to yourself, "I need an independent contractor to design my web page" or "I need an independent contractor to write more grants for us." More commonly used terms are *consultant* or *freelancer.* For example, small organizations may contract with an accountant or bookkeeper to maintain financial records and prepare financial reports.

Independent contractors aren't just a resource for small organizations: Large-scale, well-heeled nonprofits also use them. A good organizational consultant, hired as an independent contractor, can bring a fresh perspective to assessing an organization's work, a depth and breadth of experience the organization hasn't yet developed, and focused attention to a project — say the writing of a new strategic plan — that staff can't give while managing day-to-day operations.

Differentiating an independent contractor from an employee

Technical differences between employees and independent contractors are reflected in how you hire, pay, and manage them. Independent contractors are almost always paid a flat fee or hourly rate for their work, ideally on a schedule that's set out in a contract that specifies the work to be done and the fee. Although you don't have to withhold federal and state payroll taxes, you need to file an IRS Form 1099 that records the amount paid over a full year (usually a calendar year) and the contractor's Social Security number or federal tax ID number (EIN).

Proceed with caution, because there's often a thin line between an independent contractor and an employee. Just because someone works a limited number of hours each week doesn't mean that he should be considered an independent contractor. The IRS doesn't look kindly on trying to pass off employees as independent contractors. Here's a short list of factors that differentiate an independent contractor from an employee:

✔ **Independent contractors are just that — independent.** Although setting time parameters for the job is fine, contractors should be free to set their own schedules and work with little direction from the organization. They should provide their own offices and equipment.

✔ **If you have to provide extensive training for the contractor to do the job, chances increase that the contractor may be considered an employee.** In hiring an independent contractor, you're supposed to be engaging someone with specific expertise.

✔ **If a contractor is working only for your organization and is putting in many hours each week, he may be considered an employee.** If you hire a contractor with the idea that the relationship will continue indefinitely, rather than for a specific project or period, or if that contractor provides services that are a key part of your regular business activity, the IRS believes that you likely have the right to direct and control that worker's activities. To the IRS, this association looks like an employer-employee relationship.

If you think you may be pushing the envelope on this question, consult an attorney or tax specialist who can give you proper advice. Authorities are giving increasing scrutiny to the distinction between regular employees and independent contractors. The IRS may require employers who pay individuals as contractors, when they're really employees, to pay back payroll taxes and penalties.

The IRS has defined *Common-Law Rules* for determining whether someone is an employee or an independent contractor. Check IRS Publication 15A, *Employer's Supplemental Tax Guide*, for a definition of these rules. The publication is available on the IRS website at www.irs.gov.

If you want to hire someone for a short-term assignment or a limited number of hours, but if the work is taking place in your offices, using your equipment, and requiring your regular supervision, consider using a temporary employment agency. The agency handles the employee's benefits, including his employment taxes, and reassigns the employee if he's a poor fit for the job. Although using a temp agency may cost more than hiring the person directly, the agency can help you find someone who's qualified.

Seeing what an independent contractor can do for you

Independent contractors can help you with just about any aspect of your organization, from managing personnel matters to hooking up a computer network. But nonprofits most commonly bring them in to help with

- **Fundraising:** Fundraising consultants help with grant writing, planning for fundraising, special events, direct mail, and major gift and capital campaigns, among other methods of raising funds.

- **Organizational development:** Organizational development consultants may guide your board and staff through a planning process or help you develop tools needed to evaluate your organization's work, to name just two examples.

- **Marketing and public relations:** Consultants can help you spread the word about your organization's good work by handling a public relations campaign directed at the media, developing your website, creating compelling brochures and newsletters, creating short promotional films, and many other strategies.

- **Evaluation and assessment:** Evaluators can take an in-depth look at an organization's programs, bringing specialized skills to that assessment and the value of an unbiased point of view.

Have a clear idea of what you want to accomplish before you seek help. Sometimes you don't know exactly what you're aiming to accomplish, but you should still try to articulate as clearly as possible what your aim is in hiring a consultant before you go looking for one.

Finding a consultant: Ask around

We don't have a single best way to find consultants. You can certainly search the web for nonprofit consultants who work in your area, but we think one of the better ways is to make a few calls to other nearby nonprofits or funding agencies. You may also be able to find a consultant through a nonprofit support organization.

We prefer consultants who have more than one way of doing things. Not all nonprofits are alike, and what works for one may not work for another. Also, as your project evolves, you may find that you need a different kind of help than you originally imagined. Believe us, changes happen all the time. Ask the consultant whether she's willing to consider revisiting the project goals along the way and adjusting her approach if the need arises.

Some consultants work as sole practitioners; others work in consulting companies. Working with a company or consulting group may give you access to more varied expertise. On the other hand, consultants working alone tend to have lower overhead expenses, so their fees may (and we stress *may*) be lower.

Interviewing consultants

Interviewing a consultant is similar to interviewing a regular job applicant. You want to review the resume carefully to see whether the candidate's experience and expertise match your needs. Don't be intimidated just because the person sitting across the table from you has more experience than you do. He'll be working for you. Ask any questions that you feel are necessary so you can be sure you've chosen the right person.

Interview more than one person before you make your decision. As with interviewing for staff positions, having more than one person present at the interview is important because it lets you see how the prospective consultant interacts with a small group and gives you multiple perspectives on the consultant.

You may have the opportunity to use a volunteer consultant supplied by a program that provides free or low-cost assistance to nonprofits. Interview these individuals just as you would paid consultants. Remember that you'll be investing time in working with this person, so you need to be certain that she's right for your organization.

Ask interviewees to describe their method or approach to the problem or project that you're seeking to solve or complete. You shouldn't expect them to give you a full-blown plan in the interview, but you should expect a good picture of the initial steps they'll take. Also, if your project culminates with a written report, ask the applicant for writing samples.

Signing the contract

You need to have a signed contract with every consultant with whom you work. These points should be clearly stated in the contract:

- ✓ **The scope of work and expected results:** You can include more or less detail here, depending on the type of project. If you're hiring the consultant to facilitate a one-day retreat for your board of directors, be sure that the contract includes the preparation time needed. Also, will the consultant be writing a report after the retreat? Try to touch on as many details as possible. The more specific, the better. Sometimes if the scope of work is very detailed, that detail is included as an attachment to the main part of the contract.

- ✓ **Fees, of course:** Some consultants charge an hourly rate plus expenses; others charge a flat rate that may or may not include expenses per project. The contract should state that you must approve expenses over a certain amount. Or you can write into the agreement that expenses are limited to a certain sum each month. Consultant fees vary, just like salaries, from one geographic area to another and depend on the type of work to be done and the consultant's experience.

We don't recommend paying fundraising consultants a percentage of money raised. Although some consultants, grant writers, and, in particular, telemarketers work under this arrangement, percentage payment isn't considered good practice by most fundraisers and nonprofit managers. See the Association of Fundraising Professionals' code of ethics (www.afpnet.org) for more information about this issue.

- ✓ **The schedule of when you'll pay the fees:** Some consultants who work on an hourly basis may send you an invoice at the end of the month. Consultants working on a flat-fee basis may require advance payment on a portion of the fee. This is fine. It's protection for the consultant, who probably has as many cash-flow issues as you do. The final payment shouldn't come before the project is completed. Be sure to ask the consultant for an estimate of her out-of-pocket expenses and how she plans to bill you for such costs.

- ✔ **Special contingencies:** What if the consultant gets sick? What if your organization faces an unforeseen crisis and you don't have time to work with the consultant? What if you've chosen the wrong consultant? You should include a mutually agreed-upon way to end the contract before the project is completed. A 30-day cancellation notice is common.

- ✔ **A timetable for completing the work:** You and the consultant need to negotiate the timetable. Have you ever had remodeling work done on your house? You know that contractors can get distracted by other work, right? That's why having a schedule is so important.

- ✔ **The organization's role in the project:** If the consultant needs access to background materials, records, volunteers, board members, or staff, you must provide this access in a timely manner so the consultant can complete the job on schedule.

- ✔ **Required insurance:** What if your consultant injures someone in the course of working on your project? If she's not insured, the liability could become your organization's responsibility. Just to be on the safe side, many consultant contracts include standard language about the consultant's responsibility to carry liability insurance and pay workers' compensation insurance and other legally required benefits if the consulting company has employees who will be working on your project.

- ✔ **Ownership of the finished product:** This point doesn't apply to every consulting project, but if yours focuses on developing a study or report, specify in the contract whether your organization, the consultant, or both have the rights to distribute, quote, and otherwise make use of the results. Often the organization has the right to publish and produce the report if it gives proper credit to the author, and the consultant owns the copyright and has permission to make use of lessons learned in articles or future studies. Sometimes you agree to seek approval from one another before using the work.

We think that having the consultant prepare the contract is a good idea. It's the final chance to make sure he understands what you want done. You may suggest changes when you see the first draft.

Chapter 11

Showing the Money: Budgets and Financial Reports

*N*onprofit organizations are expected to spend cautiously and honor the trust placed in them by their donors. As a result, they need to be especially good at budgeting and living within their means.

Designing budgets is a critical part of program planning, grantwriting, and evaluation. Maintaining a financially stable organization is one of management's most important tasks. To achieve that stability, a nonprofit needs to keep clear records and base its decisions on accurate financial information. Asking the right questions about financial reports is one of the board's key responsibilities.

The best things in life may be free, and volunteers can accomplish a lot, but frankly, no money equals no program.

Making a Budget = Having a Plan

Because a budget is composed of numbers and because we're taught in grade school that arithmetic problems have right and wrong answers, you may panic when faced with making a budget. What if you don't get it absolutely right? It's true that you need to add and subtract your numbers correctly, but you should relax. It really isn't so bad.

Making a budget is yet another form of organizational planning (the topic of Chapter 7). Often it's done hand in hand with other types of planning. It estimates how you intend to gather and disperse money on behalf of your organization's mission. In the course of a year, the cost of utilities or postage may rise, and the cost of mobile phones and computer equipment may fall. You're not expected to employ extrasensory perception in making a budget — just to be reasonable and thoughtful.

If your organization doesn't spend more than it takes in, and if it holds onto a little emergency money at the bank, why does it need a budget? Writing and agreeing upon a budget is an important process for your staff or board because it sets priorities. Equally important is working with the budget after you've created it. After you've written your budget, make note of all the actual amounts that relate to the income you hoped for and expenditures you planned. It's a discipline that keeps your organization on solid ground.

Beginning with zero

In many businesses, the annual budget is made by looking at what happened in the preceding year and adjusting numbers up or down based on the work that lies ahead. When you're starting something new, however, you have no preceding year's results to consider. In that case, you start with zero and carefully consider each number you use to build your plan. Zero is a hard place to start, but it's where every new organization begins.

A budget has two key sections — income and expenses. (See Figure 11-1 for typical line items.) Because dreaming up expenses that exceed your organization's means is easy, we suggest that you begin with income, making conservative estimates for what you may earn and what you may attract in contributions. As you work on the contributed income estimates, you also may want to look at Chapter 13, which discusses developing a fundraising plan.

Examining income

It's common to separate your income statement into two general categories, "earned" and "contributed," also called "revenue" (contract or fee income) and "support" (grants and contributions), respectively.

Anatomy of a basic budget

INCOME
Earned Income
    Government contracts
    Product sales
    Memberships
    Interest from investments
        Subtotal
Contributed Income
    Government grants
    Foundation grants
    Corporate contributions
    Individual gifts
    Special events (net income)
        Subtotal
        TOTAL Income
EXPENSES
Personnel Expenses
    Salaries
    Benefits @ _% of salaries
    Independent contractors
        Subtotal
Nonpersonnel Expenses
    Rent
    Utilities & Telephone
    Insurance
    Office supplies
    Program materials
    Local travel
    Printing
        Subtotal
        TOTAL Expenses
    Balance (the difference between Total Income and Total Expenses)

Figure 11-1:
A sample budget showing how line items usually are named.

Illustration by Wiley, Composition Services Graphics

Ask yourself these common questions as you begin developing the income section of your budget:

✔ Will you offer services or products for which you'll charge money? How many services and how often? How many people are likely to use them? What can you reasonably charge? How soon will you be ready to offer them?

✔ Can you sell memberships to people and give them premiums or discounts in exchange for paying those fees?

✔ Are the founders and board of your organization able to contribute some start-up funds? Are they willing to ask their friends and associates to contribute?

✔ Is your organization well positioned to receive a grant or grants?

✔ Are you capable of sponsoring a fundraising event?

✔ Can you provide visibility to a business sponsor in exchange for a contribution?

Evaluating expenses

In anticipating expenses, start with anything concerning the payment of people. That list may include the following:

✔ **Salaries for employees, both full time and part time:** On your budget, list each position by title and identify the full-time salary and the percent of full time that person is working for you.

✔ **Benefits for salaried employees:** At a minimum, you need to pay approximately 12.5 percent of salaries to cover federally required benefits, such as Social Security, workers' compensation, and unemployment tax contributions. Some states also require disability insurance, and local jurisdictions may require paid sick leave. Many organizations provide paid leave to employees for vacations, illnesses, and jury duty. Your organization also may provide health insurance or a retirement plan to its employees. If so, you want to compute those costs as percentages of your total salaries and include them in your budget as benefits. Benefits come immediately after your salary expenses.

When setting up your employee benefits, check on both federal and state requirements. The U.S. Department of Labor website, www.dol. gov, is a good guide to federally required employee benefits.

Employee benefits may cost more than you think. According to the Bureau of Labor Statistics in March 2013, benefits — across all employment sectors — represented 30.9 percent of total compensation to employees. This figure was computed prior to full implementation of the Affordable Care Act, which primarily affects businesses with more than 50 employees.

✔ **Fees for services to consultants or service agencies:** You may hire a publicist, grant writer, evaluator, or other consultant to handle important tasks. Such consultants are responsible for paying their own tax and insurance costs. Show fees paid to consultants after salaries and benefits in your budget.

At this point, compute a subtotal for all your personnel costs.

Next, identify all non-personnel expenses, beginning with ongoing operating costs that allow your organization to offer programs. These expenses may include the following:

- ✔ Rent
- ✔ Utilities
- ✔ Telephone and Internet expenses
- ✔ Office supplies
- ✔ Printing
- ✔ Insurance

New organizations often have special start-up costs for the first year, including nonprofit registration and filing fees. For example, you may need to purchase desks and chairs, computers, signs, shelving, office cubicles, and even playground equipment, and you may need to pay for training for new staff members, first and last months' rent, the telephone and Internet hookup costs, and a photocopier or postage machine lease. Finally, you may have costs associated with the specific nature of the work of your organization. These expenses range widely but can include diagnostic tests, carpentry tools, classroom supplies, and printed materials.

As much as possible, keep notes in your budget files about the estimates you made while drafting your budget. Keeping a worksheet helps you remember your assumptions and follow your budget.

We present three different organization budgets in the digital files included with this book — File1101, File1102, and File1103. Two of the examples show how organizations compare budgets to actual costs. Pop in the CD or click the link in the table of contents to view these files.

Defining a good budget

In a good budget, the income and expenses are equal to one another, which is what the term "balanced budget" means. Although balance is a good state to achieve, we recommend that you work to produce modest surpluses each year so you have some capital to invest to meet emergency needs or try new things. Having said that, organizations' budgets vary widely, and no one right model exists. As a general rule, your budget looks healthy when you show multiple sources of income. Why? Wouldn't it be easier to keep track of one or two major grants and contracts? Or one annual special event?

The reason is based on the adage "Don't put all your eggs in one basket." What if a power outage strikes on the night of your gala? What if one of your major grant or contract sources changes its guidelines? Your programs could be jeopardized.

Another sound concept is "saving for a rainy day." Many organizations slowly develop a *cash reserve,* money put aside in case unexpected expenses arise. If they need to use their cash reserves, they take care to replace them as soon as possible. Often their board sets a policy for how large a reserve they want to keep and how quickly expended reserve funds must be replaced. Many organizations work to create a cash reserve that is equal to at least three months of their operating costs.

Finally, a good budget is realistic and is based on an honest assessment of the resources a nonprofit can earn and raise. In leading a nonprofit, you want to be forward-thinking and optimistic about producing high-quality, meaningful work but also bring a sober brand of that optimism to creating financial plans.

Budgeting based on your history

As your first year passes and your organization develops programs, it also develops a financial track record. After you have a financial history, anticipating the future can be easier. You need to analyze every assumption you make, but at least you have a baseline of revenues and expenses from the first year.

Here are some questions to consider when drafting future years' budgets:

- ✔ What are your earned income trends? Are they likely to continue or change? Do you face any new competition or opportunities?

- ✔ How many of your current year's grants or contracts may be renewed and at what levels?

- ✔ How healthy is the current financial environment? Will it affect your previous donors' abilities to give?

- ✔ How likely are you to increase individual giving or special-events revenues in the coming year?

- ✔ What's the duration of all employees' employment periods? Anticipate the timing of possible annual raises and the need for additional staffing.

- ✔ Do you offer benefits that kick in after an employee has worked with you for three months or six months or five years? If so, don't forget to include these increased costs.

- ✔ When does your lease obligate you to pay for rent increases or taxes?

- ✔ Have rate increases been scheduled for utilities, postage, or other services?

- ✔ Does your organization need new technology — perhaps additional or upgraded hardware, website development, or software?

Isolating general administrative and fundraising costs

Some of your organization's expenses are defined as being general administrative or fundraising costs and aren't allocated to program expenses. The expense of having an audit, for example, is allocated to general administrative costs, and mailing costs for your end-of-the-year fundraising letter are identified as fundraising. IRS Form 990, which nonprofits file annually, asks organizations to present their expenses to identify which annual costs are for general administration and which are for fundraising. (See Chapter 5 for more about preparing a 990.)

Accounting for in-kind contributions

Some nonprofit organizations benefit from donated goods and services rather than, or in addition to, contributed and earned cash. Suppose, for example, that a local business provides office space for your organization so you don't have to pay rent, 50 volunteers contribute labor to your organization each week, and a major advertising firm sponsors a free marketing campaign to promote your work. These gifts of goods and services are called *in-kind contributions.*

How can you show these valuable resources in your organization's budget? First, we encourage you to make the effort. If you don't show these contributions, your budget doesn't truly represent the scope of your organization, and you're underplaying how much the community values its work. On the other hand, mixing the in-kind materials and services with the cash can make following and managing your budget confusing.

So what's the solution? We prefer creating in-kind subheadings within the budget or summarizing all the in-kind contributions at the end of the cash budget in a separate section.

If you choose to use subheadings and include in-kind items alongside the cash in your budget, don't forget that when you receive an in-kind good or service, it's a source of income, and when you make use of it, it's an expense. Often nonprofits fail to show the expenditure of an in-kind contribution, and it can make their budget appear to have more available cash than it really has.

You'll want to keep records of volunteer time if you're going to include it in your budgets or financial reports. *Generally accepted accounting principles (GAAP;* a framework outlining standards and rules for accounting) say you should show the value of volunteers' time in your financial statements if they improved a financial asset of the organization (for example, if volunteers rebuilt a greenhouse owned by a nonprofit botanical society) or if the organization needed a task to be performed that required a special skill, the volunteer had that skill, and the nonprofit would have paid for that help if it had not been volunteered (for example, if an attorney reviewed the nonprofit's lease pro bono).

Annually, the nonprofit organization Independent Sector computes a standard average value for volunteers' labor, both nationally and by state. (In 2012, the national average was $22.14 per hour.) Check out File1114, which you can use to find a link to these charts on the Independent Sector website.

Creating Budgets for Programs or Departments

If your organization focuses on a single service, you can skip ahead to read about projecting cash flow, but if you resemble many nonprofit organizations, you manage several programs or departments. Each of these programs has a budget that must fit within the overall organizational budget.

Suppose that when your nonprofit organization begins, you offer only one program — an after-school center that provides tutoring and homework assistance for low-income children. The program really clicks, and more and more children begin showing up after school — some because they need tutors, but others because their parents are at work and the kids need a safe place to go. To serve these new participants, you add art classes and a sports program.

So now, instead of one program, you have three. Each has its own budgetary needs. A program coordinator trains and recruits the tutors and purchases books, notebooks, and school supplies. The art program requires an artist's time, supplies, space for art making, and access to a kiln. To offer a sports program, your agency rents the nearby gym, hires four coaches, employs a volunteer coordinator to recruit parents and other assistant coaches, and purchases equipment. The specific costs of a program — books, art supplies, coaches — are called its *direct* costs.

But each of the three programs also depends on materials and services provided by the people who work on behalf of the entire organization, such as the full-time executive director of your agency, the part-time development director, and the bookkeeper.

Each of the three after-school programs also uses the organization's offices, utilities, telephones, and printed materials. The costs that the various programs share — such as the executive director's salary, bookkeeping services, rent, and telephone bills — are called *indirect* costs. You can think of these shared costs as the glue that holds the nonprofit together.

When you prepare a program or department budget, you want to include both direct costs and indirect costs.

Direct costs are pretty straightforward. For example, you know what you have to pay your tutors per hour, and you know how many hours they work. But indirect costs can be sticky, and we don't say that because they're the organizational glue. They're sticky to deal with because determining how to divide them accurately among your organization's activities is difficult. Many grantmakers are reluctant to pay true indirect costs associated with programs, and, if your organization depends heavily on grants, that reluctance can put you in the awkward financial position of being able to pay for a famous basketball coach but not to turn on the lights in the gym.

After recognizing that foundations and nonprofits often don't see eye to eye on how to determine indirect costs, a group of foundations commissioned researchers at Rand Corporation to write a report titled, "Indirect Costs: A Guide for Foundations and Nonprofit Organizations." You can find a link to it in File1114.

When your organization is relatively small with just a few programs, you may be able to keep accurate records for how staff members spend their time, how many square feet in a building a program uses, and even how many office supplies each staff member checks out of the supply cabinet. Based on those records, you can fairly estimate your indirect costs.

As your organization grows in complexity and number of programs, you may compute indirect costs by using a formula you derive based on your direct costs. We outline sample formulas and steps to derive them in Table 11-1.

Table 11-1	Computing Direct Cost Percentages for an After-School Center
First, add all your direct costs:	
Program	*Direct Costs of Each Program*
Tutoring and homework assistance	$46,000
Arts and crafts	$60,000
Athletics	$164,000
Total direct costs:	$270,000
Then compute the percentage of total direct costs that each program represents:	
Tutoring and homework assistance	$46,000 ÷ $270,000 = 17%
Arts and crafts	$60,000 ÷ $270,000 = 22%
Athletics	$164,000 ÷ $270,000 = 61%

In many cases, you can reasonably assume that the indirect costs of a program correlate to its direct costs, or that a program that's more expensive requires more oversight of staff and more use of office space. In the case of the after-school center, all the indirect costs — which include a salary for the director, a contracted bookkeeper, rent, utilities, telephones, and printing — total $130,500.

Using this figure, we can put together the direct and indirect costs into a true financial picture of each program by multiplying the $130,500 in indirect costs according to the percentages we computed for direct costs in Table 11-1. We outline the proposed allocation in Table 11-2.

Table 11-2   Allocating Indirect Costs for an After-School Center

Program	Formula	Indirect Cost Amount
Tutoring and homework assistance	$130,500 × 17%	$22,185
Arts and crafts	$130,500 × 22%	$28,710
Athletics	$130,500 × 61%	$79,605

Sometimes organizations write a project budget by identifying all the direct costs in detail and then showing the indirect costs as one lump sum at the bottom of the list of expenses. But some funding sources balk at paying for indirect costs when they're presented this way. The funders want to know what actual expenses contribute to those indirect costs. We recommend that you show the specific indirect costs item by item rather than lumping them all together. For the tutoring program, for example, you would show 17 percent of the executive director's salary, 17 percent of the bookkeeper's fees, and so on.

File1104 shows the tutoring program budget with the indirect costs specified alongside the direct costs. This shows a true picture of the project's needs.

Working with Your Budget

Your budget isn't capable of getting up and walking out of the room, but it needs to be an "active document." If you simply create it once a year to keep in a file folder and submit with grant proposals, it doesn't do you much good. A good budget is crumpled, coffee stained, and much scrutinized. A good budget guides and predicts.

Numbers in your budgets are meant to be compared. One critically important comparison looks at actual income and expenses alongside the original projections you made in your budget. Most organizations create a spreadsheet that includes columns for:

✔ Annual budget

✔ Year-to-date income and expenses

✔ Current month's budget ($\frac{1}{12}$ of the annual budget)

✔ Current month's income and expenses

Pay close attention to where you're exceeding your budget and where you're falling short. Use your progress as a guide to adjust your fundraising or your expenditures.

The CD accompanying this book demonstrates two ways of tracking actual income and expenses in comparison to budgeted income and expenses. See File1105 and File1106. Also, to take a critical, long view of your financial progress, use the Five-Year Financial Trend Line in File1107.

Other useful exercises to make sure your budget is "living and breathing" include the following:

✔ Involve your staff (paid and volunteer) in the early stages of drafting the coming year's budget. If you can't afford all their dreams, involve them in setting priorities.

✔ Three months before the beginning of your new fiscal year, meet with a small committee of board members to review and refine a budget draft. Present the draft with options and recommendations to the entire board for discussion and formal approval.

✔ If your organization's situation changes significantly, prepare and adopt a formal budget revision. Budget revisions are time consuming, but don't try to proceed with a budget that doesn't reflect the size and scope of your organization. You don't want to try to find your way through Maine with a map of Utah.

✔ Provide copies monthly or quarterly to your entire board or board finance committee. Encourage your board treasurer to summarize the organization's financial situation and invite questions and discussion at each meeting.

✔ Keep notes in your budget file about changes you recommend for years ahead.

BoardSource has published a helpful article, "Key Financial and Related Questions All Boards Should Ask." You can find a link to it in File1114.

Because revenues aren't earned, grants aren't received, and expenses aren't incurred in equal amounts every month throughout the year, we recommend that you also project your cash flow (see the following section).

Projecting Cash Flow

A *cash-flow projection* is a subdocument of your budget that estimates not only how much money you'll receive and spend over the course of a year but also *when* you'll receive and spend it. It breaks down your budget into increments of time. Some organizations create quarterly (three-month) projections, some monthly, some weekly. Our personal preference is to do cash-flow planning monthly.

Although grantmaking organizations and major donors are likely to want to see your budget (and may want to see the version that compares projections to actual amounts), your cash-flow projection generally is a document for you, your board, and possibly a loan source.

If you think of a budget as the spine of an organization — supporting all its limbs — the cash-flow statement is its heart and lungs. A good cash-flow statement is in constant motion, anticipating and following your every move. Based on the careful way you developed your budget, you may know that you're likely to have enough revenue to cover your organization's expenses in the coming year. The cash flow helps you figure out whether you'll have that money at hand when you need it.

Constructing your cash-flow projection

To set up a cash-flow projection, begin with a copy of your budget and add details to the names of all the various categories. For instance, under "Foundation Grants," write down the names of every foundation from which you now receive money and of any from which you anticipate receiving a grant. Add the same kinds of details for your expense categories. For example, under "Utilities," add separate lines for each bill you receive, such as water, electricity, gas, and sewer service.

We recommend that you project forward by going backward. Sounds contradictory, doesn't it? Create columns for the most recently completed three months of your year. Go through your records. Put any income received into the appropriate periods, and write down all your expenses in the right categories and time periods. If you've forgotten any categories, you have a chance to add them. Having these actual figures for the recent past helps you see patterns of income and expenses.

Now, begin projecting: Go back to each line item and write down the estimated amount that's due during each monthly period. Begin with the "easy" items — like the rent that's a constant amount due on a certain day or the employer's share of federal payroll taxes. Then look at the consistent bills that vary over time. If your utility bills are high during winter months because your agency is using the furnace more, don't forget to project that increase. If you manage a community vegetable garden during the summer that increases water usage, project for that increase as well.

As you get into the flow of making predictions, it's easy to become too optimistic about your anticipated income. If you've applied for a grant that you're just not sure about, don't put it into your cash-flow projection. If your annual fundraising event raises between $25,000 and $32,000 each year, project $25,000 in income. The reason? You won't have any problem knowing what to do when you have more money than anticipated, but you may have a problem making up a shortfall! Your cash-flow projection is supposed to warn you if you're about to fall short.

You're almost finished at this point. As a next step, look back at your financial records to see how much money you had at the beginning of the first month of your cash-flow projection. Place this figure in a "Balance Forward" row as the first income item for your first month period. Add it to all the income for that month and subtract that month's expenses. The difference gives you the next "Balance Forward" amount that belongs at the top row for the next column of income for the *next* monthly period. And keep going. The balance for each month is steadily carried over to the top.

Table 11-3 shows a highly simplified sample of a cash-flow projection.

Table 11-3	Simple Cash-Flow Projection		
Income	*1/1–1/31*	*2/1–2/28*	*3/1–3/31*
Balance forward	$21,603	$9,845	$43,445
Government contract		$65,000	
Williams grant	$15,000		
Power company contribution			$2,500
Board giving	$4,000	$750	
Total income and balance forward	$40,603	$75,595	$45,945
Expenses	*1/1–1/31*	*2/1–2/28*	*3/1–3/31*
Payroll	$22,197	$22,197	$22,197
Health benefits	$2,111	$2,111	$2,111
Payroll taxes	$2,775	$2,775	$2,775
Rent	$2,500	$2,500	$2,500
Electric company	$675	$675	$580
Telephone	$435	$450	$475
Office supplies	$65	$120	$120
Travel and transportation		$1,322	$8,700
Total expenses	$30,758	$32,150	$39,458
Balance:	$9,845	$43,445	$6,487

See File1109 for a detailed sample cash-flow projection and File1110 for a blank form you can use to begin your own cash-flow statement.

Deciding what to do if you don't have enough

You probably won't have more income than expenses in every single one-month period throughout the year. During some periods, you get ahead, and at other times, you fall behind. Your goal is to sustain a generally positive balance over the course of time and be able to cover your most critical bills — payroll, taxes, insurance, and utilities — in a timely manner.

Some government agencies and foundations pay grants as reimbursements for expenses after you've incurred them. You may need to prepare your cash-flow plan accordingly while waiting to be reimbursed.

We want to promise that you'll always have enough resources to sustain your organization's good work. But some times will be lean. Then what? First, your cash-flow projection should help you anticipate when you may fall short. It enables you to plan ahead and solicit board members who haven't yet made gifts in the current year, send letters to past donors, cut costs, or delay purchases.

We also recommend being proactive about contacting your creditors. If you think you can't pay a bill on time, call and ask for an extension or explain that you're forced to make a partial payment now with the balance coming in a few weeks. Your ability to do business depends on your earning and sustaining other people's trust. If you can't have perfect credit, being honest and forthright is the next best thing. It's hard to do, but important.

Don't "hide" behind your bills, thinking that if you don't say anything, nobody will notice. If you're facing a period of debt, tell your board. Also, call anyone to whom you owe money and explain the situation and your timeline for paying your bills. Among other things, your honesty helps them with *their* cash flow. And when your expenses are exceeding your income, always try to cover your federal, state, and local tax obligations, because fees and interest on unpaid taxes add up quickly. If covering those obligations isn't possible, don't forget to call those agencies. Setting up a payment plan, both over the phone and in writing, can prevent your assets (or a board member's) from being frozen.

Borrowing to make ends meet

Another route to managing cash shortfalls is to borrow the money you need to cover your bills. Your cash-flow statement can help you plan the size and duration of the loan you need. Here are some of your options if you need to borrow money:

- ✔ **Ask a board member for a loan.** If the board member can help, you can probably secure the loan quickly, but borrowing from a board member is only appropriate to do if you act in accordance with your organization's conflict-of-interest policies, and if the board member can provide the loan at market rates or below market rates. Make sure to sign a promissory note with the lender and record the board's formal approval of accepting the loan in its meeting minutes.

✔ **Ask local foundations whether they know of a loan fund for nonprofit organizations.** Some associations of grantmakers and government agencies offer such loans at low interest to their grantees that face cash-flow problems. Such a program is likely to be more sympathetic to your needs than a commercial lending institution may be.

✔ **Apply for a small-business loan at your bank.** If your organization doesn't have a credit history, getting a bank loan can be challenging. However, foundations sometimes make this process easier by guaranteeing these bank loans for nonprofits.

✔ **Check to see whether you qualify for a line of credit from your bank.** A *line of credit* allows you to borrow up to a certain sum for a specified period of time. When the organization repays the borrowed amount, often it can't borrow from its line of credit again for a designated period of time. Your organization may want to apply for a line of credit even if it doesn't expect immediate cash-flow problems. Doing so can provide a safety net for emergencies.

✔ **As a last resort, borrow the money from an organizational credit card.** Do this only if you're positive that you can repay the loan quickly and cover the interest.

Borrowing money requires time and preparation and usually costs your nonprofit in the form of interest payments. However, borrowing is better than damaging your nonprofit's reputation or incurring severe penalties and interest charges — particularly on tax obligations.

Putting money away for a rainy day

Over the last five years, nonprofits, foundations, and consultants have talked and written articles about the importance of nonprofit "capitalization." It sounds dull, but we're confident that you'll like the idea, which helps your organization respond to urgent needs and take advantage of opportunities. Just as a family is better positioned to manage a flooded basement or invest in a small business if it has set some money aside, nonprofits should set goals for saving working capital.

In Chapter 18, we write about *capital campaigns,* which are intensive fundraising efforts to raise money for a specific goal; purchasing land, constructing a building, or developing an endowment are common capital campaign goals. Budgeting for *working capital* generally is more modest and less specific: It means having the discipline to set aside money for a rainy day rather than for a specific project. Raising and saving three to six months of operating expenses is a worthy working capital goal. A year's worth of operating costs could position your organization to remain strong through a major emergency.

Many grants and government contracts limit how you can spend project money, so if you want to develop working capital, we recommend turning to individual donors or setting aside a small portion of your earned revenue each month. We recommend setting tangible goals for this effort — perhaps the cost of replacing essential equipment or operating for four months without any new income while you set up programs and write grants.

Keeping Your Books Organized and Up to Date

After you've created a budget, you need to set up a system for keeping consistent, organized records of your financial information. You may choose to do your bookkeeping by hand or with accounting software. If you're interested in bookkeeping by hand, *Nonprofit Bookkeeping & Accounting For Dummies,* by Sharon Farris (Wiley), can guide you. If you prefer to have a computer do the math for you, we name some software options later in this section.

Accounting, like the world of nonprofits, has some specific ways of doing things. In the next section, we explain the two fundamental accounting approaches.

Understanding the different accounting systems

You'll encounter two standard systems for compiling and presenting information about your organization's financial history: cash and accrual. Here are some ways they differ:

- ✔ **A cash system closely resembles the way most people keep their checkbooks.** You enter income into the books when you receive and deposit a check or cash. You enter expenses when you pay a bill. Many find a cash system to be a comfortable approach because it's straightforward. When your books show a positive balance, you have money in hand or in the bank.

- ✔ **An accrual system recognizes income when it's promised and expenses when they're obligated.** Suppose you receive a grant award letter from a foundation promising your organization $60,000 over a two-year period. This grant is going to be paid in four checks of $15,000 each. In an accrual system, you enter the entire $60,000 as income in your books when that money is promised — when you receive the grant award letter. On the expense side, you enter your bills into your books when you incur them — which may be before they're due.

Each of these approaches has possible disadvantages:

- ✔ In cash books, your organization may owe money in unpaid bills, but those debts aren't apparent because they aren't on your books until they're paid.

- ✔ In cash books, your organization may have been awarded a large grant but may look poor because you haven't received the check.

- ✔ In cash books, it's more difficult to tell whether you owe payroll taxes.

- ✔ In accrual books, you may have been promised a large contribution but not yet received it. You may have no cash in hand, but your books look as if you have surplus income.

Keeping books by an accrual system is standard accounting practice for non-profits and is recommended by the Financial Accounting Standards Board, so this section of the book assumes you use an accrual system. To be honest, however, small organizations can often get by with a cash system on a daily basis and then transfer them to an accrual presentation once each quarter or at the end of their fiscal year.

Considering accounting software

If you decide to use software to keep your books, you can purchase types that are designed specifically for nonprofits, which have some different needs and use a few different terms than for-profit businesses. We recommend that you choose one of these products meant for nonprofits, though accountants differ on whether it's necessary. Some accounting software packages that many small nonprofits use include QuickBooks by Intuit, Sage 50, and Fund E-Z.

If more than four or five people at your organization will be using the accounting software, if your budget exceeds $1 million, or if you need to track many programs, you'll likely want to invest in more-complex accounting software.

Also important, if your nonprofit has multiple full-time staff members, it will need systems to manage payroll and track time and attendance. Intuit's Online Payroll is popular among small organizations, and larger nonprofits may prefer ADP (Automatic Data Processing) or time-tracking tools such as Kronos.

The online journal Idealware (`idealware.org`) is an excellent source of articles, blogs, webinars, and forums about technology for nonprofits. We include a link to a couple of its articles through File1114.

When creating your start-up budget, don't forget to include accounting software — the cost of purchasing the package or online service, of setting it up, and of being trained to use it. As your organization grows and you need more sophisticated software, the setup time will be greater.

Reviewing the Numbers: Financial Statements and Audits

Budgets and cash-flow statements predict your organization's financial future. But you also need to review each year's annual income and expenses in a financial statement. When your nonprofit organization is small and lean, your staff or bookkeeper can prepare its financial statements. As it grows and becomes more complex, you'll likely hire an outside accountant to prepare and audit its financial statements.

Preparing financial statements

If a budget is a document about the future, a financial statement tells the story of your organization's past. Nonprofit organizations keep and review their financial records throughout the year, and they prepare a financial statement at least once a year, at the end of the fiscal year. (See Chapter 4 for more information on a fiscal year.) Many organizations also prepare monthly or quarterly "in progress" versions of their annual financial statements.

Although good nonprofit accounting software can organize your financial information for you, preparing and interpreting financial statements is a special area of expertise that goes beyond the scope of this book. Many non-profits seek outside professional help for this essential task. If hiring such assistance is beyond your organization's means, we recommend that you become acquainted with *Nonprofit Bookkeeping & Accounting For Dummies,* by Sharon Farris, and *Accounting For Dummies,* 5th Edition, by John A. Tracy, CPA (Wiley). If you do choose to prepare your own financial statements, you may want to hire an accountant at year's end to review them for accuracy.

The information in your yearly financial statement resembles (but may not be identical to) the 990-EZ or 990 financial report that your organization may be required to submit annually to the IRS. (You can find more information about the differences between these types of 990s and filling one out in Chapter 5.) You'll also include your financial statement in your board orientation packets and with requests for funding. Some organizations publish it in an annual report.

Seeing the value of an audit

At year's end, your organization may be required to or may choose to have its books audited by a certified public accountant (CPA) or firm. This service involves a formal study of the organization's policies and systems for managing its finances, a review of its financial statements, and commentary about the accuracy of those statements.

The accountant may issue an *unqualified opinion,* meaning that the statements appear to be accurate. In "auditor talk," the accountant didn't find a *material misstatement* — false or missing information. If the auditors have recommendations to make about how money is managed or how finances are recorded and reported, they may issue a *management letter* to the board about how the organization can improve its practices. These letters can contain a wide array of recommendations. For example, the auditors may tell the board that the organization didn't consistently collect original receipts before writing checks to reimburse staff; that staff travel costs increased dramatically without that increase being approved by the board (and recorded in board minutes); or that the organization's employees are owed so many vacation hours that the organization's work could be jeopardized if everyone were to take his or her deserved holiday.

Although some nonprofit organizations look upon a management letter as a scolding, its point is to help organizations safeguard their financial health by strengthening their policies and recordkeeping.

If you hire a CPA to conduct your audit or financial review, make sure the person has knowledge about or expertise in nonprofit organizations. Nonprofits use some accounting terms and bookkeeping methods that differ from for-profit businesses.

Knowing whether you need an audit

When do you need to conduct an audit? Use the following guidelines to help you determine this.

> ✔ **Many states require nonprofits that receive contributions over a specified amount to conduct audits.** This varies by state. Check with the office that regulates nonprofits in your state (usually the attorney general's office) to see whether it has specific audit guidelines.

> ✔ **Nonprofits that directly spend $500,000 or more in federal funds in a fiscal year are required to conduct an OMB A-133 audit — commonly called a Single Audit.** It has a fancy name because it's based on the Office of Management and Budget Circular A-133, and it takes a particularly close look at how government funds are tracked within the organization and whether the organization complies with federal laws and regulations.

✓ **Some other kinds of government programs also require audits of specific grants or contracts.** Other funders may also require audited statements from applicants.

Even if it isn't required, your board may decide that it's a good idea to have an outside CPA examine the books. Doing so provides reassurance that financial systems are healthy and the organization is working with accurate financial information.

If your organization is required to have an audit, your board should form an audit committee. The board president, board treasurer, and paid staff members may *not* serve on this committee, however. The committee selects the audit firm, reviews a draft of the audit and any recommendations from the auditors, and, if necessary, investigates any practices that should be changed.

If you have an audit prepared for your organization, check out File1111, which contains advice for reading an audit. Pop in the CD or click the link in the table of contents to view this file.

Although your organization can learn a great deal from an audit, the practice isn't appropriate or necessary for every nonprofit. The process is expensive and time consuming. A less-expensive option is having a CPA firm provide a formalized compilation or financial review of annual statements. Smaller nonprofits often go this route to cut down on costs but still provide some level of comfort and assurance to funders that the organization has the appropriate level of financial practices and controls in place.

Many nonprofits wonder whether they should seek pro bono audits from accounting firms or ask a board member's firm to audit their books. Although we're big fans of contributed services, a pro bono audit is a bad idea, and asking a board member for assistance is a very bad idea. An audit should be prepared independently of the organization's staff and board. It loses its value as the voice of unbiased, outside validation when provided as a gift.

Reading Your Financial Statements

Audited or not, prepared by you or by a bookkeeper or accountant, your organization needs to produce financial statements, and it's critically important for you and your board members to understand how to interpret them. So in this section, we show you everything you need to know, including how to identify the two parts of a statement and how to arm yourself with the right information.

Getting to know the parts of a standard financial statement

Nonprofit financial statements include two important substatements:

- ✔ The *statement of financial position* (also called a balance sheet) provides an overview of what an organization is worth. It outlines how much money is available in bank accounts and other investments; the value of property, furniture, and equipment; immediate bills; and other debts and liabilities. The basic formula at the heart of this statement is Assets – Liabilities = Equity.

- ✔ The *statement of activities* outlines "Revenues, Gains, and Supports" and "Expenses and Other Losses," which tell you how much money the organization received in the past year, its sources for that income, and how it spent that income. The basic formula at the heart of this statement is Revenues – Expenses = Income. Statements of activities divide an organization's income and expenses into three categories:

  - • **Unrestricted funds** were available to spend in the fiscal year covered by the statement.

  - • **Temporarily restricted funds** were promised or awarded in the year covered by the statement, but they were given to the organization for it to spend in the future or for a specific task that isn't yet complete.

  - • **Permanently restricted funds** were given to the organization for permanent investments — such as endowments. Earnings on such money may be used toward the organization's costs (your board will set a policy about how much of these earnings may be used, subject to applicable state laws), but the amounts donated as permanently restricted gifts shouldn't be spent on current activities.

The statement of activities also contains a statement of *functional expenses,* which details expenses spent on programs and those expenses that were exclusively for general and administrative costs and for fundraising costs.

Many staff and board members are drawn to nonprofit organizations because they're knowledgeable about the services they provide, but their eyes glaze over when they're faced with financial statements. This lack of interest in finances is understandable but can be dangerous: The board and staff are stewards of the organization's resources, and the board accepts the responsibility of providing fiscal oversight. If your board lacks members with financial expertise, your board orientation could include training on reviewing and understanding nonprofit financial statements. BoardSource and other nonprofit service organizations also can help board members understand what they're reviewing and what questions they should ask to ensure financial integrity.

We include a sample of an audited financial statement in File1112 that you can use to become familiar with which terms are used and how the information is organized.

Asking the right financial questions

At the year's end, when you've completed the financial statement, we suggest reviewing the following points, either as a board or within the board's finance committee. You can ask different questions about the statement of position (or balance sheet) and the statement of activities. The answers arm you with a clear understanding of your organization's financial health.

Looking at the statement of position, compare some of the numbers, asking:

- ✔ **Do the cash and cash equivalents exceed the accounts payable?** If so, the organization has enough cash in the bank to pay its immediate bills to vendors.

- ✔ **Are accounts payable increasing over time?** You'll see fluctuations in amounts owed from month to month and year to year, but if accounts payable are steadily rising, the nonprofit's bills are getting ahead of its capability to pay them.

- ✔ **Do the total current assets exceed the current liabilities?** If they do, the organization has enough money readily at hand to cover all its immediate obligations, such as bills and taxes, employee benefits, and loan payments.

- ✔ **How much of the assets are made up of property, equipment, or other durable goods the organization owns, and what is the nature of those assets?** Some organizations appear to be financially healthy because their total assets are high, but they may have trouble covering immediate expenses if all of those assets are things that are hard to sell.

- ✔ **Does the current liabilities section show a high amount of payroll taxes payable?** If so, the organization may be delinquent in paying its taxes.

- ✔ **In the liabilities section, do you see an item for a refundable advance or deferred revenue?** If you see this item, it means money paying for a service was given to the organization before the organization provided that service (such as subscription income theatergoers pay in advance of attending performances). Make sure the organization has sufficient assets — preferably cash — to provide the services it has promised.

- ✔ **Has the revenue-to-date ratio changed?** To see whether income is coming into your organization in a steady and reliable way, divide the current year's revenue by the prior year's revenue at the same point in time. If your revenue is steady over time, the ratio figure you'll compute is close to 1. If the ratio is less than 1, money is coming into your nonprofit at a slower rate.

✔ **Are you using temporarily restricted funds for other purposes?**
Temporary restricted net assets consist of money from foundations,
donors, or customers for which the organization must still perform
some kind of service. For example, if your nonprofit receives a foundation grant to produce a particular play and subscribers buy advanced
tickets to that play, the money you receive from those sources is considered temporarily restricted until you produce the play. What if you need
money immediately to pay the rent? Sometimes organizations borrow
from their temporarily restricted funds for such a purpose. If you do so,
the temporarily restricted funds should be restored as quickly as possible. Otherwise, you won't have the money you need to produce the
play. To see if temporarily restricted net assets have been spent, divide
cash plus accounts receivable by temporarily restricted net assets. The
ratio should total 1 or higher.

✔ **Has the organization borrowed money?** If so, the amount appears in
the liabilities section as a loan or line of credit. Compare its total unrestricted net assets to the total amount borrowed. If the numbers are similar, the organization may have cash at hand, but all of it must be repaid
to a lender.

File1113 provides even more questions you can use to analyze the numbers on
the financial statement.

The financial statement will be dated, and the answers to the questions you
have just asked should give you a good picture of the health of your organization over its entire history leading up to that date. Now it's time to look at
the statement of activities, which illustrates what happened in the past year.
Two simple questions summarize that story. Look to the bottom of the page
to see:

✔ **Is the change in net assets a negative or positive number?** If it's negative, the organization lost money in the previous year. If the loss is a
high number, ask why it took place. If it's a modest amount, ask whether
it's part of a downward trend or something that rarely occurs.

✔ **Is the number shown for total net assets a positive number?** If so, the
organization is in a positive financial position (even if it lost money in
the past year). That's good news!

In accrual accounting, if an organization receives a multi-year grant, the entire
amount of that grant is shown as revenue in the first year. If that grant is a
major part of the nonprofit's annual revenues, it may create a high positive
net balance in the grant's first year that is followed by apparent losses in year
two and year three. You may want to footnote this situation in presenting your
finances to your board or funders. If your books are audited, you can ask the
CPA firm to include a footnote about it in the audit.

Managing Financial Systems

Even in a small organization, you want to establish careful practices about how you handle money and financial documents. If you have a one-person office, creating all the following controls may be impossible, but you should try to implement as many of them as possible:

- ✔ Store checkbooks, savings passbooks, blank checks, financial records, and cash in a locked, secure place.

- ✔ Regularly back up financial records that you keep on computers, and store a copy off-site in a safe location.

- ✔ Assign to different people the separate functions of writing checks, signing checks, reconciling bank accounts, and checking the canceled checks that return from the bank. If you can arrange for four different people to perform these tasks, that's great. If not, maybe a board member can double-check canceled checks. Look for accuracy and for anything that looks fishy, such as checks made out to vendors you don't recognize, checks canceled by people or businesses other than those to whom they're written, or canceled checks that are missing from bank statements. Embezzlement is rare but possible, and taking these steps is a way to detect it. Trust us, we've discovered such a case!

- ✔ Require two signatures on checks or bank transfers over a certain amount. We can't give you a standard amount for this practice: It depends on what qualifies as an unusually high transaction for your nonprofit. You can adopt this requirement as an internal policy and enforce it as a way of ensuring board oversight of large transactions. Although your bank probably monitors large or unusual transactions and may contact your organization if it notices unusual activity on your account, these days few banks accept responsibility for enforcing a two-signature policy on customers' checks.

- ✔ Retain in organized files, subject to a document retention/destruction policy, all paperwork that backs up your banking documents. These documents may include personnel time sheets, box office or other records for tickets sold, receipts, and invoices. You may scan and retain them as electronic documents, if you wish. If you do so, we highly recommend backing up the files and carefully protecting passwords.

- ✔ Keep an itemized list of any furniture or equipment you purchase or receive as donations (including computers), noting the date they were purchased or received and their value.

Blue Avocado (www.blueavocado.org) published a helpful article, "Treasurers of All-Volunteer Organizations: Eight Key Responsibilities," and we include a link to it in File1114.

Chapter 12

Marketing: Spreading the Word about Your Good Work

You may think that marketing has no place in the nonprofit sector. After all, if an organization's work isn't driven by the dollar, and if its focus is on meeting a community need, why does it need to sell its services? If your motivation is to do good, isn't it crass to toot your own horn?

But wait. Marketing — the process of connecting consumers to services and products — is just as critical to the success of nonprofit organizations as it is to for-profit enterprises. Both nonprofit and commercial organizations depend on getting the word out, and the message from both is the same: "Here we are, and here's what we can do for you. Come and check us out. Use our services. And, if you're truly inspired, make a contribution."

You can go far if you have the "goods" — good planning, good stories, good services, and good luck. And, of course, persistence.

Taking Care of the Basics

Before you begin tackling client surveys and media releases, you need to spend a little time making sure you have a few basic communication tools in place. These tools help you tell your clients, audiences, donors, and the general public who you are and what you do.

In this section, we provide some tips for the most basic communication tools that every nonprofit — large or small, new or old — should have.

Before we go much further, we want to introduce you to a few websites that can help you understand and use technology for nonprofit communications and management. `Idealware.org` is the place to go for information and advice about which software will work best for your nonprofit. After you decide what you need, `TechSoup.org` provides free and discounted software packages to qualified nonprofit organizations. `Nten.org` is an online community that helps nonprofits use technology tools to their best advantage. We include links in File1209.

Designing a logo and letterhead

Your letterhead should include your organization's name, address, phone number, fax number, and e-mail and website addresses. Many organizations also list their board members on the letterhead. Doing so is a great way to highlight the board members' affiliations with your organization, but if your board is rapidly changing and growing, you may be reprinting the letterhead every few weeks. You may also want to include a tag line that briefly identifies what your organization does, like *Feeding the hungry in Tuborville*. Often the tag line is a phrase drawn from your mission statement.

A logo is a graphic image that represents the mission of your organization. Many people remember pictures more vividly than words, so they may remember your logo more easily than they remember your organization's name. Try not to resort to standard computer font symbols or clip art when designing your logo. Instead, if you need to be frugal, ask around your community to see whether anyone knows a graphic artist or a printer with a good eye who can help you create something original. If you can't locate anyone, we recommend a simple solution: Choose an attractive typeface in which to present your name. You can get fancier later.

Whether it's complex or simple, as you're creating your logo, produce several drafts, spend time looking at those drafts, and show them to others, asking for feedback. You don't want to grow tired of your logo or have it confused with the logo of another group in your community.

If your organization is small and your resources are limited, don't design a logo that has to be printed in more than one color of ink. Using just one color reduces printing costs.

Preparing an organization overview or brochure

An *organization overview* is a one-page description of your organization's mission and programs. You can enclose it with news releases, grant proposals, and fundraising letters. Place copies in your lobby or reception area for visitors to read. Feature it on the home page of your website.

As you grow, your organization may want to get a little bit fancier and produce a folded brochure with photographs or graphics. An effective brochure clearly conveys the essence of your organization. You want it to be inviting and readable. Visual elements help to make a more attractive document and often enable you to tell your story in fewer words.

Keep the colors and design elements consistent between your printed materials and your website. You're creating a face and a voice for your organization, so try not to send out mixed messages.

Creating a website

Having a web presence is as important as being listed in the telephone book or printing a brochure. A basic website isn't difficult to create. You want an overview of your agency on the home page and a few additional pages where people find out more about your organization's leaders and programs. Including strong photographs of your organization's work in action can make your website more appealing to visitors.

A few key features we highly recommend include:

- A "Get Involved" page or menu of pages that lets readers know what they can do to help your cause. Involvement invitations can range from removing blackberry bushes from hiking trails to taking and uploading pictures of the playground your nonprofit is building to sharing information with friends about the organization's work.

- A contact page with phone numbers and e-mail addresses. Not only does a contact page suggest that you're available to provide more information, but it's also a means by which your organization can begin gathering e-mail addresses for further communications about events, programs, and fundraising.

- Clear information about how to make a contribution to your nonprofit — preferably a "donate now" feature for collecting donations. (See Chapter 14 for more information.)

> ✔ Icons for all your social media networks. It's an easy way for your website visitors to like or follow your organization. (We cover how to use social media to promote your organization at the end of this chapter.) You can also add the icons to the signature in your e-mail and ask your staff to do the same.

In good time, you can add bells and whistles to your website: a gallery of photographs or short videos, articles about your field, a blog or discussion board, and much more. But keep in mind that as you add features to your website, you're also increasing the number and types of things that need to be maintained. If you need to learn about designing and building a website, have a look at *Web Design All-in-One For Dummies,* 2nd Edition, by Sue Jenkins (Wiley).

If you're looking for assistance with creating a website, you may find free or low-cost help at a local college or university. Often students majoring in graphic arts, design, educational technology, and technical writing are required to complete internships or capstone projects as part of their degree programs. You may find a talented, eager designer by contacting his department or by reaching out to the campus's community-service learning program. Another option is to search online for a graphic artist through Volunteer Match (www.volunteermatch.org). If you do use such a volunteer, make sure that person leaves behind clear information about how you can continue to refresh the site in the future.

An unattended website leaves a bad impression. Broken links and out-of-date information tell the reader that your organization isn't paying attention to communicating with its constituents. If you're going to have a website, assign someone in your organization the task of checking on and updating it regularly. If your budget allows, consider hiring a web design firm or web-savvy individual to create and maintain your site.

Producing annual reports and newsletters

Begin producing an annual report after your first year of operating. The report may be published as a letter, brochure, website, or even a book. Usually, the annual report includes a financial statement for the year, along with an overview of recent accomplishments. It may also include introductory letters from the board president and executive director of your organization. An annual report conveys the image of an accomplished organization that's transparent in its communications. The messages the report conveys build trust among people seeking the organization's services or considering making contributions.

Making customer service a daily habit

The trick to providing exemplary customer service is to work at it in little ways all the time. Every staff member and volunteer needs to be aware of the importance of customer service. We offer five key areas to address if you wish to improve (or maintain) your service levels:

✔ **On the telephone:** Talk to all staff and volunteers about how to answer the phone politely and otherwise use it to maximum effect. Provide a cheat sheet with lists of extensions, instructions on how to forward calls, and any other useful information. Simple additions to a greeting, like "May I help you?" or telling the caller the receptionist's name can set a friendly, professional tone.

Make a rule for yourself to return all calls within 24 hours or, if that's not possible, within one week. Let callers know, through your voicemail greeting, when they may expect to hear from you. If you're selecting a voicemail system, make sure it's user-friendly for your callers. We prefer a small number of transfers within the system and options for modifying standard recorded announcements with more personal and pertinent messages.

✔ **At the door:** Someone needs to (cheerfully) answer the door. If you're in a small office without a receptionist and the interruptions are frequent, you can rotate this task among staff members or volunteers. If visitors must use a buzzer or pass through a security system, try to balance the coldness of that experience with a friendly intercom greeting and pleasant foyer.

✔ **Before and after a sale or donation:** If you have tickets to sell, make it easy to buy. Accepting only cash is far too restrictive. The banker managing your business account can help prepare you to accept credit card orders. Also, consider selling tickets over the web; a number of web services assist small businesses and nonprofits with web sales and online donations. If a customer isn't satisfied with your service, invite the customer to give feedback and listen carefully. Offer a partial or complete refund. Doing so wins loyalty.

✔ **With a note:** Keep some nice stationery and a rough draft of a standard message handy so that writing thank-you notes is easy. Handwritten notes are more personal and often make a stronger impression than formal, typed letters or e-mail messages. However, expressing your appreciation in a timely way is more important than the form of that appreciation. Use e-mail if you can get to it more quickly. Write a thank-you note for a contribution within a few days of receiving it.

If your organization receives *things* — like a theater group that receives play manuscripts or a natural-history museum that accepts scholarly papers for publication — have an acknowledgment e-mail ready that confirms the item's receipt and states when the person submitting it can expect to hear from you.

✔ **In the details:** An old saying suggests that the devil lurks in the details, but that's also where you find the heart and soul of hospitality and service. Keep notes in a database about the interests, connections, and preferences of your board members, donors, volunteers, and constituents. Find out the names of your board and committee members' significant others and be prepared to greet them personally at events and on the phone.

A newsletter offers background stories and information about your organization. You can publish it as a feature page on your website, as a PDF document linked to your website or attached to an e-mail, or as a printed or photocopied document. Issuing a newsletter is a great way to keep in touch with your organization's constituents. It can take them behind the scenes of your organization. You may use a newsletter to profile members of your staff, board, and constituents; alert followers to upcoming events; summarize research; and announce news about your organization's work.

Taking care of customers — your most important marketing tool

If your constituents, audiences, patients, clients, volunteers, and board members aren't treated well, you can make major investments in advertising and public relations but still struggle to find new customers and keep your old ones. Small adjustments in customer service can make a big difference to your organization's image.

If your agency is likely to receive calls from people requiring counseling or emergency assistance, make sure that everyone answering the phone is thoroughly trained in how to calm a caller and provide a referral.

Discovering Who You Are: First Steps to Marketing

You've put your basic tools in place and your programs are up and running, but you sense that something is wrong. You know that you're addressing a need and that your agency is highly regarded. Why aren't your programs full? How can you engage more people in the important work that you do?

If a marketing program is what you need (and we believe it is), the first step is understanding your current situation — what you do, whom you serve, who admires your work, and who is willing to support it. When you know the answers to these questions, you can begin to build marketing strategies that highlight your agency's strengths and are tailored to all your key audiences — the people who walk through your doors every day to receive your services, your board members and staff, your donors and volunteers, and the community at large. Blend in your budget constraints (we all have to do that!), and you're ready to roll.

Your A-to-Z references on marketing and public relations

Whole books — hundreds and hundreds of whole books — have been written on the topic of marketing and the related field of public relations. Our job in this chapter is to take you on a quick flyover of marketing for non-profit organizations so you get the big picture and know where to turn for details. For all the details on marketing plans, surveys, public relations, news releases, the use of electronic media, and related topics, we recommend four other books from Wiley: *Marketing Kit For Dummies,* by Alexander Hiam; *Small Business Marketing Kit For Dummies,* by Barbara Findlay Schenck; *Public Relations For Dummies,* by Eric Yaverbaum, Ilise Benun, and Richard Kirshenbaum; and *E-Mail Marketing For Dummies,* by John Arnold.

Defining your current market

If you want to improve the way you reach the public, you first need to know how your current marketing works. Who are your constituents? How did they find out about your organization? Why do they make use of your programs? The following sections help you answer these kinds of questions.

Surveying your constituents to gain important info

You may never discover who reads about your organization in the newspaper or sees your sign every day on the bus, but some people — those with whom you directly communicate — can be identified. Start by defining your core group — your most important constituents — and work out from there.

Suppose that your organization is a small historical society that organizes exhibits and panel discussions at three libraries in your town, publishes a quarterly newsletter, and maintains a website featuring news and information about its collection. Your current constituents (or stakeholders, if you want to use a common nonprofit term), working from the core to the outer boundaries, include the following:

- ✔ Your board and staff (and their friends and relations)
- ✔ Your docents and volunteers
- ✔ Families and organizations that donate materials to your collection
- ✔ Local library staff and board members
- ✔ People attending your panel discussions

   ✔ Schools and other groups visiting your exhibits

   ✔ Scholars and other archivists writing to ask about your holdings

   ✔ Patrons of the three libraries

   ✔ Subscribers to your quarterly newsletter

   ✔ People visiting your organization's website

Drawing up this list of interested people is easy enough. But for marketing purposes, you need to know as much as possible about the characteristics, backgrounds, and interests of each group. Some things you can do to collect this sort of information include

   ✔ Creating a database of your supporters by gathering names and addresses from every possible source within your organization — items like checks from donors, subscription forms from newsletter subscribers, sign-up sheets from volunteers, and e-mail messages sent to the "contact us" address on your website. Enter these names and addresses in a database that can sort them by last name, type of contact, and date of entry; if you're planning to send traditional mail to them, sort them by zip code. Articles on the website `Idealware.org` can help you choose a database software program.

Review the zip codes appearing most frequently on your list. If you're in the United States, you can visit the U.S. Census Bureau website (`www.census.gov`) and get demographic information about residents in those zip code areas.

   ✔ Asking the three libraries whether they collect demographic data when visitors apply for library cards and whether they can share that information with you. (Some public agencies offer information about their constituents on their websites.)

   ✔ Asking a few standard questions of schools or other groups when they call to sign up for a tour. Don't engage in a lengthy interview, but find out how they heard about your program, why they want to visit it, and whether they have other needs you may be able to address. You can gather similar information when collecting registrations online.

   ✔ Inserting clearly worded and inviting surveys in the programs at your public events. At the beginning and end of an event, make a brief public pitch explaining why it's so important for people to respond to the surveys. Make pencils or pens available. Create incentives for completing the form, such as a free museum membership for a person whose survey is drawn at random. Include the same survey as part of your mailed newsletter. Provide a return envelope to make it easy for readers to respond. Similarly, make it easy for visitors of your website to subscribe to announcements or services, and send a brief survey to them by e-mail. The higher your response rate, the more accurate and useful the survey information will be.

Be aware that there's an art and a science to writing an effective survey: The way questions are worded can influence the answers you get, and you want to receive clear, candid responses. If you want help developing your survey, check with local colleges and universities for faculty members or graduate students who understand survey techniques and who may be willing to give you some guidance. You can also find survey subscription services and sample surveys on the web that give you ideas about wording questions. Two such services are SurveyMonkey (www.surveymonkey.com), and SurveyGizmo (www.surveygizmo.com), which is a more expensive choice that enables you to embed photos and videos in your survey. For a fee, such sources will distribute your surveys by e-mail and tally the results for you.

On the CD that accompanies this book and in the e-book's table of contents, you can find two sample surveys (File1201 and File1202) that may suggest wording for your survey questions.

Organizing and interpreting the responses

After you have survey results, you can compile the responses by hand or use a spreadsheet program such as Microsoft Excel or Google Spreadsheet to tally responses.

If your survey responders identify themselves and you want to keep track of information and opinions they share to inform your fundraising or volunteer-recruitment staff, you want to incorporate their information into a database. Microsoft Access and Filemaker Pro are commonly used tools that will serve you well if you or your staff knows how to adapt them to your needs. Another option is to invest in contact-management software, which is designed to create a record for each person who responds and each event at which surveys are gathered.

You may discover that you serve several distinct groups of people. For example, low-income students may use the library after school and visit your exhibits while they're there. Middle-income mothers from the immediate neighborhood may bring their toddlers to the library for afternoon story time and take advantage of your programs. And wealthy older adults may volunteer as docents, serve on your board, and attend your organization's panel discussions.

With this valuable information, you may be able to recognize ways to reach more people who resemble the ones you're already serving. The more challenging task is to reach and entice new groups of people.

Do people you don't know gather at your organization's programs? Sponsor free drawings in which contestants compete for prizes by filling out forms with their names, addresses, and phone numbers.

Designing a useful survey

Developing a picture of your current constituents is critically important to creating a marketing plan, and a good survey can be your camera. If you're going to go to the effort to conduct a survey, it needs to have a purpose and must be clear and direct. Here are some general guidelines to keep in mind:

✔ If your survey is long, fewer people will complete it.

✔ You probably want to include some multiple-choice questions, but be sure to have one or two open-ended questions as well so people have a chance to speak their minds.

✔ Be careful not to ask *leading questions* — questions that suggest the answers you hope to hear.

✔ Explore different kinds of information by asking how convenient and appealing your events and services are and by asking your patrons what other kinds of programs they would enjoy.

✔ Ask your current constituents how they found out about you. The answers tell you which forms of your current marketing are effective and begin to suggest how you may best further spread the word about your programs.

If you discover that your target audience likes your program offerings but finds the times you offer them inconvenient, do you want to experiment with new times and formats? For instance, do people find Sunday afternoons (when the library is closed) to be more convenient? What other barriers inhibit their involvement? Maybe mothers with toddlers want to come to your lectures but need childcare. Perhaps you charge a modest admission fee for lectures but students find that charge to be too high.

One of your most difficult marketing tasks is analyzing the very basis of what you do and how you do it. You may feel that your historical society's close working relationship with libraries is its greatest asset, but the surveys may point out that those libraries are cold and musty during winter months. You may do better by taking over a neighborhood restaurant and creating a "warmer" atmosphere — even offering hot gingerbread and beverages.

Using focus groups to gain detailed feedback

Surveys are useful for providing you with general information. You read them looking for an overview of what most people think and feel. Focus groups are another common tool for gathering information from constituents. Because they're based in conversations, they often give you more specific, nuanced responses. Perhaps you want to know what small business leaders think of your agency; a focus group of businesspeople can help you uncover their attitudes and needs.

When producing a focus group, remember to limit the number of questions asked to fewer than ten (five or six is ideal). Provide refreshments to create a convivial environment. The conversation will likely be more candid if it's led by a volunteer facilitator, not someone clearly identified with your organization. Seek permission from participants to record their discussions.

Defining whom you want to reach and how

Armed with information about the people who already know about your nonprofit, you're now ready to extend your reach by defining target groups you want to serve and discovering how best to reach them. In general, it's better to begin with your current constituents and work to expand within their demographic group or to others who are similar to them.

How market research can open your eyes

A small nonprofit alcoholism treatment center for women was started in San Francisco in the late 1970s in response to studies that found multiple programs to help alcoholic men but few focused specifically on women. No local service of this type focused on helping Spanish-speaking immigrant women.

The program's mission was to provide comprehensive counseling and alcohol treatment services to low-income women, particularly those originally from Mexico or Central America. Four years into the nonprofit's history, its programs were full and effective, and it had won prestigious contracts from the city. The center had even launched a capital campaign to create a permanent home. It appeared to be very successful. With one exception. The women being served were mostly middle class and white. A few were African American. None came from the neighborhood where the program was based.

The board realized that the center needed to change its image and marketing strategy. Through interviews with women from the center's target population, the board and staff realized that the stigma associated with alcoholism was particularly strong among Mexican and Central American families, and women from these cultural groups were struggling with alcoholism in private.

The center began a multifaceted campaign to change this situation, beginning with cultural sensitivity training for counselors. When the center hired new staff, an aggressive effort was made to find Latinas to fill positions. The group published all brochures and other informational materials in Spanish and held news conferences for the Spanish-language press. The center hired a Latina outreach counselor to meet with community groups, churches, and schools and to develop connections and a system of referrals to the agency.

Within two years, more than one-third of the women served were low-income women from Mexico and Central America. The marketing aimed at this community was well worth the investment. Fulfilling the organization's mission depended on it.

Marketing on a shoestring

Effective marketing doesn't have to be expensive. It can be based on multiple grassroots efforts that are small in scale and specifically targeted. *Guerrilla marketing* is the term for marketing that's cheap, creative, and effective. Jay Conrad Levinson's website (www.gmarketing.com) is a good place to find out more about low-cost marketing.

The guerrilla approach may use sandwich boards with provocative messages, cards passed out to people waiting in ticket lines, or enticing online offers. A famous guerrilla marketing example from the business world includes an Internet start-up company that offered families $5,000 if they named a child after one of its products. The point of guerrilla marketing is to get customers talking about your organization and its products to develop powerful word-of-mouth advertising.

Google AdWords has a nonprofit component. Qualified organizations can apply for up to $10,000 a month in keyword advertising. We haven't used this feature, but you may want to check it out at www.google.com/grants. The program isn't available for government entities, schools, or hospitals.

As you shift your attention to reaching new groups, be cautious. You may alienate and lose current followers. The more different demographically your new target groups are from the people you now serve, the more difficult and expensive your marketing task may be.

If you run a local history archive and have audiences of low-income students, middle-income mothers of toddlers, and affluent docents and volunteers, logical new target audiences may include the following:

- ✔ Family members and classmates of the students using the libraries
- ✔ Mothers and toddlers from a wider geographic area surrounding the libraries
- ✔ Docents and volunteers who assist other local cultural institutions
- ✔ Friends and acquaintances of the docents

Your marketing plan should then be tailored to reach these groups. To succeed, you may need to change both how you present your work and how you spread the message about that work. Consider some of the ideas in this list to reach the following groups:

- ✔ **The students' classmates and friends:**
  - Contact local history teachers and work with them to link their lessons to archival materials in your collection. Invite them to bring their classes to see your exhibits.

- Offer student internships and then use your interns as docents for the school tours.

- Invite the students who currently use the library space to help in planning, researching, and presenting an exhibit. Honor them for their involvement at the exhibit's opening and provide them with invitations for their friends and acquaintances.

✔ **More mothers and toddlers:**

- Advertise or place articles about your organization's work in local newsletters for parents of young children.

- Post fliers about your organization's work at parks, playgrounds, local stores that sell goods for small children, and other cultural institutions with children's events.

- Provide childcare at lectures and weekend programs.

✔ **Docents and volunteers who also help other organizations:**

- Advertise or place articles in your local volunteer center's newsletter.

- Contact local parent-teacher organizations and offer their members special tours or presentations.

- Exchange e-mail lists of docents and volunteers with other local cultural organizations, and then use the new lists to extend invitations to a special get-acquainted-with-us event.

✔ **Friends and acquaintances of your current docents:**

- Hold a volunteer recognition party and provide each of your volunteers with ten or more invitations for friends and acquaintances.

The cost of implementing new programs and spreading the word about them can add up quickly. Consider what resources you have available (including your time) before committing to big changes in your organization.

Using Mass Media to Reach Your Audience

What if you want to reach all the people, all the time? We're sorry, but you can't. You can, however, extend your reach beyond the contacts known by your friends and family by approaching mass media — newspapers, magazines, radio, television, and the web. Although some nonprofits pay for advertising to spread the word, most organizations rely on free publicity from the media.

The art of shaping a news story

A few years ago we were involved as grant makers in supporting the creation of a mural on the exterior of a community center next to a small urban park. One of San Francisco's best-regarded mural artists led the project. She spent a great deal of time talking about images to use in her mural with the park's neighbors and people who used the building. People kept mentioning a young couple who had been killed in the park in a random, accidental shooting several years earlier. Although it wasn't her original subject idea, she included the couple's portraits in the painting surrounded by images representing peace and renewal.

The story of the mural's unveiling was presented to the media as a public memorial event for the neighbors and families of the young couple. Front-page, color images of the piece appeared in both the morning and evening papers the next day, and five television stations covered the event that evening. An acclaimed artist completing another mural wouldn't have been a story, but a neighborhood mourning two lost teenagers was hot news.

We hope your nonprofit never needs to tell a tragic story, but we give this example to show that not all good work is news. Tragedy is news. Drama is news. Breakthroughs are news. Surprises are news. Stories that connect to current trends are news.

Planning for effective publicity

Before contacting the media, first decide what story you want to tell and whom you want to reach with that story. What's distinctive and important about your organization's work? Why is it newsworthy? Be honest: Analyze your idea as if you're a news editor who has to choose among many different stories from many sources. How does yours stand up to the competition?

Ask yourself about your proposed story's relevance: Will it affect the lives of its readers? Is it timely? Does it contain conflict, intrigue, or prominent people? The journalism column at about.com (journalism.about.com) includes useful articles about how to decide whether something is newsworthy and how to structure a story.

Reporters often have more story ideas than they have time to cover them. You can increase your chances of coverage if you write (or record or film) a basic document and vary it to address the different media interests that you appeal to, making use of your multiple story angles.

Developing a media list

A *media list* is a compilation of names, addresses, e-mail addresses, and phone numbers of contacts at local (and maybe national) newspapers, radio and television stations, magazines, and websites.

Your media list is a valuable tool that you refine and expand over time. Some metropolitan areas have press clubs and service organizations from which you can buy membership lists, providing a basis for your list. Cision (us.cision.com) is a comprehensive online media service. Its databases encompass contacts at online, print, radio, and television outlets. A full membership to Cision can be expensive, but one-time searches are reasonable.

Journalism is a rapidly changing field with frequent layoffs and employee turnover, so it's important to update your media list often.

For all the nuances of media-list development and management, we recommend that you take a look at *Public Relations For Dummies,* by Eric Yaverbaum, Ilise Benun, and Richard Kirshenbaum (Wiley). In general, your objective is to build two working lists, one that you use with practically every news release you send out and the other for specific opportunities for publicity. The latter group may include the following:

- Social and entertainment editors to whom you send news of your annual benefit gala

- Social and business editors to whom you announce new members and officers of your board

- Opinion page editors for letters to the editor

- Sunday magazine supplement editors for in-depth profiles of leaders in your field of work

- Features columnists for amusing anecdotes or unusual news

- Writers of blogs on topics related to your work

Understanding the media's timeline

Different media outlets require different amounts of lead time. In an ideal situation, you want to begin your efforts to reach the media four or five months — or even longer — in advance of that hoped-for coverage. The first two months are spent creating news releases and public service announcements and shooting photographs. Always check with the publication beforehand to find out how much lead time is necessary.

Many organizations create a media section on their website where they post news releases, background information, and high-resolution images with captions and photo-credit information. This tool enables your media contact to expand upon the information you send and download the photos he prefers for publication.

After you've done the initial legwork over the first couple of months, then you start distributing the materials:

- ✔ Most monthly magazines need to receive your news release and photographs at least two — preferably three — months in advance of publication (even earlier if they're published quarterly or bimonthly).

- ✔ At the same time that you're e-mailing your release to magazines, send advance notice to your most important daily and weekly outlets.

- ✔ We recommend sending public service announcements (see the section "Putting together public service announcements" later in this chapter) two to three months prior to the time when you hope they'll be used. Although most stations have set aside time for broadcasting nonprofits' announcements, they need time to rotate through the many announcement materials they receive.

- ✔ News releases to daily and weekly papers should be sent four to six weeks in advance of the event you want covered. You may also send follow-up releases approximately ten days prior to the event. You certainly want to make follow-up phone calls.

- ✔ Releases inviting members of the media to attend a news conference or witness a special event or announcement may be sent three to ten days in advance of the event. If a news outlet is reluctant to cover your announcement, invite a reporter to visit your program and see your good works firsthand.

Take rejection graciously if your media contact decides not to use your story. You need to be able to go back to these people in the future. If you receive a rejection, ask the reporter for honest feedback about the kinds of stories that would better fit her needs.

Submitting materials to your media contacts

Each section of a newspaper and each part of a TV or radio program is made up of materials from multiple sources that are competing for time and space. You improve the odds of receiving attention in the media by providing clear, accurate, and provocative materials in time for consideration and possible use by reporters and broadcasters.

We recommend the following steps when you submit material to the media:

1. **Even if you've purchased a reputable media directory, call to confirm the most appropriate contact person for your story at the newspaper, radio station, TV station, or online outlet, and ask about the format that each wants you to use in your submission.**

   Most media outlets want your news release, photographs, and recorded materials to be sent via e-mail. Paste the news release into the body of the e-mail so the recipient doesn't have to mess with an attachment.

2. **Submit clear and accurate written materials and labeled, good-quality photographs.**

   The media generally want photographs to be in the form of high-resolution JPEGs, which work well in print.

3. **Call to see whether your materials have been received.**

   Take this opportunity to ask whether more information, further interview contacts, a different format, or additional photography are needed.

4. **If requested, submit additional information immediately and call to confirm its receipt and clarity.**

5. **If you don't receive a clear response (either "Yes, we'll cover it" or "Sorry, I don't see the story here") to your initial release, call again in a few days.**

6. **If a member of the media covers an event you've announced, provide a media packet (generally on a CD).**

   A media packet commonly contains a news release, fact sheet, background information, and photographs. It briefs the reporter about your event and makes it easy for him to check facts when writing a story. If a reporter is covering your event, introduce yourself and be available to answer questions or introduce the reporter to key spokespeople, but don't be a pest. Let a reporter find his own story.

   You can help the reporter write a better story by recruiting ahead of time constituents who have benefitted from your program and are willing to be interviewed.

7. **If your situation changes and the news release is no longer accurate, immediately call in the change and, if necessary, revise and resubmit your original release.**

When making calls and sending e-mails to members of the media, recognize that they're busy and often working to meet deadlines. If you ask brief, clear questions that they can respond to quickly, you'll find it easy to engage them.

For example, "How many photographs would you like?" is easier to answer than "What do you want a picture of?"

A sample news release (File1203), media alert (File1204), calendar release (File1205), photo caption (File1206), and photo permission form (File1207) are on the CD and in the links in the e-book's table of contents. They help you understand the approaches and formats to use.

Getting listed in the calendar

Getting your organization's events listed in newspaper calendars and broadcast on TV and radio can be critically important to attracting a crowd. Readers, viewers, and listeners use these calendars to help decide how they're going to spend their time on, say, a Thursday night. If your event is listed clearly and accurately, you're in the running.

Larger newspapers and many other media outlets assign the preparation of calendar sections to specific editors. When you put together your media contact list, make sure you identify the calendar editors. And to improve your access to this important source of publicity, contact the calendar specialists in advance and ask for instructions about how they prefer calendar listings to be formatted and how far in advance of the event they want to receive your information. Sometimes publications provide these explicit instructions — or the specific form you need to complete — on their websites.

Putting together public service announcements

Many radio and television stations allot a portion of their airtime to broadcasting public service announcements (PSAs) on behalf of nonprofit causes. Although these stations rarely give away their best viewing and listening hours to this free service, sometimes they do tack PSAs onto the end of a newscast or special program during prime time. But even an announcement played during the morning's wee hours can reach many people.

Public service announcements are brief. Most are 15, 30, or 60 seconds long. You may submit them as written text to be read by the stations' announcers, or you may submit them recorded or filmed on a CD or DVD or as an e-mailed podcast for direct broadcast. Many stations are more willing to use PSAs that are already recorded or filmed, but this isn't universally true. If you submit a prerecorded PSA, also include a print version of the text. Some stations string several announcements together in a general public announcement broadcast, and it's easier for them to work from text.

If you choose to submit a prerecorded PSA, make sure it's of broadcast quality with excellent sound and/or images. If you're the narrator, spit out your gum! If you mumble or if the images are blurry, stations can't use it. Using the voice of a celebrity — even a local luminary — for your prerecorded PSA can be particularly effective.

The challenge to writing public service announcements is to clearly convey a lot of information in a short time. Write your message and test it against the clock. If you're rushing to finish it in time, it's probably too long. Ask someone else to read it back to you and time that person. You don't want to be the only one who can finish it in 15 seconds.

File1208 is a sample public service announcement addressed to a media outlet.

Using Social Media for Fun and Profit

How many people do you know without a Facebook account? Probably not many. Facebook has penetrated our culture and enables us to view photos of the children of our cousins and the pets of our friends and acquaintances. It doesn't matter if you think Facebook and other social media platforms are a positive step forward or the first step on a slippery slope toward the total destruction of personal privacy. Social media is here, and it's not going away.

It's not a surprise that nonprofit organizations are working to turn Facebook and other social media applications to their advantage. After all, what could be better than the opportunity to communicate easily with clients, volunteers, and donors — and to recruit more of the same? You can let people know what you're doing without the hit-and-miss efforts of trying to place articles in mass-media publications.

In this section, we give you an overview of the most popular social media tools and some tips for getting the most out of the time you spend on Facebook, Twitter, LinkedIn, and other sites that may become popular in the future.

Developing a social media policy

If you have staff and volunteers posting on your organization's social media platforms, you're wise to establish guidelines for what is and isn't appropriate to reveal to the public and to use a tone that builds a positive image for your nonprofit.

In your social media policy, include the following points:

- ✔ **Be professional.** Blog posts, status updates, and tweets determine your organization's online face. Review your posts before posting. Spellchecker is your friend.

  Keep your personal social media play separate from your organization activities.

- ✔ **Post regularly.** Update regularly to keep your content fresh. We recommend creating a calendar and assigning responsibility for updates so your information is routinely refreshed.

- ✔ **Know what's appropriate to post.** Announcements, awards, milestones, and general news about the day-to-day activities of your organization are all worthy of posting. Rumors, gossip, bad news, and the like should never be circulated through social media. Here are some other tips about posting:

  - Ask questions. Engage your audience in conversation.

  - Respond to comments as soon as you can. Don't be defensive about negative comments.

  - Photos and videos typically draw more comments and "likes" than text postings. You can add images to your website, or, if you have more images than your website can hold, open a Flickr account for still photos and upload videos to YouTube or Vimeo. Let people know when you've added new material by posting links on your social media pages.

  - Get permission to post photos and names of people who work at your organization or clients who receive services.

- ✔ **Respect copyrighted material.** Ask permission to repost (if you can't just post a link) and give proper credit.

- ✔ **Use good judgment.** Don't post anything you wouldn't want your mother to see or you wouldn't want to read on the front page of your local newspaper.

In addition to questions of taste and tone, you want to be sure that employees and volunteers understand that any 501(c)(3) organization must be cautious about taking stands on political campaigns, especially campaigns for political office. And although you can't ban your staff and volunteers from using their own social media accounts for personal activities, remind them that their friends probably know where they work and that a tasteless or vulgar post can reflect badly on the organization.

We provide links in File1209 to information to help you develop your social media policy.

Planning your social media posts

Because social media can swallow up a lot of time, especially if you're distracted by cute cat videos, you should develop a plan before jumping into promoting your nonprofit through social media channels. Knowing what outcomes you want to achieve through social media helps you post or tweet information that is useful to both your organization and your followers.

Here is a list of questions you should ask yourself:

✔ What is your primary goal? Do you want to make more people aware of your services? Do you want to recruit volunteers? Do you want to raise money? Do you want to drive people to your website?

✔ How will you achieve that goal? After you determine your goal, set an objective. For example, you may decide to recruit ten new volunteers over the next three months.

✔ Whom will you target? If your nonprofit is a community theater, for instance, you want to look for people who enjoy the dramatic arts, either as audience members or performers.

✔ How much time can you spend implementing your plans? Can you spend an hour each day? Three hours a week? Do you have volunteers who can help?

We don't think it's necessary to create a formal plan document, but the more specific you can be about your goals and objectives, the more successful you're likely to be. We suggest *Social Media Marketing All-in-One For Dummies,* by Jan Zimmerman and Deborah Ng (Wiley), for good information about using social media marketing.

 It's important to track visitors' activity on your website and social media networks so you can see how you're doing and make adjustments as necessary. Google Analytics (`www.google.com/analytics`) can help you do this. As you use these analytics and observe which features and posts attract the most attention on your social media pages, you can shape future content and campaigns to reach maximum numbers. You also want to keep an eye on qualitative information, such as whether influential people follow you on Twitter, whether your contacts share and re-tweet your material, and whether the comments you attract are thoughtful and well-informed.

Choosing your social media platforms

We doubt that anyone has been successful in developing a complete list of all social media applications because so many exist and because new ones are being launched almost on a daily basis. However, in the following sections, we list three that can't be ignored.

Facebook

For a company that is barely ten years old, it's amazing that Facebook can be called the granddaddy of social networking. If you do nothing else, you should create a Facebook page and begin collecting fans and likes. The company claims more than one billion users worldwide. And although it's unlikely you'll generate interest from more than a very tiny percentage of users, it's the best place to find the niche for your nonprofit.

Facebook provides advice, including a resource guide and examples of how nonprofits are using the platform to advance their work. Visit www. facebook.com/nonprofits to find good ideas that you can adapt for your nonprofit's page.

Keep your organization's page separate from your personal account. Facebook provides a handbook to guide you through setting up a page for your nonprofit. *Facebook For Dummies,* by Carolyn Abram (Wiley), is a useful resource.

Facebook used to manage a "Facebook causes" feature that can now be found on a discrete platform, www.causes.com. Causes.com guides its users to organize boycotts, raise money, and build volunteer involvement.

Twitter

Twitter has fewer users than Facebook, about half as many according to estimates at the time of this writing, but it can be a powerful driver for traffic to your website and Facebook page. Your tweets are limited to 140 characters, so don't plan on publishing any essays on Twitter. On the other hand, it's perfect for writing a snappy headline and including a link to the essay or blog post on your website.

You build Twitter followers more quickly if your tweets have an authentic voice that sounds like a person who wants to have a conversation with followers — not someone who's reading a news release or shouting slogans.

Re-tweeting Twitter posts that you want your followers to see is an effective way to participate in the Twitter community. Don't forget that photos can be a part of your tweet and can be a fine way to promote a program or event. You can find a guide for nonprofit use of Twitter at www.twitter4good. com. Also, check out *Twitter For Dummies,* by Laura Fitton, Michael Gruen, and Leslie Poston (Wiley).

LinkedIn

LinkedIn is frequented by business folks and professionals, and who could be better to network with, especially when you're looking for potential board members or corporate connections? You want to create a company page for your organization. Remember, this is a professional network, so, you know, keep it professional. *LinkedIn For Dummies,* by Joel Elad (Wiley), provides in-depth information about the ins and outs of LinkedIn.

LinkedIn groups can be a good way to exchange information with people who share your interests. If you're feeling adventurous, you can open your own group for your board members and volunteers. While you're at it, encourage those board members and volunteers to identify their participation in your nonprofit in their profiles. Declaring their affiliations with your organization can be a subtle but effective way to introduce their professional associates to your work.

Protecting your online reputation

Not all the information that people find about you online is generated by your organization. A number of online services rank and rate nonprofit organizations against such criteria as financial health, use of resources, transparency, and constituent feedback. Just as none of us can control gossip, you don't have the power to change the data these services use or their ways of interpreting that data. However, you can provide them with information, remain vigilant so you're aware of any critiques, and be proactive if your nonprofit is criticized.

Here's a list of major sites that review nonprofits so you can provide them with up-to-date information:

- ✓ The Better Business Bureau's Wise Giving Alliance (www.bbb.org/us/wise-giving) rates approximately 1,300 national nonprofits. Local BBBs also review nonprofits — approximately 10,000 of them. They use a range of standards to grade nonprofits. You can strengthen your rating by building your board of directors and making sure it meets more than three times a year, paying attention to the balance between your management costs and program expenses, being honest and transparent in fundraising materials, and providing options for donors who don't want their names to be disclosed. You can also gain a seal as a BBB Accredited Charity, for which you'll have to pay a fee on a sliding scale of $1,000 to $15,000 per year.

- ✓ Charity Navigator (www.charitynavigator.com) analyzes the finances, apparent effectiveness, and transparency of approximately 6,000 of the United States' largest charities with revenues of more than $1 million, and assigns 0- to 4-star ratings. If you are a new, emerging nonprofit, you're unlikely to be included on this charity rating site, but it might be helpful to understand how nonprofits are assessed so you can plan for the future.

On the homepage of Charity Navigator's website, you can find information about how it analyzes nonprofits. Apart from the long-term hard work of growing your organization and containing overhead costs, your nonprofit can improve its rating by having conflict-of-interest and whistle-blower policies and publishing a donor privacy policy on your website.

✔ GuideStar (www.guidestar.org) offers an array of nonprofit information and is particularly valuable for posting three years of nonprofits' most recent 990 tax forms. You can strengthen your presence on GuideStar by writing the profile of your organization and checking to be certain that your most recent 990 forms are posted. The IRS provides the 990 forms to GuideStar directly, and occasionally there's a delay.

Collecting donations through crowd funding

Crowd funding (also called crowdsourcing) is a form of online fundraising that can benefit from the social networks you've developed. Kickstarter (www.kickstarter.com) and Indiegogo (www.indiegogo.com) are two of the best-known crowd-funding sites.

Kickstarter is all about projects and isn't specifically designed for nonprofits. You can't use Kickstarter to raise funds to support the ongoing costs of your nonprofit, for example. But if your work involves making a film or producing a play, Kickstarter may be the place to go. Indiegogo lets you raise funds for a cause, as long as your organization is recognized as a 501(c)(3) public charity. Fundly (fundly.com) is just for nonprofits and works well with

Facebook. So if your organization has a lot of Facebook friends, and you're eager to try out crowd funding, Fundly may be a useful fundraising tool. For more details about these innovative funding initiatives, check out *Crowdsourcing For Dummies,* by David Alan Grier (Wiley).

Using crowd-funding platforms does involve some costs, so be sure to research carefully before you commit your organization to any one of them. Also, don't expect the contributions to flow into your organization's bank account without lots of work publicizing the campaign to your friends and followers. If you need a review of the principles of raising money from individuals, look at Chapter 14.

Part III
Successful Fundraising

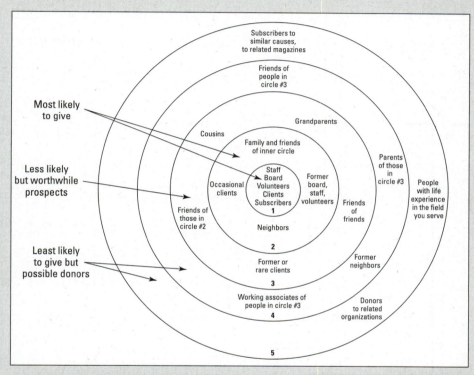

Subscribers to similar causes, to related magazines

Friends of people in circle #3

Grandparents

Cousins

Family and friends of inner circle

Most likely to give

Parents of those in circle #3

Staff
Board
Volunteers
Clients
Subscribers
1

Less likely but worthwhile prospects

Occasional clients

Former board, staff, volunteers

People with life experience in the field you serve

Friends of those in circle #2

Friends of friends

Neighbors

2

Least likely to give but possible donors

Former or rare clients

Former neighbors

3

Working associates of people in circle #3

Donors to related organizations

4

5

Illustration by Wiley, Composition Services Graphics

In this part . . .

- ✔ Know where your money is coming from by writing a detailed fundraising plan.

- ✔ Check out the many ways you can ask individuals to donate money to your organization. Many small donations can add up over time.

- ✔ Go big and plan a special event that will draw in the dollars. The event may take a lot of work, but the payoff can make it worthwhile.

- ✔ Nonprofits often receive grants as a source of income. Find out where to look for grants and how to apply for them.

- ✔ Capital campaigns provide large amounts of funding for specific purposes — often property or buildings. Figure out how to establish a realistic plan.

Chapter 13

Crafting a Fundraising Plan

*I*f an organization is going to provide a public service, it needs money. Plain and simple. It may be run by volunteers and need just a little money, or it may need lots of money to pay for employees, office space, and formal research. If it's a brand-spanking-new organization, it needs start-up money, or what's called *seed funding*.

Any nonprofit — whatever its purpose — grows out of someone's idea or passion (maybe yours!) to make the world better. Raising money is inviting others to share in that belief and passion.

Successful fundraising is based on a plan, and a good plan is based on understanding an organization's likeliest sources of funding. After all, different kinds of causes appeal to different people or institutions. For instance, your organization may get most of its money from the government, grantmaking foundations, businesses, or individuals. A good plan is also balanced. No organization should put all its eggs in one basket or imagine its entire omelet coming from one generous chicken.

In this chapter, we show you how to create a plan for gathering your funding eggs from a number of nests. For those of you whose organizations are new, we offer some ideas for where to begin.

Recognizing Who Can Raise Funds

Federal tax codes designate more than a dozen different kinds of nonprofit organizations (which we discuss in Chapter 2). This book focuses on those that are authorized under section 501(c)(3) of those tax codes and that qualify as public charities. Such nonprofits are exempt from paying some kinds of taxes, and their donors can take tax deductions for making contributions to them. Because many individual donors, foundations, and corporate foundations are motivated, in part, by that tax deduction, this chapter and the fundraising chapters that follow are written about 501(c)(3) nonprofit organizations with public charity status.

Churches and very small organizations (if their annual gross receipts are less than $5,000) that are performing a public service can receive contributions that are tax-deductible to their donors even though they may not have applied for and received 501(c)(3) status from the Internal Revenue Service (IRS).

Thirty-nine states and the District of Columbia require charities to file registration forms before engaging in fundraising solicitations. Each state defines its registration requirements differently. For example, some don't require universities, hospitals, or churches to register. If your state requires charities to register, make sure you do so before you start soliciting funds. After all, not filing the forms can cause your organization to lose its nonprofit status or even lead its officers and board members to be charged criminal penalties. If you hire a fundraising consultant, both that consultant and your organization may need to file. See File0402 to link to the state offices that regulate nonprofits.

Naming Possible Funding Sources

Before plunging ahead, we need to introduce some of the terms we use in this chapter to describe the different kinds of contributions an organization may seek. Here's what you need to know:

- **Grants:** *Grants* are formal contributions made to an organization by foundations, corporations, or government agencies, often to help the nonprofit address defined goals or manage specific programs. Some grants, called *project* or *program grants,* are for trying out new ideas or enhancing existing programs. Others, called *general operating grants,* support the overall work of an organization.

- **Corporate contributions:** Some corporations create their own foundations (that award grants), and some award contributions directly through corporate giving programs — most often out of their public affairs, community relations, or marketing departments. Many corporations give *in-kind gifts* — contributions of goods and services — rather than or in addition to cash contributions.

- **Individual contributions:** Gifts to organizations from private individuals represent the largest portion of private money given to nonprofit organizations (more than 72 percent in 2012). Individual donors may support specific activities or the nonprofit's general costs. You may seek these contributions through the mail, over the phone, through your website or social media, in face-to-face visits, or at special events. Common types of individual contributions include the following:

- **Annual gifts:** A contribution written once a year to a charity is called, appropriately enough, an *annual gift*. The consistency of such gifts makes them of great value to the recipient.

- **Major gifts:** As suggested in the name, a *major gift* is a large amount of money. For some organizations, a major gift may be $500, and for others it may be $50,000.

- **Memberships:** Similar to an annual gift in some ways, a *membership* is a contribution made once a year. The difference is that you often make a membership gift in exchange for a benefit or service from the nonprofit, such as a discount on tickets or a free tote bag. Some nonprofits are structured so their members play a role in their governance, but that's a different, more formal relationship than calling a contributor a member because she paid to join. (See Chapter 4 for details on having members in your organization.)

According to IRS regulations, if a donor contributes $75 or more to your organization in exchange for a good or service, your nonprofit must inform that donor in writing about the value of the good or service she received and the portion of her contribution that she can claim as a federal income tax deduction. Your nonprofit also must acknowledge in writing to a donor any gift of $250 or more. It is best to acknowledge contributions within seven to ten days.

- **Planned giving/bequests:** These gifts are contributions that donors make to nonprofit organizations through their wills or other legal documents specifying what happens to their money and property after they die. Generally, the donor works with a trust officer at a bank or law firm to design her planned giving. Large nonprofits often employ staff who specialize in providing donors with technical assistance in this area.

- **Special events:** From marathons to chicken dinners to online auctions, fundraising events generate income that supports organizations. Contributors can deduct from their taxes the portion of any event ticket that's above and beyond the cost of the value of the goods received at the event. Individuals, corporations, and small businesses are the likeliest supporters of special events. We talk more about special events in Chapter 15.

Analyzing Your Potential

Different approaches to raising funds work best for different kinds of organizations. When you make a fundraising plan, you have to be both ambitious about your goals and realistic about what's likely to work for you. As you try to figure out how much money you can glean from each possible funding source, answer the following questions:

✔ **How far do your services reach?** Do a lot of people understand, care about, and benefit from your organization's cause? Do you focus on a small geographic area or work at a national or international scale? The answers to these questions tell you whether your nonprofit should be casting its net close to home or all over the country or world.

✔ **Are you one of a kind?** If you're unique, you may have a more difficult time explaining to potential donors who you are and what you do. But you may have an advantage when you appeal to foundations that like model programs and new approaches to solving community problems.

✔ **How urgent is your cause?** When a river floods a community or famine breaks out in a refugee camp, if your nonprofit is on the scene providing emergency shelter and food, you'll find that social media tools can be particularly effective in raising money from people who understand the importance of responding quickly.

✔ **Does your cause elicit strong feelings?** Even if it doesn't appeal to large numbers of people, a hot topic with a few passionate believers can still attract major gifts. However, organizations that focus on potentially controversial topics — such as family planning, use of pesticides, or incarceration of juveniles — may find that corporations and businesses are uncomfortable with having their names associated with the cause.

✔ **How well-known and highly regarded are your leaders?** Most people feel better about supporting an organization when they believe in its leaders — whether they're famous research scientists or well-liked next-door neighbors. People give money to people they trust, so your organization's leaders (both staff and board) are critically important to its fundraising.

✔ **How well-known is your organization?** Just as any commercial company with a well-known brand name has an easier time selling its products, a nonprofit with a widely recognized name often has an easier time attracting contributions from individuals. On the other hand, an agency with a low profile that's recognized by experts for doing good work may be more successful with foundations.

✔ **Whom do you know?** Your nonprofit's contacts are important to its ability to raise money, especially when seeking funds from individuals. Knowing somebody who may write a big check is great, but knowing a lot of people who may write small checks is just as beneficial.

✔ **What can you provide to a donor?** Many donors appreciate when they benefit from their gifts to you, so look at what your nonprofit can provide. Maybe your organization can offer contributors the best seats in a concert hall, print their names in the programs, and introduce them to visiting musicians. Organizations that are easily able to give tangible items and special recognition to donors may be particularly successful with membership drives or corporate campaigns.

✔ **Can you cover the needed fundraising costs?** Special events and *direct mail* (fundraising letters sent to large numbers of people) are expensive forms of fundraising. Grantwriting takes time, but its cost is relatively low. We say more about fundraising costs in the later section "Estimate fundraising costs."

✔ **Do you have fundraising expertise?** Do staff members, board members, or volunteers have experience with raising money? If not, can your organization afford to hire expert help?

✔ **How does this year's fundraising climate compare to last year's?** Apart from the value and importance of your wonderful organization, donors give money according to their capabilities, and those capabilities change with the times. Corporate mergers, natural disasters, and economic downturns all affect how much money your organization can raise.

Drafting a Fundraising Plan

Setting out to raise funds is a lot easier when you have a guide to follow. After you analyze your nonprofit's fundraising potential, we recommend that you take the following steps to create a fundraising plan for your organization:

✔ **Set preliminary goals.** Ask yourself how much you need to raise to cover your organization's costs in the year ahead. Naming a clear and reasonable goal is the first step in your planning.

✔ **Ask whom you know.** Brainstorm lists of contacts — both the ones you and your board have now and the ones you want to have in the future. As you gather names, ask yourself the best way to approach those contacts — whether it's through formal proposals or a game of golf — and how much those prospects might give.

✔ **Research.** Your research phase asks both who might contribute and how much they might give. Using directories, the Internet, and advice from others, find out as much as you can about your potential sources. Continually build your lists of prospects and then refine and edit it as you go.

✔ **Estimate costs.** List the tools you need for your fundraising — perhaps a simple brochure, a "Donate" button on your website, or pancake batter for a breakfast at the firehouse. Estimate the costs of those tools, the staff time devoted to fundraising, and the fees for consultants if you use them. Also remember to invest in a good record-keeping system.

✔ **Get real.** Draft a schedule of what needs to be done when. Assign staff members, board members, or volunteers to different tasks and — this is important — agree to a system of checking in with one another to make sure you're all completing your assignments. (We address this step in the later section "Getting Down to Business: Moving to an Action Plan.")

The following sections outline these steps in greater detail.

Set a preliminary goal

A first step in your fundraising plan is to look at your estimated expenses for the year ahead. Spending this money should allow you to do the work your nonprofit has laid out in its organizational plan (see Chapter 7). For help connecting expenses to activities, see Chapter 11.

You want your fundraising goal to be aspirational, but you also want it to be realistic. Have you ever daydreamed about winning a lottery and how you would spend your millions? In that frame of mind, you might daydream a fundraising goal that depends on your nonprofit receiving seven-figure grants or gifts. That's great fun to imagine, but it's not a good model for setting a fundraising goal.

Look at the competition and the amount of funds your organization has raised in the past. Set goals that allow you to cover your essential costs but that also seem reasonable based on the experience of your staff and board. This step grows easier over time as your organization develops a track record and solid donor relationships.

Ask whom you know

If your organization is brand-new, brainstorm with your founding board members the names of people and organizations they know who may support your cause. If your organization has been around for a while, begin by listing its previous contributors. Annotate your list by identifying which supporters are likely to contribute again. Then stretch your thinking to consider new prospects — people who know you or who support other causes that are related to yours. You may even ask a few loyal donors to contribute to this brainstorming exercise.

After you begin this effort of generating names and ideas, you'll start to notice prospects all around you. A good fundraiser is ever vigilant, collecting names from newspaper stories, athletic event programs, public television credits, donor display walls in buildings, and related organizations' websites and annual reports.

This kind of brainstorming is best for identifying possible individual donors, but don't restrict your thinking at this stage. Go ahead and name all the prospects you've observed and thought of, including

✔ The foundations and government programs that fund other organizations like yours

✔ The corporations where your board members or volunteers work or those that make products that relate to your nonprofit's work

✔ The business associations or clubs that raise money for good causes

✔ The churches and places of worship in your neighborhood that offer community support and volunteers

Research and refine your prospect list

Professional fundraisers will tell you that the three keys to raising money are research, research, and research. To see what they mean, consider this scenario: You know that your next-door neighbors' child plays music. After all, her band rehearses at all hours in the garage. That leads you to put them on your list as good prospects for your community music school. But you may not know what your neighbors' other interests and hobbies are or where they work (which may be for a business that matches its employees' charitable contributions). A little research can go a long way!

Professional list brokers and services can provide data about donors, but you don't need to follow that expensive, formal route. Local news media, the Internet, social media, and informal conversations can tell you a great deal about your neighbors' affiliations and interests. You just need to pay attention and take notes.

After you've brainstormed a list of individual donor prospects (see the preceding section), go back through your list of names with board members, volunteers, and trusted associates. Mark which of your prospects seem to be highly likely, somewhat likely, and not very likely to donate to your efforts, based on what their interest appears to be in your organization's purpose, whether someone you know can contact them personally, and how much they've given to other nonprofits.

Researching institutional sources

If you want to raise money from foundations and government agencies, you'll likely begin by using the directories, databases, and websites specifically geared toward helping grant applicants. However, if your brainstorming session uncovers institutions as prospects, be sure to check out their websites or printed annual reports for info on their current guidelines and giving priorities. You can find details about institutions that don't have their own websites by subscribing to the Foundation Center's online directory at `www.foundationcenter.org`. Search for federal government agencies and programs at the Grants.gov website (`www.grants.gov`). See Chapter 16 for more information about conducting foundation research.

As you conduct your research, you're likely to uncover other prospects that you didn't think of when brainstorming, and you may also eliminate many that you discover are inappropriate.

Estimate how much your prospects will give

Identifying names of possible donors is just the beginning of the puzzle. You also need to estimate the amounts your prospective donors may give. For this estimate, you have to continue your research. For example, you may find clues by tracking down the approximate amounts of their contributions to other organizations that publish their donor lists.

For your foundation prospects, you can look up sample grants awarded to similar projects in the "Grants" section of *The Foundation Directory* book or online version (find it at `fconline.foundationcenter.org`). This book lists grants of $10,000 and higher. You can find grant lists for foundations that award smaller amounts by downloading their IRS Form 990 tax reports from the Foundation Center (`www.foundationcenter.org`) or GuideStar (`www.guidestar.org`) websites.

Estimating how much money you'll receive requires research into each type of donor. They're also based on overall goals that you set, including attracting new donors, sustaining many of the contributors your organization has had in the past, convincing some donors to increase their gifts, and continually expanding your contacts and resources.

Estimate fundraising costs

As you probably already know, raising money costs money. No organization receives every grant or gift that it seeks. So before you put your fundraising plan into action, you need to make sure that your organization can afford its potential fundraising costs and that the possible returns outweigh those costs.

Fundraising costs should be a modest part of an organization's budget. The costs will be higher when the organization is starting up or launching a major new fundraising effort. Costs likely will decline after a few years. Generally speaking, recruiting a new donor costs more than securing a second gift from a past supporter, and raising money through special events, mass mailings, and telemarketing are expensive fundraising methods. However, all of the above may be worthwhile if they bring visibility, new donors, or unrestricted support to your organization.

Consider the time and money you'll invest in fundraising

Here's a quick look at the costs — in terms of both time and money — of the fundraising activities your organization may consider using:

✔ **Grants and contracts:** Most of the costs of securing grants and contracts are labor costs for planning and writing the grant proposal. Sometimes you need to travel to meet in person with the agency awarding the money, so don't forget to budget that, too.

Pay attention to each grant maker's requirements for reporting the results of a project and make sure you can afford to complete the report. Some grants require the collection and analysis of extensive data. Some require audited financial statements.

✔ **Corporate sponsors:** Businesses and corporations may require visible recognition for their contributions to nonprofit organizations. Such support is often called a *sponsorship,* and the nonprofit and corporation agree upfront to the type of acknowledgment that they expect — whether it's a corporate logo printed on volunteers' t-shirts or a 6-foot banner announcing a company's support of a museum exhibit. Costs of printing t-shirts, banners, and other promotions generally are incurred by the nonprofit organizations.

✔ **Individual contributions:** Costs related to securing individual contributions include salaried staff members' time spent compiling lists of possible donors and the tools used for making successful donation requests. Common tools include solicitation letters and e-mails, brochures, and printed reply envelopes. Adding capacity to your website so it can accept online contributions may be another good investment.

Often when you think of solicitation letters, you probably think of *direct mail* — hundreds of thousands of letters sent to purchased lists of potential donors. Although direct mail can be a very successful form of fundraising for some causes — medical emergencies, animal rescue, and civil rights, just to name a few — it's also very expensive. A new, emerging nonprofit can make good use of letter-writing by targeting a small mailing to people who already know its work well, asking its board members and volunteers to make personal appeals to people they know, or by using e-mail rather than snail mail.

Some organizations hire companies to handle telephone solicitation campaigns. Be cautious if you take this step: Some of these companies charge a high percentage of the money raised in exchange for providing this service. Others are reputable and valued by the nonprofits they serve.

✔ **Special events:** Special events can be a great way to introduce new people to your organization, but producing such events can be one of the more expensive ways to raise funds. Spending 50 percent or 60 percent of the income from an event to pay for costs is common. After all, printing, advertising, food, and entertainment all cost money. Also, special events are labor intensive, so make sure you have an experienced volunteer group or detail-oriented staff to work on special events if you go this route.

✔ **Planned giving:** If your nonprofit isn't familiar with tax laws regarding wills and estates, it may need to employ or hire on contract a planned giving expert (or attract one as a board member). Bringing this person on board can be expensive in the short term, but doing so can yield important long-term support for your agency.

Planned giving works best for organizations that have been around for a long time and that show good prospects for continuing. Universities, museums, and churches come to mind. Small, new groups have a difficult time attracting bequests.

Keep good donor records

Before it starts to raise money, you need to set up a system for keeping timely records on all of your nonprofit's donors. This system usually is a Microsoft Excel spreadsheet or a specialized electronic database, but it can even be as simple as a handwritten card file and datebook. For foundation grants, such a system can help you remember deadlines for applying for grants and submitting final reports.

For individual donors, a good records system can help you keep information up-to-date about when and how you've contacted them, who in the organization knows them, how and why they gave their gifts, and whether you promised them any special recognition or invitations when they contributed. Because nonprofits hope to talk to or keep in touch with their donors over time, recording their spouses' and children's names, their interests, their business affiliations, and any other pertinent personal information also is worthwhile. File1301 provides a donor information record that you can use to record these details.

If you decide to use an electronic database system to manage your donor records, you can choose a program that focuses specifically on fundraising, or you can keep track of every connection you have with anyone and everyone, including clients, ticket buyers, professional peers, donors, and volunteers.

Specialized fundraising software can really increase your efficiency in record keeping, but be careful when you choose your program because it can be quite costly. Consider the purchase price, setup charges, and availability of technical backup support. For example, open source software — which is made available for free use by anyone — may not charge you to download and use their software, but they also may not provide consistent technical support if you run into problems.

You can find reviews and articles to help you choose among different kinds of donor, member, and constituent management systems at www.idealware.org. To help you start your search, here's a quick look at some of your options:

- ✔ CivicCRM (www.civicCRM.com) is available license-free to nonprofits. Although it's an excellent tool, you'll likely need someone with technology skills to set it up for you. It integrates easily with Drupal and Joomla content management systems.

- ✔ DonorPerfect (www.donorperfect.com) focuses on donors but has some support for members, volunteers, and other contacts. It offers an online version for a reasonable monthly fee.

- ✔ eBase (www.ebase.org) is a good, inexpensive option. This program runs on FileMaker Pro, but you don't need FileMaker unless you want to customize eBase.

- ✔ eTapestry (www.etapestry.com) offers a 30-day free trial for trying out its system. You can subscribe at different levels and prices based on your estimated number of donor records. (The basic service accommodates up to 1,000 records.) eTapestry is aimed primarily at managing donors.

- ✔ GiftWorks (www.missionresearch.com) is a reasonably priced software option with a reputation for being easy to use. It's primarily designed to track gifts and donors.

- ✔ Salesforce.com (www.salesforce.com) offers a high-end product for free to nonprofits with up to ten users. Salesforce offers a growing body of features for tracking donors and other constituents.

After you choose the system that's right for your organization, check out www.techsoup.org to see if you can find it at a discounted price.

Initially, when you urgently need grants and gifts to start up your organization, keeping good records may seem to be a time-wasting activity, but in the long run, thorough records allow you to raise more money. You can start with a simple approach and upgrade it over time, but every time you shift to a new system, make sure you invest time in the change.

Getting Down to Business: Moving to an Action Plan

A good fundraising plan includes the practical details that move it from being a list of goals, contacts, and costs to being a road map for your fundraising direction. The following steps help you incorporate these practical details:

1. **Assign tasks, gather tools, and make a calendar.**

   For each of the revenue areas in your plan (government, foundations, corporations, and/or individuals), indicate who's going to work on raising the money, how many prospective sources you need, and which tools you need to meet your goals (such as fundraising letters, photographs, web newsletters, social media campaigns, membership cards, or an online donation system). Then outline a general time frame for how long your fundraising efforts will take and research specific deadlines for government, foundation, and corporate grants.

Include in your calendar a schedule for staff, board, and volunteers to check in with one another on progress made toward completing their assigned tasks.

2. **Link your cost estimates to each fundraising goal.**

   You've already estimated costs of the time and tools you'll need to raise funds (see the previous section "Drafting a Fundraising Plan"). Now you need to create a fundraising cash flow outline that shows when you need upfront money and when you can expect to secure income from your efforts. Keep in mind that some foundations have a rather lengthy time from letter of intent to grant funding, sometimes up to 18 months. Individual donors may have one time of year (before the end of the year, for example) when they make charitable contributions.

3. **Put the fruits of your labor together in one document — this is your funding plan!**

   Your finished plan likely consists of the following elements:

   - Sources sought and fundraising goals (for example: foundation grants, $75,000, and special event revenues, $2,200)

   - Prospects identified (both current and prospective contributors), along with amounts you expect them to give

   - Number of prospects you need to achieve your goals in each category

   - List of who's responsible for making particular contacts or contributing other services to raising the funds

   - Estimated costs of pursuing the contributions in each category

   - Timeline and cash flow projection

 Many agencies create an optimum fundraising plan as well as a bare-bones fundraising plan — one based on their hopes and one based on what they must secure to survive. During the course of the year, they rebalance and adjust their plans.

 Check out the two sample fundraising plans (File1302 and File1303) and two sample fundraising budgets (File1304 and File1305). One set is for a small school music organization, and the other is for a slightly larger neighborhood park improvement organization. Pop in the CD or click the link in the table of contents to view these files.

Planting the Seeds for a New Organization

One tried-and-true rule of fundraising is that people give money to people they know. They also give money to causes they care about. However, making a contribution is an expression of trust. That means the likeliest contributors to a new nonprofit organization are people and agencies that know and admire its founders and their work.

Hitting up people you know

We know of a few people who have launched their organizations with the help of major grants from a government agency or a large, national foundation, but many more of them start close to home with gifts from their founders, their founding board members, and the people who know them. They then build out from that inner circle of relationships, gradually creating networks of associations with the friends, family members, and business associates of their initial contributors.

We asked some people who founded organizations how and when they got their first sources of income. One invited 20 people to her house and, after a convincing pitch and some good wine, got most of them to write checks. Another started a youth mentoring program out of his dorm room when he was a college student. He talked his college into paying him a work-study stipend to begin his project, and then he charged his volunteer mentors modest membership fees to cover basic costs. Another noticed a city department's neglect of small city parks after budget cutbacks and, by knocking on local politicians' doors, secured a city grant to involve volunteers in park cleanup days.

Many organizations start up with contributions from individuals, in part because individuals often make up their minds more quickly than businesses or foundations.

Branching out with special events

Although special events are one of the more expensive ways of raising money, you probably can see real advantages to including them in the fundraising plan for a new organization. Events create a way to inform dozens or hundreds of people about your organization at the same time. The best part is that those people then begin to spread the word about your good work. Remember that events don't have to be elaborate. A gathering of a dozen people can be a good start.

Approaching foundations

When approaching foundations, you may think that you're at a disadvantage because your project doesn't have a track record. On the contrary, some foundations specifically like to support start-up projects and organizations. If your agency is new, when you're using *The Foundation Directory* (either the book, which is available in many libraries, or the *Foundation Directory Online,* which is available through subscription), check the "types of support" listings to see whether the foundation you're looking at awards *seed funding* — that is, support for new activities. If the foundation makes grants in your field of interest and geographic area, it may be a good prospect for helping you launch your organization. Find out more information about conducting foundation research in Chapter 16.

Considering government grants

Government grants and contracts may provide significant underpinnings for a new effort, but they come with three distinct disadvantages for new nonprofit organizations:

- ✔ **In general, they take longer to secure.** The review and approval process may be slow, and many government agencies have only one annual deadline.

- ✔ **They often require grantees to comply with rules and regulations regarding permits, board policies, hiring practices, and financial reporting.** Although their rules may be good rules, when you're just starting out, your organization may still be working out its systems and policies.

- ✔ **They sometimes require their funded organizations to spend money upfront and then submit invoices in order to be reimbursed for an agreed-upon amount of money.** If you have few sources of income, you may not have any funds available for this upfront spending.

If your organization is applying to the federal government, you must first register with Grants.gov (www.grants.gov). This registration ordinarily takes three to five days, but to be safe, plan on two weeks for completing it in case questions arise about your organization.

Chapter 14

Raising Money from Individuals

- -

In This Chapter

▶ Figuring out why donors give

▶ Writing a case statement

▶ Tracking down possible donors

▶ Asking for major gift contributions

▶ Soliciting donations via mail

▶ Securing funds online

▶ Raising money through telemarketing

- -

*E*veryone has had some experience with asking for money. Maybe you sold cookies for a scout troop when you were a child. Maybe you asked neighbors to sponsor you in a summer read-a-thon for your school library. Maybe you once had to call Mom and Dad when you were stranded at a bus station in Toledo and couldn't get home for Thanksgiving.

These moments can be awkward, but asking for money for yourself and asking for money for an organization you believe in are very different. Organizational fundraising can feel good because it helps you do something important for a cause you care deeply about. The hard part is finding the right words to say, the means for conveying those words, and the audience who's receptive to those words.

Responding to the right cause, the right message, and the right person, individual donors give to many kinds of organizations. In fact, they represent the largest portion of private contributions in the United States. According to Giving USA, financial contributions from individual donors accounted for 72 percent of all charitable giving in 2012. This chapter shows you how to flex your own fundraising muscles and persuade individual donors to give to your organization.

Often when people think of raising large amounts of money for organizations, they think of securing major grants from foundations or sponsorships from corporations. But we recommend that your nonprofit also include individual giving as a part of its fundraising plans. In total, individuals give more to nonprofits than do foundations or corporations, and most individuals allow you to use the funds contributed for whatever your greatest needs may be. That kind of flexibility adds considerable value to a contribution — even if it's just $20.

Knowing Why People Give and Asking Accordingly

The key rule of fundraising is "If you don't ask, you won't get." Taking the step of asking is critical, but so is knowing how to ask. According to marketing experts who study motivations for doing just about everything, people contribute to nonprofit organizations because they want to

- Feel generous
- Change the world
- Exercise compassion
- Have a sense of belonging to a group
- Feel a sense of well-being, of safety
- Be recognized

By understanding these underlying donor motivations, you can phrase your request in the most effective way. Appeals to new donors often ask them to "join" or "become part of" a movement or cause in order to touch upon the desire for belonging. Appeals also call upon donors' compassion and idealism, and they commonly link the needs of particular constituents served by a nonprofit to the well-being and security of an entire community. That's making the most of asking.

Registering to solicit donations

Many states, the District of Columbia, and some local jurisdictions require organizations that solicit charitable contributions to file registration forms before soliciting. This registration is meant to protect the public from solicitors touting illegitimate causes. The regulations differ from state to state. Typically, the rules don't apply unless the nonprofit raises more than $250 a year (which we hope you will!). Check with your state's attorney general's office to be sure your nonprofit is in compliance with all laws. It's also important to check local laws when raising money through what is known as charitable gaming (bingo, raffles, pull tabs, and

so on). Laws regulating these activities often differ from county to county and city to city.

What if you're raising money online? Guidelines adopted in 2001 by the National Association of State Charity Officials (NASCO) state that any nonprofit that uses fundraising tools to target donors in a specific state must register in that state. Plus, the 990 tax form for nonprofits asks organizations where they are registered to fundraise. If you're seeking donations nationally, take all relevant states into account and remember to renew your registrations annually.

When you find yourself hesitating to ask someone for a contribution, keep in mind that you're not begging, you're offering him an opportunity to be part of something worthwhile. Giving your organization a gift can make him feel good.

Stating Your Case

A *case statement* is a tool nonprofits often use when asking for a contribution. It's a short, compelling argument for supporting the nonprofit that can be presented as a brochure, one-page information sheet, or glossy folder filled with factsheets, photographs, budgets, or charts. It should be professional, factual, and short enough that readers will read it all the way through.

A good case statement can be used in many ways in fundraising:

✔ After talking about the agency with a potential donor, you leave behind a copy of your case statement for her to consider.

✔ If you need to phone a potential donor, you keep the case statement close at hand as a reminder of the key points to make about the agency.

✔ If you mail or e-mail a fundraising letter, you can borrow wording from the case statement to write that letter or include a copy of the case statement with the letter.

Instructions for writing a case statement resemble a recipe for stew or soup. A few basic ingredients make any version of this dish delicious, and the cook can spice it up with whatever other quality ingredients she has at hand. Follow these steps:

1. **Make notes about the following subjects. Be selective; allot no more than 100 words to any of these items:**

   • The mission statement of the organization

   • The history of the organization

   • The services it offers

   • The organization's key accomplishments

   • Affidavits, reviews, or quotes from enthusiasts who have benefited from the organization's work

   • The organization's future plans

2. **Toss in no more than 50 words on each of these topics:**

   • The organization's philosophy or approach to providing service

   • The pressing needs the organization works to address

   • The ways the organization will measure or recognize its success

3. **Stir in whatever else you have on hand, including**

- Compelling photographs of the organization's work

- Quotes and testimonials from clients, partners, donors, and others

- Charts or maps illustrating growth — for example, the increasing numbers of clients the organization serves or the expanding geographic area it serves

- An overview of the organization's budget and finances, particularly if the budget is balanced and the finances are healthy

- Anything else that shines a light on the agency, such as publications completed, awards received, and so on

4. **State the giving opportunities your nonprofit offers.**

The giving options must be clear and not too complicated. Donors want to understand how their contributions can make a difference. Sometimes giving opportunities are linked to the cost of providing services, such as the following:

- The cost of immunizing one child against a deadly disease

- The cost of replacing one chair in a symphony hall

- The cost of rescuing and rehabilitating one injured wild burro

- The cost of planting one acre of trees in a reforestation area

Sometimes opportunities are linked to premiums or gifts the donor receives in return. For example:

- For a gift of up to $50, the donor receives a coffee mug as a token of thanks. A larger gift is acknowledged with a tote bag.

- For a gift of several hundred dollars, the donor's name appears on a brass plate on the chair the gift has paid to refurbish.

- For a gift of $1,000, the donor receives quarterly progress reports from the scientist whose research the gift is supporting.

- For a gift of several thousand dollars, the donor's name is etched on a tile in the lobby of the organization's new building.

- For a gift of several million dollars, the lobby is named after the donor.

For a contribution of $250 or more, you must acknowledge the gift in writing and specify the date of the contribution and the amount. If you give that donor something of value in exchange for the contribution, you should mention the value of that premium in your acknowledgment letter (because the donor must deduct the fair market value of that gift if she itemizes her contribution to your organization in her tax filing). See File1401 and File1402 for examples of acknowledgment letters.

Recognizing your donors

Before acknowledging a donor in print, on a donor wall, or in another public manner, always ask him for permission and ask how he wants to be listed.

When choosing how to recognize your donors, you want to consider the cost of the recognition, the nature of the activity supported, and the way the donor recognition advances (or doesn't suit) your organization's purpose and mission. A simple, printed list of names is dignified and inexpensive. Although donor gifts cost money, having your organization's name printed on t-shirts or tote bags that your donors wear or carry throughout the community may be an effective way of promoting your work. However, if you spend too much on gifts, you can annoy donors or leave them wondering how much you really need their contribution.

When writing your case statement, you don't need to follow the exact order in which we list the elements. Lead with the strongest points and leave out the less compelling items. Choose a strong writer to draft the piece and then test it on others — both within and outside your agency — to see whether it tells a clear, impressive story.

When your case statement is written, produce it for distribution and make sure to match its look to your nonprofit and its intended audience. If your nonprofit is a modest, grassroots organization, your case statement should be simple and direct in its presentation. If it's an environmental organization, you may want to produce the case statement online instead of using paper. If it's an internationally known opera company, your case statement should look dramatic and elegant.

Identifying Possible Donors

Your doorbell rings, and you open the door to greet an adorable child you've never met. The child is selling candy bars to raise funds for band instruments at school. You played in a band when you were young, so you buy a candy bar, wishing the little fundraiser success.

A few minutes later, the doorbell rings again, and you open the door to greet a second adorable child. You know this child because he lives next door. You remember when his mother brought him home as a newborn, and you watched him ride his first bicycle down the sidewalk. He's selling the same candy bars to benefit the soccer team at his school: They need equipment and uniforms. You buy *five* candy bars.

Rich or poor, most of us are influenced in our charitable giving by how well we know the people, either directly or indirectly, who are doing the asking.

Mapping the personal connections of each member of your organization is a key first step in identifying possible donors.

Drawing circles of connections

Figure 14-1 represents a common brainstorming exercise that nonprofit organizations use to identify possible individual donors. This exercise is most effective if both staff and board members participate. Follow these steps:

1. **Identify the people who are closest to the organization — those within the "inner circle."**

   This inner circle includes staff and board members and active volunteers or clients who frequently use the organization's services.

2. **Identify those people who have the second-closest relationship to the organization.**

   This second circle may include family and close friends of those people in the inner circle, former staff and board members, neighbors of the organization and its inner circle, volunteers, and clients who sometimes use its services.

3. **Take one more step backward and identify the people who make up the third circle.**

   These folks may include grandparents or cousins of those people in the inner circle, old friends whom they haven't seen recently, friends of former staff and board members, and former or infrequent users of the organization's services.

4. **Identify the friends, relatives, and other associates of those who make up circles #2 and #3.**

5. **Search for your cause-related friends and associates.**

   Look for people who may not know anyone involved in your organization but who demonstrate an interest in the subject and the purpose it represents (as indicated by their memberships, their magazine subscriptions, or their contributions to similar organizations). Follow the local media and watch for people who take an interest in your cause because of their personal experiences. For example, maybe their child was born with the congenital disease your nonprofit is studying, or maybe they come from a forested part of the state and care about the preservation of old-growth trees.

You can continue enlarging your circle of connections, but with every step you take from the center to the outside, the bond between the organization and the potential donors weakens. As that occurs, the cost of raising money from the people who inhabit those circles increases. Eventually, the cost of securing gifts from an outer circle becomes higher than the likely amount of income to be gained, and it's time to stop.

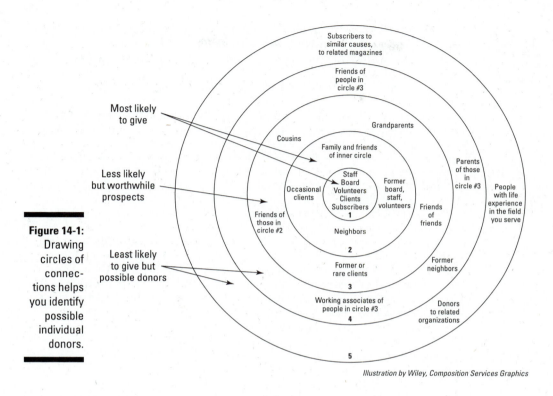

Figure 14-1:
Drawing circles of connections helps you identify possible individual donors.

Illustration by Wiley, Composition Services Graphics

How do you know when it's time to stop and back up? Most organizations try to keep the cost of their overall fundraising at or lower than 20 percent of their organization's budget. However, when you're starting out, particularly with some kinds of fundraising strategies, such as mailings or special events (see Chapter 15), your percentages may be higher in the first few years. These approaches generally begin to bring in significant contributions as they're repeated and donors renew their gifts. If you're still just "breaking even" in year three, it's time to back up and refocus your approach.

Getting a list of contacts from your board of directors

Every year, or before you start work on a special event or letter-writing campaign, ask each of your organization's board members to provide the names of ten or more people they know. This exercise is useful for developing a solicitation list.

Most people can sit down and list ten friends and associates off the top of their heads. However, when you ask your board members to produce a list in that way, it's unlikely that they will exhaust all their connections and relationships. If you hand board members starter lists of people they may know and then ask them to edit and add to that list, you're likely to get many more names.

To develop this "starter list," think about your board members and their probable networks and connections. Say, for instance, that your nonprofit is lucky enough to have a local business leader on its board of directors. Searching online and scouring the business sections of local newspapers can reveal a variety of connections, such as the board member's business partners and suppliers; members of his professional associations, clubs, or other boards; and his close neighbors. Everyone, no matter how modestly he or she lives, has a web of professional and personal connections.

The next step in developing your organization's network of connections is to address personalized letters from your board members to the people on their lists, providing each of those people with an opportunity to find out more about your organization and to contribute. When asking for their help, make it easy for your board members' contacts to respond: Provide a simple form for them to fill out and a self-addressed, stamped envelope, or link an e-mailed request to an easy-to-use donation page on your website. If you send your query by e-mail, make sure the subject line is compelling and the sender is someone the recipient knows.

After you have your list of contacts, you can use it as the basis for a face-to-face individual donor campaign, as well as for mail and e-mail campaigns and event invitations.

Growing a Major Gift

Face-to-face visits are the best way to secure larger contributions, what fundraising professionals call *major gifts* (see Chapter 13 for more information on major gifts). Rarely does one knock on a door, deliver a short speech, and depart with a check for a large amount. Generally, several contacts must take place before a major donor is ready to make a commitment. This process is often called "cultivation," and the comparison of planting the idea, tending the relationship, and harvesting the result when it's fully grown is an apt one. It takes time. In this section, we break down key steps and tips for growing a major gift.

Before you talk yourself into making a phone call or sending a letter rather than sitting down to talk to a donor face to face, remember that it's more difficult for donors to say no to someone sitting in front of them.

Deciding who should ask

If possible, the board member or staff person who knows the potential donor should make the visit. If that's not possible, the visiting team should be made up of two people who are peers of that person — perhaps a board member who's a local business leader and the executive director. Be careful not to overwhelm a potential donor with a huge group. Two or three people are plenty.

Preparing to put forth your request

Gulp. It's time to ask someone for money. In preparing for this moment, you need to remember that you're not asking for something for yourself. You're inviting the potential donor to belong, to be part of something worthwhile. When planning how to describe the reason for the gift, step back for a moment and remember why volunteering for the organization is important to you. How did you become involved? What lives have you seen changed with the organization's work? Sally forth armed with your personal story and your case statement, which will remind you of the key points you want to mention.

Breaking the ice

Open the conversation with easy material. What did you find out about this person while conducting research, and how do you know her? Maybe your kids attend the same school or you're both baseball fans. Try to use something low key to open the conversation instead of forcing yourself on your "victim" with a heavy sales pitch. The key is creating rapport.

Brief small talk can ease the conversation's start, but don't waste a potential donor's time. Let her know how you became involved in the organization, and then briefly give an overview of its attributes and current situation. Team members should take up different pieces of the conversation, remembering to let the potential donor talk, too, and paying close attention to the signals she sends. Keeping the meeting comfortable for the prospect is critical.

Adopting the right attitude

When soliciting gifts, be firm and positive, but not pushy. Pay attention to how the potential donor is acting or responding and step back if you discover he isn't feeling well or his business has taken a difficult turn.

Just as you can see signs of when not to press the case, you also may notice signs of readiness when the discussion is going well. The potential donor may express interest in attending an event at the nonprofit. He may display pride in his familiarity with the organization. Be a good listener as well as a good presenter.

Asking someone to contribute to an organization is easier when you've already made a gift yourself. Even if you can't make a large contribution, you'll feel more confident about asking others if you've already contributed — and the potential donor will find you more credible. In general, it's a good idea for the people in the agency's inner circle to contribute before asking outside individuals to give. (Refer to the earlier section "Drawing circles of connections" for more on those who make up the inner circle.)

Timing the request: An inexact science

Many people don't believe in asking for a specific contribution at the first meeting. They believe in setting the stage — letting a prospective donor know that a campaign or special program is coming up and that the organization will be seeking her help in the future. At a second visit, they try to get this person to see a program in action or meet other board members at an informal gathering. The goal is building a relationship, inviting the potential donor to feel as if she wants to belong with the people leading your agency.

For some major gift campaigns, fundraisers use a feasibility study. In such a study, someone from outside the organization interviews board members and potential major donors, seeking their impressions of the organization and getting an idea of the size of the contribution they may make. This process both helps the organization to set realistic goals and warns the "research subjects" that the agency plans to come knocking at their doors.

As with any cultivation, the timing of the harvest is critical. When the time is right, it's like recognizing a piece of fruit that's ready to be picked. Make a date for a follow-up visit. Plan a setting where the conversation can be congenial but focused. Don't rush (a common failing), but don't leave without asking. If the answer is disappointing, ask for feedback on your visit and try to figure out which aspects of your case statement the potential donor finds most (and least) compelling. Maybe the donor wants a naming opportunity that you didn't present, or maybe he wants to see the program in action first. Or maybe the timing isn't right for the donor, but next year he'll be able to make a sizable gift. Sometimes contributors come around at a later time, so it's always good to seek permission to stay in touch.

Determining what to ask for

Before asking a potential donor for a contribution at one of your follow-up meetings, find out everything you can about the person's gifts to similar causes. (To do so, you can scour donor lists and ask board members who know this person.) This information helps you ask for an appropriate amount.

Many people believe that you should ask for an amount that's somewhat higher than what you expect to get, because making a request for a generous gift is flattering to the donor. However, you don't want to ask for so much money that the potential donor feels that whatever he gives will be a disappointment. Donors commonly say something like, "I can't do $50,000, but I'll consider $25,000 if that would be a help." (Add or subtract zeros as appropriate.)

In most cases, when the donor suggests a level, you don't want to haggle; you may become annoying and cause him to back out of contributing. You *may* gently push for a higher amount by using the personal connections angle, however: "We were hoping you might become one of our $50,000 donors, along with Joe Schmoe and Sally Smiley, but whatever you can provide would be a big help."

Minding your manners

One of the most important parts of your major gift campaign is thanking your contributors. Do it very soon after the pledge is made or the gift is received. We recommend an immediate phone call or e-mail and a handwritten note. If you acknowledge a donor thoughtfully and graciously, and follow up that thank-you note with a newsletter or information about the organization's accomplishments, you're strengthening your future relationship with that contributor and making her feel as if she's part of your organization. That's good manners and smart fundraising.

Raising Money by Mail

Direct mail, the practice of soliciting donations through large-scale mailings, grows out of a sophisticated and fascinating area of fundraising. Your organization may be much too small to make investing in a direct-mail campaign worthwhile, but you can use valuable tips from the "big guys" and develop small-scale letter-writing efforts that yield good results.

Taking the direct-mail route

If you want to try large-scale direct-mail fundraising, we strongly recommend that you hire a direct-mail consultant or firm to handle your campaign. Direct-mail fundraising can be an expensive investment, and you want the best, most up-to-date professional advice available.

Successful direct mail depends on the following:

- ✔ A cause that's meaningful to many thousands of people across your state or the country

- ✔ A compelling, well-presented letter that makes its reader believe that your nonprofit can make a difference

- ✔ A well-chosen mailing list, usually purchased from a list broker

- ✔ Nonprofit bulk-rate postage, which can save you a significant amount over commercial mailing rates

- ✔ Easy, clear ways your letter readers can respond to the request by using a return envelope, response card, or website

- ✔ Testing your letter and list at a modest scale before sending the letter to hundreds of thousands of names

- ✔ A mailing schedule through which you solicit donors several times each year

When writing a fundraising letter, remember that many potential donors will read your letter's P.S. before they read the body of the letter, so include compelling information there, such as a testimonial from a client, a statistic that demonstrates your organization's accomplishments, or information about a matching gift.

To secure a nonprofit bulk-mail permit, you must apply to the United States Postal Service, completing PS Form 3624. You can find a link among the web resources at File1409.

Successfully raising money through the mail depends on gradual development of a loyal cadre of donors who respond by mail. Fewer than 1 percent of the people you initially mail to may send contributions, but after they give, you add them to your *donor list* — a precious resource you develop after an investment of time, effort, and postage. You can send mail to these generous folks in the future and expect a higher rate of return (between 6 percent and 12 percent).

Donors who make repeat contributions are likely to stick with your organization for several years, making three or four (or more!) contributions in that time, and they'll likely increase the size of their contributions. Adding to this value, you'll uncover prospects for major gifts and planned gifts (contributions from bequests) among these donors.

Before your donor list develops into a significant and loyal resource, a direct-mail campaign on your organization's behalf may only break even on the cost of the initial letter-writing campaign. You may even lose money. That's why direct mail may not be appropriate for a small or start-up organization: The financial risk is too high. You need to be able to cover significant upfront costs and not expect a strong return on that investment for several years.

Trying your hand at a letter-writing campaign

Given the risks and costs of direct mail, we recommend that you borrow some of its techniques and work on a more affordable scale, using your organization's small but mighty contact list and your own writing skills. The key to success is targeting donors to whom the staff, board, and volunteers are already connected in some fashion.

Your fundraising letter isn't just a letter; it also includes a mailing envelope, a reply envelope and card, and sometimes a brochure, a copy of a newspaper clipping, or a photograph. All these pieces should relate to one another and convey a clear, compelling message.

The outer envelope should be inviting to open. For instance, did you use a first-class stamp? Did you handwrite the address and add a special message? Is the envelope a different color and size than standard envelopes to draw attention to its importance? The letter itself should give readers enough information that they feel involved in the cause. Most of it should be dedicated to describing the problem that the organization is trying to solve. After that, it should discuss how things can be turned around for the better and the organization's specific method or program for doing so. Make the tone personal by using "I" and "you." The letter should close with a vision for how things will look if the plan succeeds. Keep paragraphs short and emphasize key points with underlined or bolded text.

Always make it easy for your donor to respond by offering postage-paid envelopes and clear information about how to give through your website. Always include your mailing address, website, and phone number on the letter in case a donor misplaces the envelope or other materials included in the mailing.

Your nonprofit can get a permit from the post office to offer postage-paid return envelopes.

See File1403 for an example of a solicitation letter sent to individual donors.

Try out your letter first on your organization's internal lists of board contacts, clients, and donors. Then continually build your potential donor list by making it a habit to collect names, addresses, and e-mails at events you present and meetings and conferences you attend.

Just as important as collecting names for your list is taking care of those names — especially of those who become donors. You want to develop a good system for recording information about new donors in order to thank them, keep in touch with them, and ask for their support again in the future. You'll find that database programs to manage your donor information come in various degrees of complexity and prices (see Chapter 13). Choose the one that's best for your needs.

Treating donors well for great results

Good fundraisers recognize the importance of treating donors well. In fact, the Association of Fundraising Professionals has even developed a thoughtful Donor Bill of Rights that offers standards to follow (`www.afpnet.org/Ethics/EnforcementDetail.cfm?ItemNumber=3359`).

Good treatment of your donors includes allowing them to tell you if they don't want their addresses shared with other organizations. You can include a check box on your reply card where they can indicate their preference for keeping their information from being traded or sold. If you send e-mail solicitations, be sure to include a safe unsubscribe option for donors who want to be removed from the mailing list.

Raising Money the "E" Way (Easily and Electronically)

Just as your website and electronic-communications system are tools for serving your constituents and marketing your work, they are tools for raising money. According to the "2010 Online Giving Report," produced by Network for Good, approximately 80 percent of charities raised money online, but online giving represented only about 8 percent (or less) of total money contributed to charities. Although online giving increases every year, we don't recommend that it be your only fundraising approach: It's a good tool only when it's used in combination with other methods.

Given that more and more of us make online purchases and read electronic media, why is online giving so tepid? Part of the answer lies in who is giving online: They tend to be younger donors who make smaller gifts. Part of the answer is relationships: Most people find the Internet to be relatively impersonal and are unlikely to make a major contribution online. And part of the answer is the fault of nonprofits that haven't marketed their online giving option and haven't made it easy for donors to make online donations.

Gradually, online giving is expanding, and online fundraising has worked very well in some contexts — especially disaster and emergency relief campaigns, for which donors want to respond quickly. People also respond well to online fundraising by organizations they know well, such as their college alumni associations.

Using e-mail and related tools to build and maintain relationships

Fundraising is about building relationships with people. It's in a nonprofit's best interest to thank donors regularly and keep them informed about what the organization is doing. It can't hurt to get to know the people who give money to your nonprofit, either. Here's where the Internet can be of help.

The most frequently used feature of the Internet is e-mail. It's easy to use, and it's cheap and fast. Many nonprofit organizations produce monthly (or more frequent) online newsletters about their work. Distributing these bulletins to donors is a great way to keep them informed about how their contributions are making a difference.

 If you're going to send bulk e-mails, you may want to use an e-mail marketing service that can help you build your list, set up your message in an attractive format, and make it likelier that your message is received (and doesn't land in a spam folder). Some of these businesses allow nonprofits to send a certain number of messages without charge.

As a first step, obtain an organization e-mail account and address that enables people to contact you (and enables you to build an online mailing list). You can use e-mail messages to compel readers to click through to your website, where they can read more about your organization and find out how to contribute to it. Remember to mention your online donation option in every piece of mail and e-mail you send, and place your "Donate" button in a prominent place on your site.

Related online tools you want to have at hand include the following:

- ✔ **A website:** Your site should feature clear, timely information, calls to action that encourage readers to get involved, a "Contact Us" option linked to your e-mail address, and an easy-to-use click-through "Donate" button that enables website visitors to make contributions online. If you have a wish list of in-kind items that people can donate, place a link to that list in a prominent location (perhaps accompanied by a link to your online wish registry at a website like Amazon.com (`www.amazon.com`), where donors can make a quick purchase that's delivered straight to your organization's door). You can read more about creating a website in Chapter 12.

- ✔ **A brief electronic newsletter:** This e-newsletter about your organization's work should feature an intriguing subject line and be highly readable. Imagine your typical reader: *If* she opens it, she'll scroll through it quickly. You want to write a compelling sentence or two about each topic, inviting the reader to click through to your organization's website and read more about it (noticing the "donate" button while she's there).

- ✔ **An organization blog:** Blogs (and group discussion lists, called *listservs*) are great tools for inviting comments and feedback. Both tools are available for free at a number of websites.

- ✔ **Social-networking accounts:** Social marketing options include Facebook, LinkedIn, Google Groups, Twitter, Pinterest, Instagram, and many others. These social-networking tools remind people of your organization and urge them to take action on your behalf. Some of them provide features for raising money (such as Facebook's "Causes").

File1404 and File1405 provide sample e-solicitation letters, and File1406 shows how a nonprofit uses e-mail correspondence to develop a relationship with a potential donor. File1407 offers tips on how to solicit donations through your website and social media outlets. For tips on writing an e-solicitation letter, head to www.dummies.com/extras/nonprofitkit.

Building your e-mail address lists

When corresponding with people who contact you through e-mail or your website, consider them prospective donors. If you're e-mailing a new correspondent, ask whether he wants to be added to your mailing list. Make this invitation a habit and respect those who decline. Others will accept, and slowly and steadily you'll build your list.

E-mail address lists, like mailing address lists, can be purchased, traded, or borrowed. A nonprofit may be willing to lend or trade its list with another nonprofit with a similar mission. When using a borrowed list, it's important to respect the privacy of the people listed. Don't pass it along to others without permission and always offer an "unsubscribe" option.

Making your website a cultivation tool

A website can never replicate a face-to-face encounter with another person, but if you design your site to grab and hold a visitor's attention, you can succeed at attracting donors. Strategies may include:

- ✔ Short profiles of clients, donors, volunteers, and staff members

- ✔ Strong visual features — graphic-design elements, photographs, and short videos

- ✔ Behind-the-scenes tours of the organization's activities (Our local zoo's website currently has a feature story about a newborn tiger cub.)

- ✔ PDFs of studies your nonprofit has conducted or curricula it has developed and links to information and resources about the field in which your agency works

  ✔ Invitations to readers to provide contact information — and promises of specific, enticing rewards if they do so

  ✔ Blogs and chat rooms on subjects related to your work

  ✔ A clear and easy-to-use donation feature for making contributions and information about how donations will be used to make a difference

The longer a website keeps visitors involved, the likelier it is to build their trust and interest.

Most websites include a "contact us" page. Make sure this option is user friendly and that someone on your staff is responsible for replying to queries quickly and courteously. Include opportunities for readers of the website to sign up for your electronic newsletter or other publications and to leave a mailing address and/or telephone number.

You may build the most amazing website on the planet, but if readers aren't finding it, it's not fulfilling its role for your organization. One critical question is how to attract the notice of search engines. Some agencies sit back and wait for a web spider to find their page; some submit their page to search engines one by one, which can be time consuming; and some hire a service to submit their information to the leading search engines. See *Search Engine Optimization For Dummies*, 5th Edition, by Peter Kent, for information on getting your site noticed by search engines.

Gathering money online

A key first step to raising money through the Internet is to add a "donate now" button to your organization's website. If you have good technology support and a website that includes a system for securely collecting money, you can insert your own "donate now" button. However, many nonprofits find it easier to contract with a "donate now" service. The number of options available can be daunting. We recommend checking Idealware's website (`www.idealware.org`) for helpful, updated articles about choosing online donation and credit-card processing tools.

If you hire a marketing service to develop and maintain your organization's website, consider the breadth of the services you're purchasing. Will the agency design your website for you? Will it thank your donors? Will it manage a donor database for your online contributions?

Also, look carefully at how and for what an agency charges fees. Most online contribution services charge a setup fee, a monthly fee, and a per-contribution fee. Sometimes you can avoid the monthly fee, but when you do, you often pay a higher fee for each contribution you receive. Some less-expensive nonprofit technology services charge lower fees but send you your contributions in a lump sum, so you only receive the money, not the donor records. On the other hand, some services charge for keeping the donor records or for allowing you to upload them onto your computers.

If your organization is sending fundraising appeal letters by e-mail, you should know that the federal CAN-SPAM Act makes it unlawful to send unsolicited commercial e-mails unless the e-mails contain a "clear and conspicuous identification that the message is an advertisement or solicitation" (this information doesn't necessarily have to appear in the e-mail subject line), an ability to opt out of future e-mails, and the valid postal address of the sender.

Finding financial support from a crowd

A new method of raising money online, called *crowd funding* or *crowd sourcing,* involves seeking donations from people who may have no connection to your organization but are willing to support its mission.

Online crowd-funding platforms provide individuals and enterprises with tools to conduct focused, time-sensitive campaigns to raise money. Someone seeking contributions must name a specific amount to be raised and a specific project to be launched or completed. Some sites are "all or nothing," meaning fundraisers don't receive any of the pledged gifts until they meet their goal. Crowd funding isn't exclusively for nonprofit organizations, but platforms that include nonprofits among their clients are Fundly (www.fundly.com), Indiegogo (www.indiegogo.com), Kickstarter (for creative projects; www.kickstarter.com), and Weeve (www.weeve.it).

Distributing your fundraising through volunteers

Technology provides novel ways for your organization's supporters to help raise money. In *distributed fundraising,* an individual supporter creates an online donation account for your organization, and through that account speaks directly to friends and family about your organization's work, urging them to contribute or volunteer. This is a great thing to ask your board members or tech-savvy volunteers to do for you.

As is true with your organization's website, a "donate now" button can be added to a distributed fundraising site. However, the volunteer fundraiser often uses an existing service to set up the page and collect contributions. Some of these services are Network for Good, Change.org, Changing the Present, FirstGiving, and Facebook Causes. Your volunteer will want to pay attention to the comparable setup fees and percentages of contributions collected by these services.

Soliciting text-message donations

Many charities now accept donations made via mobile phone texts. Text message contributions have been particularly strong for natural disasters and other emergencies. In 2010, the American Red Cross raised some $12 million through its text-to-give campaign for Haitian earthquake relief. Mobile phone services waived texting fees for donors who gave.

A typical texted donation is modest in size, but a nonprofit may secure a new donor who is motivated by being able to take action immediately and by the relative ease of remembering a code word and phone number rather than a long website address or street address. A text-to-give campaign works best when your nonprofit has an active social-media network or highly visible public event (such as a benefit concert) through which it can spread the word.

Nonprofits should be aware of some disadvantages — the biggest one being that it's difficult to form a relationship with a texting donor. Your nonprofit and the donor will be working through a processing service such as mGive (www.mgive), and your organization won't gain access to the donor's information. Other disadvantages include:

- ✓ **Upfront costs.** Leasing a short code from the Common Short Codes Administration can cost $1,000 upfront for a "vanity" code word you choose or $500 for a randomly selected code. Furthermore, mobile vendors will charge a one-time set-up fee of $3,000 to $10,000 for a unique "vanity" short code and $1,500 for a shared short code.

- ✓ **Small contributions.** Nonprofits are legally permitted to ask only for modest gifts of $5 to $10, and donors can't give more than five times monthly.

- ✓ **Fees charged.** The processing service will charge a modest fee for each donation.

- ✓ **Delays.** It can take up to 90 days for the donor's gift to reach the nonprofit.

A growing alternative to texted donations is the use of QR codes (two-dimensional barcodes that appear on numerous products). Nonprofits can feature their QR codes on newsletters, letters, t-shirts, and invitations. Donors scan these codes with their mobile devices to make contributions.

Telemarketing: Dialing for Dollars

In the mid-1980s, direct mail was a wildly successful means of fundraising for many organizations. In the late 1980s, it declined. Households were receiving too much direct mail, making recipients less inclined to read it, and the costs of printing and postage rose. That's when the dinner hour began to be interrupted by incessant telemarketing calls.

Now, with many people using Caller ID on their phones, and with cellphone numbers being difficult to collect for calling purposes, it's harder to succeed with telemarketing. Yet the phone is a powerful tool for connecting with others, and it's not yet time to abandon it in fundraising.

The advantages of telemarketing are:

✔ It's hard to ignore. A human voice engages you in a conversation, and you must respond. It's not like a letter that you can throw into the recycling bin without the author noticing.

✔ It can be less costly than a mail campaign. If you use trained volunteers to make the calls (rather than a commercial telemarketing firm), you can manage a campaign at a very reasonable cost.

✔ As with direct mail, you can use some of the elements that shape a large-scale, professional telemarketing project for a modest campaign.

The disadvantages? Donors grow annoyed and may stop contributing if called too frequently. Plus, if you don't have volunteers to make the calls, some commercial telemarketing firms take a very high percentage (as high as 75 percent!) of any funds raised, making it a poor return on investment for donors who want to keep fundraising costs low.

Citizen complaints about intrusive telemarketing have led to the creation of the National Do Not Call Registry, which makes it illegal for businesses to make telemarketing calls to people who register. In 2008, Congress passed legislation to make enrollment on the do-not-call registry permanent. At present, nonprofit charitable organizations and their third-party fundraisers are exempt from these rules. However, if an individual asks to have her name removed from a nonprofit's call list, the nonprofit must comply. Check the status of these regulations before embarking on a telemarketing campaign. Public policy articles on the Association of Fundraising Professionals website (`www.afpnet.org`) are a good place to check, as is the National Do Not Call Registry website (`www.donotcall.gov/faq/faqbusiness.aspx#ExemptOrg`).

The key steps to running a telemarketing campaign are writing a script, training volunteers, organizing follow-up calls, and — of course — thanking, cultivating, and upgrading donors over time. We explain everything you need to know in the following sections.

Writing a script

Every call should open with a clear, direct, personal greeting: "Hello, Mr. I'm-Getting-the-Person's-Name-Right, I'm Ms. Call-a-Lot, and I wanted to talk to you about the Scenic Overlook Preservation Fund Committee's work."

Having connected with the call recipient, the caller then tries to link that person's interests and behavior to the reason for the call:

- ✔ If she's a past donor, begin with a hearty thank you.

- ✔ If she's been involved in a related cause or effort, mention how important that work is.

- ✔ If she lives near the scenic overlook, mention how beautiful it is and the community's concern for the fragile surrounding environment.

You may notice a tricky moment in the call when you want the potential donor to relax and listen so you can tell your story and not be interrupted. To increase the caller's chances of keeping call recipients on the line, the script should be

- ✔ Engaging and information packed (to hold the listener's attention)

- ✔ Upbeat about the possibility of improvement or change

- ✔ Deeply concerned about the current situation

- ✔ Specific about the time frame in which things need to change

- ✔ Specific about the amount of money the caller hopes the listener can contribute

On the CD accompanying this book and through the link in the table of contents, we include a set of telemarketing "do's" and "don'ts" and a sample telemarketing script. See File1408.

Coaching your callers

Telemarketing can be an excellent board or volunteer group effort. If someone involved with your organization works in an office that has multiple telephone lines, see whether you can borrow the office for an evening. Early evening (6:00 to 8:30 p.m.) on weeknights is generally considered the best time to call, but — as you've probably noticed — telemarketers now frequently call during the day and on weekends as well.

Gather your volunteer team an hour before beginning. Feed them a good meal and give them a pep talk. Building camaraderie among the callers can relax anyone who's nervous. Setting a group goal for the evening and mapping it on a big chart can build morale.

Inform callers that they must deliver the message in a crisp, clear, and friendly voice. They shouldn't rush, but they also shouldn't leave holes in the conversation that the call recipient can close before the caller can ask for a contribution. They should ask for a specific contribution and confirm the amount. They also should tell potential donors that they're volunteers; this may make call recipients more likely to pay attention.

Provide your callers with information about each household they're calling, including a recommended gift request. You base your request on the potential donor's past contributions to your organization and others. Sometimes you're just guessing. That's okay so long as your callers are good listeners and deftly adjust the amount they're requesting in response to what they hear. If, after a gift is pledged, you feel that you asked for too little money, don't despair. You can ask the donor to upgrade his gift next time.

Collecting the pledges

If a pledge is made, the caller should thank the donor and try to get her to either provide credit-card information over the phone so the gift can be charged immediately or promise to return the contribution within a certain time. Ask the caller to confirm the spelling of the donor's name and address before saying goodbye.

At the end of the evening, everyone present should write brief, personalized thank-you notes. For contacts who promised gifts but didn't charge them over the phone, send the thank-you notes with pledge forms (indicating the specific amount of the promised contribution) and return envelopes.

Every telemarketing campaign suffers from a percentage of unrealized promises, and callers want to keep that percentage as low as possible. You may ask a small number of your volunteers to reconvene for a short follow-up calling session two months after the initial campaign to jar loose any contributions that haven't yet been received.

Chapter 15

Making the Most of Special Events

*F*rom glamorous dances under the stars to pancake breakfasts at the local firehouse, social gatherings are part of the fundraising mix for most nonprofits. Special events don't just raise money. They're often credited with raising friends along with funds. New donors — who don't know the organization — may come forward because the event itself sounds fun and interesting, because of who invites them, or because someone they admire is being honored. Special events can be a wonderful catalyst for attracting businesses that like to be recognized when they make contributions, or for attracting people who like to socialize and be seen.

At their best, special events raise substantial amounts of money, draw attention to an organization's good work, and attract new volunteers. If fundraising is about cultivation, a special event can be a greenhouse for nurturing growth. You hope to create a special event that becomes an occasion that people look forward to, an annual tradition. Still, a special event can be one of the most expensive ways to raise money. Expenses may eat up half or even more of the gross event income. Putting together a special event draws upon all your nonprofit management skills and can drain staff and board time and energy away from other important activities.

Bottom line? Special events need careful planning. In this chapter, we show you how to plan a successful special event — and steer clear of obstacles.

Thinking through the Whole Event

If you think a special event is in your future, we recommend sitting down with staff and board members and raising such questions as:

✔ **What would our organization's followers enjoy doing and how much would they pay to do it?**

✔ **Whom does our organization know who can provide event elements —** donated goods, auction items, entertainment, or printing services?

✔ **Whom do we know who can be honored at the event or serve on an event committee?** The event leadership and volunteer committee are critically important to attracting donors to the occasion.

✔ **When can we focus attention on a special event?** The last six weeks before an event are generally the most labor intensive. Look for a relatively clear six-week block of time in which you don't have grant deadlines or other commitments.

✔ **When can we hold an event without competing with our other fundraising drives?** If you have an annual fund drive in October, for example, why not plan your special event in the spring?

We offer some additional advice regarding these questions in the following sections.

Using your budget to guide decisions

Special events can be produced on bare-bones budgets, for princely prices, or for any amount in between. As with most kinds of investments, event planners expect a higher return in exchange for a higher investment. But don't exceed your means. In this section, we outline some ideas for tailoring an event to your organization's budget.

When deciding on an event, we recommend avoiding anything that can make your guests uncomfortable or deter them from coming, such as:

✔ Events that limit your guests' ability to come and go as they want — like a soiree on a boat in the middle of a lake.

✔ Events at which your intended audience finds the attire, time, or place awkward.

✔ Events that are designed to reach an audience that's completely unknown to your organization or its supporters. Do you like to go to a party where you don't know anybody?

After you've sketched out an idea for an event, go to your staff and board members and ask them directly: Would you attend this event? For this price? At this time of year? At this location? If your core followers and supporters aren't enthusiastic, the event isn't going to raise money. If the idea excites them and they're willing to play a role in the event planning, you're on your way to success.

Low-budget special events

Most nonprofit organizations have a wealth of talent simply waiting for a showcase. Some of the following suggestions won't work for your organization, but they can get you thinking about similar events that would be perfect for your nonprofit:

- ✔ **Sign up neighborhood children for a summer read-a-thon that benefits the library or an after-school literacy program.** By sending forms home to parents in advance, you can secure their permission and help with collecting pledges.

- ✔ **Offer a bake sale with a distinctive theme celebrating a cultural group or holiday.** Organize your volunteers around three primary activities: setting up and pricing, selling, and taking down the sale. Plan in advance what to do with items that don't sell.

- ✔ **Hold a cocktail party in a board member's home, focused on a theme or honoring a special guest.** Although a cocktail party for 15 people may not raise much money, don't rule out this idea. If every one of your board members signs up to host such a party over the course of a year, the cumulative amount raised may pleasantly surprise you.

Many nonprofit organizations produce raffles or prize drawings as low-cost activities to raise funds. If you plan to do so, proceed with caution. Such activities are defined as gambling or gaming in many states. Some states permit nonprofits to hold raffles, but in other states or jurisdictions, they may be illegal or may be presented only if you follow steps to secure a permit. You can find a quick guide to states' regulation, prohibition, or permission of raffles at the Association of Legal Professionals (NALS) website: www.nals.org.

Mid-budget special events

If you can afford a few more features in your special event, you may want to do something like one of these ideas:

- ✔ **Identify an up-and-coming performer and ask for a donation of a performance in exchange for the promotion that your event will bring to him or her.** The club or theater rental is likely to be your highest cost. If you choose an unusual site that's donated to you, make sure it can accommodate your performer's needs — acoustics, lighting, electrical outlets, and the like.

- ✔ **Sponsor a daylong cleanup of a coastal area, park, or preserve.** Volunteers can be sponsored by having their friends sign up to pledge a certain gift amount to the organization for each pound or bag of trash that they remove. Offer prizes for the most unusual refuse items found and the most sponsorship sign-ups.

✔ **Produce an online auction.** Volunteers can help you reach out to friends to secure donations to be auctioned and draw attention to the event and auction items through social media. To build and hold interest in the auction, you'll want to post regular updates and news about the event (with pictures).

High-budget special events

If money is no object — at the front end, at least — these events may be of interest. All require more upfront cash:

✔ **Hire a major speaker or entertainer from a lecture bureau or theatrical agency and use that person as the focus of a dinner party or private concert.** Honor one or more business and community leaders at the event. Form an event committee of people who will invite their friends and people who may want to come for the sake of the honorees.

✔ **Present a dance featuring a live band.** Decorate festively. Make sure your crowd likes to dance and that your musicians' repertoire suits the moves that the crowd knows.

✔ **Organize a celebrity athletic event.** Celebrity golf, bowling, and ping pong — you name it — are all possible. Create teams pairing professional players with amateurs or local celebrities with donors. If you use professional athletes, liberally handicap the amateurs so everyone has a chance of winning. Provide trophies or certificates for many kinds of "achievements" — the longest drive, the bowling ball most often in the gutter, the quickest victory, and so on. Often these events end with celebratory dinners.

Sticking to your budget

The bottom line is very simple: Your total earnings from a special event must exceed your total cost — by a lot, you hope. But how do you get a handle on revenue and expenses? In this section, we offer some thoughts.

If you're staging an event for the first time, it's particularly important *early in the process* to ask your core supporters — board, volunteers, and event leadership — how much they intend to give. Because these people are the most likely to give generously, knowing their intentions helps you forecast the overall results.

Sometimes fundraising events take a couple of years to garner high-level support, so budget exactly how much you intend to make in years one, two, and three. It's not uncommon to break even the first year of an event or to have small net proceeds from your first venture.

Another way to estimate the fundraising potential of an event is to check with organizations that produce similar events. If they've presented a program year after year and yours is a first-time outing, ask them where their income levels began. Try to objectively weigh your event's assets against theirs. Are your boards equally well connected? Is your special guest equally well known?

The digital files accompanying this book include three sample special-event budgets — File1501 for a tribute dinner, File1502 for a concert or performance, and File1503 for an online auction.

Figuring the income side

Try to design your event so it generates income in more than one way. A rummage sale may also include the sale of baked goods. An auction may include advertising in a printed program along with tickets to the event and the income generated from the sale of the auction items. Standard event income categories include:

- ✔ Individual ticket sales
- ✔ Table or group sales (usually for parties of eight or ten)
- ✔ Benefactor, patron, and sponsor donations (for which donors receive special recognition in return for contributing higher amounts than a basic table or seat costs)
- ✔ Sponsorships of event participants (for instance, pledging to contribute a particular amount per mile run by a friend)
- ✔ Food and/or beverage sales
- ✔ Sales of goods and/or services
- ✔ Advertising sales (in printed programs, on banners, and so on)
- ✔ Purchasing a chance (raffle tickets, door prizes, and so on)

Capturing expenses — expected and unexpected

Unless a wonderful sponsor has offered to cover all your expenses, your event will cost money to produce. The general categories can include the following:

- ✔ Building/facility/location (space rental, site use permits, security guards, portable toilets, tents, cleanup costs)
- ✔ Advertising and promotion (save-the-date postcards, photography, posters, invitations, event programs, publicist costs, postage, event website with a ticket purchase feature)

- ✔ Production (lighting and sound equipment, technical labor, stage managers, auctioneers)

- ✔ Travel and per diem (for guest speakers, performers, or special guests)

- ✔ Insurance (for example, liability insurance in case someone gets hurt because of your organization's negligence, or shipping insurance to protect donated goods)

- ✔ Food and beverages (including permits for the sale or serving of alcohol, if necessary)

- ✔ Decor (flowers, rented tables and chairs, linens, fireworks, banners)

- ✔ Miscellaneous (prizes, awards, talent treatment, name tags, signs, t-shirts)

- ✔ Office expenses (letter writing, mailing list and website management, detail coordination)

- ✔ All other staff expenses

Always inquire about nonprofit pricing, and let vendors know that your organization is tax-exempt.

In spite of your careful planning, certain expenses can appear unexpectedly and cause you to exceed your budget. If you plan to serve food at your event, keep these tips in mind to avoid surprise charges:

- ✔ Confirm that all service and preparation charges are included in the catering budget.

- ✔ If you need to add additional meals at the last minute, find out whether your caterer charges extra. If meals that you ordered aren't eaten, you probably still need to pay for them. Check on your caterer's policy.

- ✔ If some of the wine that you've purchased isn't consumed, is the store willing to buy it back from you?

- ✔ If wine has been donated to your event, find out whether your caterer charges corkage fees for opening and serving it.

Soliciting in-kind gifts for your event

When you think about what your event will cost and how you can pay for it, think about the business contacts that your board, staff, and outside supporters have. Often, a business's contribution of *in-kind* (non-cash) materials is more generous than any cash contribution to your event. You may need to be flexible about timing and willing to drop things off or pick things up, but don't overlook in-kind gifts. Donated auction items are one example. Other examples include the following:

✔ Businesses in your community that have in-house printing equipment may be able to print your invitations and posters, saving you thousands of dollars.

✔ A florist may contribute a roomful of valuable centerpieces in exchange for special recognition in the dinner program.

✔ A donor may let you use her beautiful residence as your event site.

You may not want or need all the in-kind gifts that are offered to you. In cases such as these, do look the gift horse in the mouth! Don't accept an in-kind contribution if it's not up to the standards that you need for your event. Also, consider the implications of accepting the gift. For instance, if your agency helps young people recover from drug or alcohol addiction, don't accept a sponsorship from an alcoholic beverage company. If you're afraid of offending the donor or hurting a relationship, you can ask to use the gift in another context and — unless it's inappropriate — acknowledge the donor publicly at your event for his generosity.

Your donors will want to claim tax deductions for their in-kind contributions. It's their responsibility to tell you the value of the gifts they give, and it's your responsibility to acknowledge that value in a prompt thank-you letter. If they make a contribution of non-cash property worth more than $5,000, generally that item must be appraised before a value is assigned to it. For more information, see the IRS website at www.irs.gov.

Building your event committee

Strong volunteer leadership is the backbone of special-events fundraising. Some of the most important work you and your board will do as event organizers is to recruit a chair or co-chairs for an event committee. Choose people who are well connected and who bring different contacts to their committee work — perhaps one community volunteer, one business executive, and one local athletic star. Many organizations include a board member on the event committee, but they also use the event as an opportunity to recruit beyond their boards, bringing in new, short-term volunteers.

We strongly recommend having a co-chair who has planned a fundraising event in the past and can help guide you and your committee through the process. Events are detail-heavy, and someone who has done this before can make sure that all details are addressed. Keep an event binder or online folder and document everything including meeting notes, invoices, timelines, budgets, and attendees.

Your co-chairs' job is to build a network of support for the event. Usually they invite other well-connected people to join them as members of an event committee. Perhaps your board recruits three co-chairs, and those co-chairs recruit 25 event committee members. Your committee members and co-chairs then send personalized letters, e-mails, and invitations and make phone calls urging people to support and attend the event. If each of them brings 20 people, you'll have quite a crowd!

You'll find two related sample letters on the CD and through the link in the table of contents. File1504 is written by an event co-chair and addressed to someone who's being invited to join an event as a committee member, and File1505 is written from a committee member to a potential donor.

Setting a date and location

You don't want to plan an event on Super Bowl Sunday or during your city's largest parade of the year. Apart from avoiding holidays and other obvious dates when you would be competing for your guests' attention, check around town to find out whether you're planning your event on the same date as one organized by another nonprofit agency. Be as thorough as possible in this date checking. Competing for the same audience on the same date — or even dates that are close to each other — hurts both organizations' results.

While the idea may not seem very innovative, good hotels are generally excellent sites for special events. They often have several banquet rooms, and catering, podiums, sound systems, and parking valets are all available at the site. All these extras leave you with fewer details to manage.

Some of the best special events we've attended have been inside the nonprofit organizations that they supported or in sites thematically linked to the cause being supported — such as a historic building, a maritime museum, a public park, or an art gallery. Outdoor locations, such as vineyards, formal gardens, and mountaintops, can be beautiful but require backup plans for variable weather, and climbing rocky pathways or crossing uneven lawns may make your event inaccessible to some of your hoped-for supporters.

Another creative angle on choosing a location is to match it to an event theme. We've put on a great Halloween party in a former mortuary.

If you're running short on ideas, ask your friends and colleagues about interesting places they've attended events, or hold a brainstorming session with your board. Make sure your constituents will feel comfortable going to the location you're considering.

Setting Up Your Timeline

Although events vary greatly in size and complexity, and although we've pulled off adequately successful events in two or three weeks, we recommend working against a six-month schedule. This section outlines a scheduling checklist for a gala dinner. It can easily be modified to fit other types of events.

The first three months

The first three-month period is, not surprisingly, the slowest part of event planning. You may wait several weeks to hear back from an invited celebrity, and you may need several more weeks to find a replacement if you get turned down.

✔ Develop the plan and recruit the event's leadership.

✔ Secure entertainment and a location.

✔ Select a theme and a caterer.

✔ Send a save-the-date postcard and e-mail announcement.

✔ Create an event webpage and social-networking site.

✔ Apply for any necessary permits (for charitable gaming, serving alcoholic beverages, street closures, and so on).

Months four and five

As the event draws nearer, you let others know about the upcoming event and begin contacting volunteers.

✔ Recruit an event committee or a core group of volunteers.

✔ Visit the site at which the event will be held, checking out all the regulations and recommendations for its use.

✔ Solicit in-kind contributions of materials you need for the event.

✔ Send initial news releases announcing your speakers, celebrities, and/or event leadership. (See Chapter 12 for more details about a marketing and public relations program.)

✔ Call all potential committee members.

✔ Develop your invitation design. All the text on the invitation should be ready for final design, printing, and online posting by six weeks before the event.

✔ Select your menu and start working on decor ideas.

✔ Mail and e-mail the invitations.

Four weeks before the event

Spend the month before the event generating excitement and finalizing the details.

✔ Build interest with frequent website and social-media updates featuring photos and news bits.

✔ E-mail a second batch of news releases.

✔ Make phone calls to the media and to invitees to confirm coverage and travel plans.

✔ Design the printed program to be passed out at the event.

✔ Assist honorees with their speeches (if necessary).

✔ Gather the elements — baskets, banners, confetti, and so on — needed for decor.

In designing your event's promotional materials, you want the look of the invitation, program, event web page, signage, and audio-visual templates to be consistent. Schedule time to solicit logos from corporate sponsors and double-check spelling of donors' names and how they want to be recognized.

The week before the event

Don't get too stressed in the days before the event. You should have only a few last-minute details to attend to.

✔ Confirm the number of guests you expect. A few days before the party, call *everyone* who has made a reservation and confirm whether he or she is coming. A few people will have changed their plans, and you don't want to pay for uneaten meals or run out of food. When ordering food from your caterer, assume that under normal circumstances, 5 percent of your expected guests won't attend. If the event is free, 10 percent of them won't attend.

✔ Plan the table seating at the event (if necessary).

✔ Prepare place cards and table cards.

✔ Decorate the site.

We include additional event timelines on the CD and through the link in the table of contents. See File1506 for a timeline for a tribute dinner or luncheon and File1507 for a timeline for a benefit performance.

You may think that nobody can rain on your parade, but have emergency backup plans anyway. What if your performer is ill, a blizzard shuts down roadways, or your permits aren't approved on time? You need to quickly move, replace, reschedule, or cancel your program. The faster you can communicate any changes, the better your constituents feel about sticking with you and your cause.

Issuing a memorable invitation

Make your invitation something your potential guests will open and remember. Addressing the envelope by hand and using stamps rather than printed postage makes it look more personal, and an intriguing phrase or logo on the outside may lead to its being opened.

What do recipients see first when they open your invitation? Most invitations are made up of an outer folded piece, a reply card, and a reply envelope. Want some more attention? What if a compelling photograph slips out of the envelope? Or a small black cat, spider, or bat sticker falls out of your Halloween invitation?

In spite of our recommending these bells and whistles, we are firm believers in clarity. Make sure the reader of your invitation can easily see who's extending the invitation, what the event is, where and when it's being held, how much it costs, and how to respond to the invitation. If people have to search for these basics, the invitation will land in the recycling bin. And remember that people look forward to your event more if other people they know are going to be there. Make sure the names of the people on your event committee are clearly and prominently presented. Also list top sponsors (cash and in-kind) on the invitation so invitees can see what businesses are involved in the event. If the

invitations are being printed for free, make sure you list the printing company's name in a prominent location. These tips are equally true for the electronic version of your invitation: Make it easy for your invitees to make reservations and send contributions.

Print the address, phone number, and/or website to which your guest should respond somewhere on the reply card, even though it's also printed on the reply envelope. Sometimes the pieces of an invitation become separated. You want your guests to readily know where to send their reply (and money!).

For informal and low-cost events, you may want to send only an e-invitation, using a service such as EventBrite or Paperless Post, which will distribute your invitation, collect reservations, send reminders to your guests, and urge them to invite others through social media. If you have good e-mail lists of your donors and contacts, this approach can save you postage costs and reduce paper waste. A few disadvantages are that these invitations may get caught up in your recipients' spam protection systems, it can be challenging to include full credit to sponsors, and the perception that electronic invitations are informal may make your event seem less important to recipients.

Spreading the Word

If the mantra of fundraising is "If you don't ask, you won't get," the mantra for special-events fundraising is "Nobody will come if they don't know about it." Your invitation list is likely the most valuable tool you have at hand for reaching out to event guests, but don't overlook the role that social media and traditional media can play.

In recruiting your volunteer committee members, ask them which forms of social media they use and arm them with tools to spread the word to their networks. For example, every time you create a post on the event's web page, e-mail them and ask them to share it. You can also arm them with good photographs and background information and urge them to use the materials to blog or post social-media updates.

Good photographs are essential to your announcements being noticed on social media. Often we think of hiring a photographer for the event itself, but photographic work done before the gala may be even more important.

If your event has a newsworthy angle, send news releases to the media in the hopes of their writing about it or broadcasting the news. (You can find information about writing news releases in Chapter 12.)

Finding a news angle

Think about all the angles you can exploit for publicity. Try to look at your event from the point of view of every section of a newspaper or newscast. Modify your basic news release to suit the content of appropriate newspaper and magazine section editors, producers of radio feature shows, and TV newsrooms. Follow up your e-mailed release with a phone call. A few possibilities include:

- ✓ **Entertainment section coverage of performers.** You may be able to arrange interviews between your special guests and local entertainment reporters.

- ✓ **Business section coverage of your event chair or honoree.** Many papers run a column highlighting the activities of local business and corporate leaders.

- ✓ **Feature stories about the community improvements that your agency has helped to bring about or human interest stories about individuals who have benefited from its services.**

✔ **Food section coverage of your picnic lunch or the gourmet food trucks serving guests at your outdoor benefit concert.**

✔ **Health advice connected to your event.** If your organization is sponsoring a 10K run, what's the current advice about dietary preparation for long-distance running? If local celebrities or unusual teams (for example, six cousins, or all the elementary school's teachers) have signed up, a local paper or news station might interview them in advance.

✔ **Society page coverage of your honorees, event committee members, or other guests at your event.**

✔ **Radio broadcast of your honoree or guest speaker's speech.**

✔ **Fashion page or television coverage of attire worn to your gala.**

Getting a mention on radio or TV

The media need great gobs of news, announcements, and other content every day. You can get some media exposure if you, for example:

✔ Invite an anchor from the local news channel to serve as the emcee for the event and ask her to promote the event and/or provide an on-air mention about the event.

✔ Prepare a prerecorded public service announcement (PSA) for broadcast by radio stations. (See Chapter 12 for guidelines on PSAs.)

✔ Donate free tickets to your event to radio stations to use as prizes of various kinds. If a station picks up on the idea, you get a free mention — maybe a number of free mentions.

✔ Invite live weather or traffic reporters to cover conditions from your location. It can be a novel way to draw attention to your event.

After the ball is over . . .

Write thank-you notes soon after the event to all your committee members and volunteers and make them as specific and personal as possible. They don't have to be long. Many people find handwritten notes of two or three lines to be much more sincere and memorable than boilerplate letters.

The thank-you letters you send to the attendees should clearly define how much money was donated and the cost of goods and services for the event. For example, if you host a dinner and the ticket cost is $50 per person and the food and beverage cost is $25 per person, the thank-you letter should thank the attendee for the $50 contribution and mention that the tax-deductible amount of the donation is $25. Thank-you letters for purchasing auction items should reference the amount paid for an item and the fair market value for the item. It is a good idea to add language like, "Please consult your tax advisor for specific tax advice." Event donations can be tricky, and this can keep you out of the business of providing tax advice.

Thank-you letters also should be sent to any person or business that made an in-kind contribution to the event that includes the value of the contribution. If you held an auction at the event, you can note that the auction generated $10,000 that wouldn't have been possible without the generous donation from the XYZ Gift Emporium.

We also recommend holding a brief gathering for your key organizers and volunteers a week or two after the event. You can thank them personally again for their effort, but the real purpose is to get their ideas about what worked, what needs to be improved, and what should happen in the future. You may want to invite a few attendees to this meeting and solicit feedback from their perspective. Good records of this wrap-up meeting are a jumping-off point for planning the following year's program.

Chapter 16

Finding the Grant Givers

· ·

In This Chapter

▶ Tracking down private grant sources

▶ Recognizing different types of private foundations

▶ Using directories and databases to research grant opportunities

▶ Exploring options for public funding

· ·

Great mystique has been woven around the writing of grant proposals. Consultants have built entire careers on that mystique. Don't be
fooled by the smoke and mirrors, however! Securing a grant is a competitive
process, but small organizations with volunteer grant writers can succeed if
they have good plans and sound nonprofit practices and if they do thoughtful
research into the interests of funding sources.

A classic rule for effective writing of any kind is to know your audience and
keep that audience in mind. Grantwriting is no different. In shaping a proposal, the grant writer considers the known and likely traits of the funding
agencies she's addressing.

This chapter shows you how to find sources of grants and figure out your
approach to a grant giver. (Chapter 17 covers writing a grant proposal.)

Planning a Grant Proposal to a Foundation

Grant sources can be grouped into two broad categories: private and public.
Private sources are generally foundations and corporations, and public
sources are based within some level of the government — city, county, state,
or national. We write about public sources later in this chapter; here we provide the scoop on foundations and corporations.

When you look at the entire nonprofit sector, you'll notice that gifts from individuals provide the largest portion (more than 70 percent) of private contributions. Because they play a smaller role, many foundations see themselves as resources for innovation or program-improvement funding. When your nonprofit has a new idea, wants to expand to a new location, or wants to compare and evaluate different methods, foundations are often a good place to turn for assistance.

It's tricky to generalize, however. Some foundations do provide flexible dollars — general operating support — that your nonprofit can use for rent and light bulbs. In fact, we've seen a gradual trend toward more funding for "gen op." Other grant makers only want to build buildings or provide new computer systems. Grantseeking can resemble putting together pieces of the puzzle that represent an organization's total needs.

Sometimes foundations actively seek grant proposals addressing particular regions or community needs. When doing so, they may issue a *request for proposals,* often called an RFP. Most foundations send their RFP announcements to *The Chronicle of Philanthropy* and The Foundation Center. At the *Chronicle of Philanthropy's* website (www.philanthropy.com), you can find these under "deadlines" in the "fundraising" menu. The Foundation Center announces RFPs in its *Philanthropy News Digest* (see "PND" at www.foundation center.org).

Foundation research generally has two phases: Developing a broad list of prospects, and then refining that list until you find the likeliest sources. We discuss both of these phases in this section.

Your time as a grant writer is better spent when you use some of it to study the priorities and behaviors of the foundations you're approaching. *Shotgunning,* or sending the same proposal to a large number of foundations, is a waste of effort. *Targeting,* or focusing your attention on your most likely sources and writing to address their preferences, is much more effective.

Knowing whom you're dealing with: Different kinds of foundations

Foundations are formed and governed in different ways. These differences may affect the way you address them as a grant seeker. The four basic kinds of foundations include the following: independent foundations, company-sponsored foundations, community foundations, and operating foundations. In this section, we describe how you can figure out which is which.

Independent foundations large and small

Most foundations in the United States are classified as *independent* — also called *private* — foundations. Some of the country's largest foundations, such as the Bill and Melinda Gates Foundation, the Ford Foundation, and the Lilly Endowment, Inc., are independent foundations, but many small- and medium-sized grantmaking foundations also fall into this category.

When conducting your research, note whether the foundations employ paid staff members who can answer your questions: If they do, they're more likely (but not guaranteed) to consider grant proposals from organizations previously unknown to them.

Although they vary widely, the key characteristics that independent foundations share include the following:

- ✔ They're established with funds donated by individuals, families, or a small group of people.

- ✔ Their purposes and modes of grantmaking are set by their boards of trustees, who may be family members (in which case, they're called *family foundations*) or their appointed representatives.

- ✔ Many (approximately 70 percent) of these foundations award grants primarily in the communities where they were formed, but they also may award grants in multiple locations.

- ✔ They must file a 990-PF with the Internal Revenue Service (IRS) each year.

Company-sponsored foundations and corporate giving

Corporations and businesses may support nonprofits by creating company-sponsored foundations, or they may award money directly from their company budgets. Some do both!

Whether the business manages its giving through a foundation or directly from company coffers, the staff members who coordinate grantmaking also may play other roles within the corporation — such as public affairs director or human resources manager. You may notice that many — both company-sponsored foundations and direct corporate-giving programs — give away goods and services or provide technical assistance, and many of them support educational causes.

Common characteristics of company-sponsored foundations include the following:

✔ They're established with funds that come from a business or corporation.

✔ Some of them maintain assets that they invest, and then they award grants from the money they earn on those investments. Many of them add to their grantmaking budgets when their business is having a profitable year. For this reason, their grantmaking budgets can fluctuate dramatically.

✔ Often they're governed by a board made up of company executives.

✔ Most of them award grants in the communities where their employees live and work, and they see their grant giving as part of their role as good citizens.

✔ Sometimes a company's grants support organizations where its employees volunteer or contribute or that its employees recommend.

✔ Some companies are cautious about supporting controversial causes that could alienate their employees or stockholders.

✔ They must file a 990-PF with the IRS each year.

Corporations' and businesses' direct-giving programs share characteristics with company-sponsored foundations, but they have a slightly different profile. Consider some of the following characteristics:

✔ All funds available for grants come directly from company budgets and depend on the business's available resources. In lean years, the business may not support charitable causes.

✔ Like company-sponsored foundations, businesses with direct-giving programs tend to award grants in the communities where their employees live and work.

✔ Many corporate-giving programs want to receive public recognition for their gifts. They justify their charitable giving to their owners or stockholders as "cause-related marketing" and "good public relations."

✔ Gathering information about grants awarded through these programs may be more difficult because the businesses don't need to specify their support of charities in their financial statements.

Because companies often want their gifts to be visible, you may want to consider the company's policies and practices regarding such issues as domestic-partner benefits, staff diversity, energy consumption, or greenhouse gas emissions. The "Search Companies" section of the Foundation Directory Online provides links to an array of these corporate social-responsibility measures.

Many corporate-giving programs match contributions that their employees make to nonprofit organizations. When seeking information about your individual donors, ask whether they work for a company that will match their gift.

In your neck of the woods: Community foundations

The first community foundation, the Cleveland Foundation, was created in 1914. Today, more than 730 such foundations exist nationwide. Community foundations have a different, advantageous tax status from other kinds of foundations. The IRS classifies them as *public charities.* Other characteristics that they share include:

- ✔ They're started with funds contributed by many sources, such as local trusts and individuals living in the communities they represent. Those communities may be as large as a state (Hawaii and Maine have community foundations), or they may be a county or city (Sonoma, California, or Chicago, Illinois).

- ✔ Community foundations focus their grantmaking on the geographic areas in which they were established.

- ✔ They're governed by boards of directors made up of people who represent the communities they serve.

- ✔ To keep their desirable public charity tax status, they must raise money as well as give it away. For that reason, even a very small community foundation has paid staff members.

- ✔ Donors to community foundations may contribute to general grantmaking programs or may create donor-advised funds within their community foundations and play a role in recommending how to award grants derived from their contributions. The number of donor-advised funds in the United States is growing rapidly.

When reviewing a grants list for a community foundation, if you see a grant that doesn't seem to fit within the foundation's published guidelines, realize that it may have been awarded by a donor from an advised fund.

The grantmaking public charity category is broader than the community foundation category, but community foundations are the most common type. Some public charities focus on addressing specific topics or population groups rather than defined geographic areas. They, too, must raise money as well as give it away. One example is the Global Fund for Women.

Operating foundations: Locked doors for grant seekers

Operating foundations don't award grants. They're formed to provide an ongoing source of support for a specific nonprofit institution — often a hospital or museum. When you come across an operating foundation, skip right over it!

Using the Foundation Center to assemble a broad list of prospects

During the past 60 years, the public has gained increased access to information about funding sources. One milestone in this movement was the creation of the Foundation Center in 1956. Originally intended to collect information so foundations could learn about one another, the Foundation Center quickly became a leading source of information for grant seekers. We explain everything you need to know in the following sections.

Understanding the basics about the Foundation Center

The Foundation Center manages five libraries across the United States and a number of official cooperating collections within other libraries and nonprofits. (See the article about nonprofit resources at www.dummies.com/extras/nonprofitkit for more information.) It also publishes several directories in print and on CDs, along with online databases of information available by paid subscription.

 If you can't find a nearby Foundation Center branch library or cooperating collection, check with reference librarians at your local public library or nearby college and university libraries. These places often have copies of some of the Foundation Center's materials. The books and CDs can be expensive for individuals to purchase, so if you can't find them in a nearby library, we recommend that you purchase a short-term subscription to the Foundation Directory Online.

 The Foundation Center directories are dense with information, but each of them contains a helpful introduction and annotated sample listing to help you identify where you can find answers to your questions. The foundation's website can also guide you with articles, webinars, and online tutorials. Visit the site at www.foundationcenter.org.

The number of foundations in the United States grows and shrinks; as we write this book, the estimated number is 110,000. Reading profiles of all of those funders is daunting (and a waste of your valuable time!). You want to find the best options for your organization and project, so what are you looking for when you use these search tools? You'll begin by asking whether a foundation satisfies the following four criteria:

- ✔ **Geography:** Does this foundation award grants in the area where your nonprofit is based?

- ✔ **Fields of interest:** Does this foundation award grants in the subject area of your organization's work?

- ✔ **Type of support:** Does this foundation award the kind of grant you want?

✔ **Application process:** Is this foundation open to reviewing proposals from grant seekers, or does it only give to preselected organizations? Some 50,000 foundations don't accept applications.

If you answered yes to all four, good work! You've found an entry for your broad list of prospects. Strive to come up with a list of about 15 or 20 foundations.

If you find too few choices, broaden your search (for example, looking for funders in your state — not just in your city). If you find too many choices, narrow your options, perhaps by adding a keyword search. But, wait, we're jumping ahead in the process. First you need to be familiar with these search tools.

Discovering the center's information and resources

The Foundation Center organizes its information in nine databases. If you're creating your broad list of foundation prospects, you'll be most interested in five of them:

✔ **Search Grantmakers:** Brief profiles of foundations

✔ **Search Companies:** Brief profiles of companies

✔ **Search Grants:** Indexes of grants of $10,000 or more

✔ **Search 990s:** Foundations' 990 tax forms

✔ **RFPs:** Announcements of foundations' requests for proposals, inviting applications that address particular subjects or community needs

These five databases are incorporated into the Foundation Directory Online, and all are available to people who subscribe to the Professional version of that online tool. Some are incorporated into published directories and CDs. Here are the titles of some of the books and materials you may use if you're not using one of the online versions of this data:

✔ The *Foundation Directory* and the *Foundation Directory, Volume 2,* are books featuring brief profiles of the 20,000 largest foundations in the United States. Most profiles include several sample grants awarded.

✔ The *National Directory of Corporate Giving* profiles more than 3,300 company-sponsored foundations and 1,700 corporate-giving programs. In addition to describing companies' grantmaking programs, it describes their business products and identifies their subsidiary companies.

✔ Twenty-five focused digital *Grant Guides,* produced as PDFs that you may purchase to download and print. These allow grant seekers to hone in on a particular nonprofit field (such as arts, culture, and the humanities or disaster relief and recovery). These guides describe actual awarded grants of $10,000 or more in each featured field.

The information contained in the Foundation Directory Online is updated weekly, and the *Foundation Directory* (the book) is published once a year with a midyear supplement. It's great to have access to the most recent information with the online service, but you should use the tools that best serve your research style and are most readily available to you.

The Foundation Center's resources aren't your only options. Some states and regions publish their own guides, and some universities have excellent databases. Another research approach is to investigate who is funding other nonprofits in your area. Compile a list of organizations with a similar focus and search for their donor lists in their annual reports, newsletters, and 990s. This can lead you to funders that may be interested in supporting your organization.

Effectively searching the center's information

Here are a few pointers to help you cast your net using the Foundation Center tools:

- **Practice searching using the free tutorials on the Foundation Center's website** (www.foundationcenter.org).

- **Start with the larger foundations first.** Although the United States has more than 110,000 foundations, many of them are very small. As you begin your research, focus on the larger ones by working with the *Foundation Directory* or sorting by size the foundations you find when using the Foundation Directory Online.

- **Take advantage of indexes and search functions.** If you're using the printed directories, you'll find indexes that allow you to search by geographic focus, type of support, and subject area. The CD and online tools offer search functions that pull out the same information and point you toward foundations that match your project's context, focus, and needs.

  Say, for example, that you want a grant for "capacity building" to strengthen your organization. If you want to search for that specific term, enter it in the keyword search box on either the "Search Grants" or "Search 990s" feature of the Foundation Directory Online. The "Search Grants" feature culls through actual grants of $10,000 or more that foundations have awarded. The "Search 990s" feature reviews more than a million records culled from foundations' 990 and 990-PF tax returns.

  File0101 is a synopsis of the types of nonprofits that make up the National Taxonomy of Exempt Entities, which is a formal index of all possible nonprofit fields.

- **Determine whether you or your board members have any contacts who serve on foundation boards.** You can gather this information using the Trustees, Officers, and Donors search box in the "Search Foundations" section of the Foundation Directory Online.

✔ **Don't forget that corporations also award grants.** The *National Directory of Corporate Giving* and the "Search Companies" section of the Foundation Directory Online present company-sponsored foundations and giving programs that are managed directly by corporations (rather than related foundations). Many companies award materials or services — often products they produce. You may find that these in-kind gifts are more valuable to your organization than the cash grants they also award.

For a step-by-step guide to the foundation research process, see File1601. For each entry on your broad list, jot down notes and questions on a *foundation prospect evaluation sheet.* You can find a sample evaluation sheet on the CD or through the link in the table of contents; check out File1602. Through cross-checking and deeper study — as we explain later in this section — you can narrow your broad list down to the five or six best potential sources.

Digging deeper to narrow your prospects

It's time to take your broad list of prospects in hand and find out more about each of them. (Check out the preceding section if you haven't yet compiled your list of prospects.) See what you can discover from the following sources:

✔ **Websites and annual reports:** Some foundations (approximately 29 percent of them) produce websites or printed annual reports with detailed information about their grantmaking guidelines and grantees. These websites and annual reports can be particularly helpful for grant seekers. They often include brief statements or introductory letters from the foundation's leaders that provide insight into a foundation's philosophy or its current direction. You can find announcements of new annual reports in the *Chronicle of Philanthropy* (www.philanthropy.com), explore printed annual reports in some libraries, or call the foundations and ask to have the reports sent to you.

✔ **Blogs and tweets:** Some foundation leaders post blogs or tweets about their work and grantees. Some have Facebook pages. You can find their social-media identities through their websites and "follow" or "like" them to get ongoing updates.

✔ **Form 990s:** Foundation 990 forms may be the only place to find a list of sample grants for a small foundation or a list of every single grant a particular foundation has awarded. Foundations are required to make their three most recent 990 or 990-PF reports available to the public. Many of them do so by including them on their websites. Other places to find 990s include the Foundation Center (www.foundationcenter.org), NOZA 990-PF Database (www.grantsmart.com), and GuideStar (www.guidestar.org) websites. Some state agencies also provide online access to 990s. Finally, you can request a photocopy of a foundation's 990-PF either in writing or in person. The foundation may ask for a reasonable photocopying fee.

A 990 is the type of tax form filled out by a 501(c)(3) nonprofit or public charity (such as a community foundation), and a 990-PF is the type of tax form completed by a private foundation.

Approximately half of the foundations in the United States don't review grant proposals from organizations that are unfamiliar to them. They only give to nonprofits chosen by their trustees or staffs. To identify these foundations, watch for the phrases "no unsolicited proposals" or "gives only to preselected organizations" when reviewing the "limitations" sections of their profiles. If you're searching with the Foundation Directory Online, you can avoid wasting time on such foundations if you use the "Search Grantmakers" feature and check the box next to "exclude grant makers not accepting applications." If you're searching through 990 and 990-PF documents to find a possible funder, check Part XV, Question 2. Foundations that don't accept unsolicited proposals will check a box here indicating that practice.

A foundation's 990 may be the only place you can see a complete list of grants, but PDF files for the nation's largest foundations are enormous. We recommend against downloading a 990 from one of the larger foundations. Reviewing 990s or 990-PFs is more useful when you're studying small foundations whose grants lists may not otherwise be available.

✔ **The foundation's contact person:** If a foundation listing includes a contact person and phone number — and if it doesn't say you shouldn't call — feel free to call that person to confirm information and ask any questions you may have. However, we recommend that you do so only after you've read as much as you can find about that foundation. This way you can be focused, clear, and knowledgeable as you seek additional information.

Going for a Government Grant

Before you start daydreaming about massive state or federal funding, compare the pros and cons of private funding and public funding. Table 16-1 sorts things out for you.

Table 16-1   Comparing Private and Public Grant Sources

Private Sources	Public Sources
The purpose of the grant-giving entity is set by donors and trustees.	The purpose of the grant-giving agency is set by legislation.
Most funders award grants to 501(c)(3) nonprofit organizations, some give to public agencies, and others give fellowships and awards to individuals.	Most agencies award grants, contracts, and loans to nonprofit and for-profit entities, to individuals, and to other government entities.
Most grants are awarded for one year, and, in general, grants are smaller than those awarded by public sources.	Many multiyear grants are awarded for large amounts of money.
The application process requires a limited number of contacts with individuals within the funding agency.	The application process is bureaucratic and may require applicants to work with staff at multiple levels of government.
Grants are sometimes awarded in response to simple two-page letters with backup materials.	Many proposals are lengthy (as long as 100 pages).
Agency files are private; applicants may not have access to reviewer comments or successful grant proposals submitted by other organizations. Review panels and board meetings may be closed to the public.	Agency records must be public. Applicants may visit many review panels; reviewer comments and successful proposals submitted by other nonprofits may be available.
Foundation priorities may change quickly according to trustees' interests.	Agency priorities may change abruptly when new legislation is passed or budgets are revised.
Developing personal contacts with trustees or with foundation staff may enhance your chances of securing a grant.	Developing personal contacts with congressional aides for state or national representatives may enhance your application's chances.
After accepting a grant, the recipient is usually required to file a brief final narrative and financial report.	After accepting a grant, the recipient may be required to follow specified contracting and hiring practices and bookkeeping and auditing procedures. It may have to prove other compliance with federal regulations. Grants can be relatively costly to manage.

If, after reviewing the info in Table 16-1, you decide you're up to the task of seeking government grants, read on.

You may have heard that finding government money is difficult. But remember that one or two major government grants can provide general operating or program support for as long as five years. The time you spend wading through bureaucratic red tape can be worthwhile.

Federal grants

To pursue government funds, you want to study a different set of research guides from those that help you with foundations and corporations. The publication that's most likely to help you is online at www.grants.gov.

Grants.gov only covers federal grant programs. If you're seeking personal financial assistance, follow the links on the "For Applicants" page of Grants.gov.

Determining the pros and cons of Grants.gov

The bad news about Grants.gov is that it's written in bureaucratic language, and the site has so much information that it can be overwhelming. But the bad news is far outweighed by the good: Grants.gov is the only source you'll need for information about all federal grants. It incorporates more than 1,000 programs representing $500 billion in annual grant awards. After you get past the initial shock of wading through the mass of information, the site is relatively easy to search.

Supplementing your search with the CFDA

Federal agencies provide 15 different types of funding, including program grants, insurance, loans, and "direct payments for specified use." For information about all 15 types of federal assistance, turn to another federal publication, the *Catalog of Federal Domestic Assistance* (CFDA), which can be found online at www.cfda.gov.

We steer you to Grants.gov because, if grant support is what you're seeking, it's more tailored to your needs and, perhaps, less cumbersome. However, the CFDA website is a powerful tool that you also may want to explore. The two websites use the same catalog numbering system to identify funding opportunities.

Beginning your search with Grants.gov

As you begin your search, pay attention to whether your organization is eligible to apply to a particular program. Some kinds of federal grants are available only to state and local governments, federally recognized Native American tribal governments, and other specified groups — not necessarily nonprofit organizations.

When opening the home page of Grants.gov, you're invited to search by

- Agency (which is useful if you know you're interested in reviewing the programs offered by the Institute of Museum and Library Services, the Department of Homeland Security, or another specific agency)
- Categories (broad subject areas such as "environment" and "health")
- Keywords

When you're ready to move beyond browsing, select Grants.gov's Advanced Search page, which allows you to check on coming deadlines, confirm applicant eligibility, and search by funding category. If you happen to know the CFDA number for a specific program, you can enter it and — voilà — the program description will appear.

Grants.gov can tell you which agencies and offices manage the funds for different grant opportunities. After identifying federal programs of interest, experienced grant seekers usually call, write, or e-mail those offices to confirm the information. That's because even though Grants.gov information is updated frequently, it also goes out of date quickly.

We outline more information about searching for federal grants and contracts and suggest further steps to take in your research in File1603.

Before you apply for a federal grant, you need to register with Grants.gov. The process, which involves several steps outlined in File1603, can take up to two weeks. Begin this process as soon as you decide to apply for federal funding so delays don't cause you to miss a critical deadline.

Nonfederal government grants

Information about state, county, and municipal grants (which state or local tax dollars generate money for) can be trickier to find than those awarded through federal agencies. That's because the information isn't always compiled in resource guides. Some, but not all, state and city government offices do a good job of informing their constituents about funding opportunities.

During your research process, check the websites of state and local agencies related to your project (such as agencies overseeing education or child services) and visit with local government officials and congressional office staff members. Also, check to see whether your governor's website includes information about available grant programs.

Chapter 17

Writing a Grant Proposal

*E*ven though grantseeking is highly competitive, writing a good grant proposal isn't particularly mysterious or difficult. First you identify a problem and make it compelling, then you set goals for solving that problem, and last you propose a possible solution and a way to test the results. In the course of laying out the plan, you also want to assert the special strengths of your organization and a sensible financial plan for the project, both in the near term and later. You present your proposal in a readable form that tells a story and conveys your vision in terms both inspiring and practical.

Some proposals are quite long and elaborate. Some are just a few pages. Some are presented on paper, and others are submitted online. Your research into funding sources (which we describe in Chapter 16) will uncover the preferences of different foundations and government programs, so you can figure out the best mode of presentation, level of detail, and method for submitting your proposal. You'll encounter many variations, but this chapter shows you the basics of how to write the grant proposal.

The Windup: Completing Pre-Proposal Tasks

Generally, a grant writer develops a proposal by talking with staff members, volunteers, or the board about a project idea. Before setting fingers to keyboard, the writer should investigate the following:

- ✔ What is the demonstrated need in the community for the project?
- ✔ Who are the constituents who will benefit from the project? (Find out everything you can about them.)
- ✔ What are others doing in this field?
- ✔ What particular strengths does your nonprofit bring to the project?
- ✔ Specifically, what do you want to accomplish?
- ✔ What will it cost to do this work?

Sometimes a funding source announces a specific initiative for which it's inviting proposals — called a request for proposals (an "RFP") or a program announcement. When you respond to an RFP, you're trying to convince the foundation or government agency that your nonprofit is the best one for the job.

Asking for permission to ask

Many funding sources screen proposal ideas before they receive extensive, detailed documents. This enables them to encourage only truly promising proposals, saving both themselves and grant seekers the time and effort that goes into reviewing and writing longer proposals.

When you encounter a request for a *letter of inquiry,* boil down the essence of the proposal — all eight areas covered in the later section "The Pitch: Writing Your Proposal" — into a readable, compelling letter. The letter doesn't ask for a grant directly, but it asks for permission to submit more detailed information. Most letters of inquiry are two or three pages long. Follow the foundation's stated preferences.

File1701 offers a sample letter of inquiry, and File1702, File1703, File1704, and File1706 show samples of full proposals. File1705 illustrates a detailed project budget for the File1704 proposal narrative.

Passing the screening questionnaire

Some funding agencies screen potential applicants by asking them to respond to questionnaires, which are often found on funders' websites. Questions may determine specific eligibility — such as whether the nonprofit organization serves a particular geographic area — or ask for substantive answers to questions. Like a letter of inquiry, this questionnaire keeps unlikely applicants from wasting their time and effort.

Don't pass off the letter of inquiry or questionnaire as an inconsequential hurdle: First impressions can be lasting impressions.

The Pitch: Writing Your Proposal

Deep down, every good proposal is based on a well-considered plan, and designing that plan is a creative, even fun, part of the task. The differences from funder to funder are in how to pitch that plan and the order in which its parts are assembled. But the parts themselves are fairly standard:

- ✔ **Cover letter and summary:** Provide a brief overview of the entire project and its costs, linking the project to the interests of the funding source.

- ✔ **Introduction or background:** Present the strengths and qualifications of the nonprofit organization.

- ✔ **Statement of need:** Describe the situation that the proposed project will try to improve or eradicate.

- ✔ **Goals, objectives, and outcomes:** Outline a vision for success in both broad and pragmatic terms.

- ✔ **Methods:** Describe the project activities, who will manage them, the time frame for the project, and why the proposed approach is the best.

- ✔ **Evaluation:** Explain how the organization will measure whether it met its goals, objectives, and outcomes.

- ✔ **Budget:** Present the project's costs and sources of income.

- ✔ **Sustainability:** Explain how additional funds will be raised if a grant is awarded but doesn't cover all costs. If the program is expected to continue beyond the grant period, how will future project costs be covered?

In this section, we cover each of these parts in detail.

File1704 and File1706 illustrate two kinds of proposals — one for a project grant and another for a general operating support grant.

Just like other nonprofit organizations, foundations have mission statements and goals. As a grant writer, you're working to convince your reader of a clear connection between the funder's mission and your organization's work.

Starting out with the cover letter and executive summary

Technically, the *cover letter* isn't part of the proposal narrative. It's attached to the top of the proposal, where it serves as an introduction to the document's primary points. One of its key roles is to convey how the proposal addresses the foundation's stated priorities. Cover letters often require a signature from the executive director and/or board president.

The letter mentions any contact the organization has had with the funding source. For example, you may say, "When I tripped over your umbrella last Tuesday, I couldn't help but notice you were reading a book about frogs. Here at the city park aquarium, we've planned an astounding amphibian exhibition."

Although you always want to lay out the basics of the request — how much money is needed and for what — you can also use the letter to say something about your personal connection to the cause. The letter should close with clear, specific information about the contact person to whom the funding source should direct any questions.

The body of the actual grant proposal begins with an executive summary (similar to an abstract for a report) containing an overview of its key ideas. You'll usually begin the summary section with a one-sentence overview of the project and how much money is being requested in the proposal. Next you include the primary ideas from every section of the proposal (boiled down to one or two sentences per section). Finally, close the executive summary with the prognosis for future funding for the program.

Don't use the exact same wording to describe your project idea in the cover letter and in the project summary. You don't want to bore your reader, and you don't want to miss the opportunity to write in a more personal manner in the cover letter.

Introducing your agency

Some proposals contain *introductions*. Others call this section *background information*. However you label it, this part of the proposal describes the nonprofit organization that's seeking money.

Usually this section begins with a brief history of the nonprofit, its mission, and its major accomplishments. Then you describe the current programs as well as the constituents. After including these standard ingredients, you can draw upon whatever other credentials recommend the organization for the work you're about to propose. Here are some things you can mention:

✔ Media coverage

✔ Citations and awards

✔ The credentials and/or experience of the nonprofit's leadership

✔ Other agencies that refer clients to the nonprofit

✔ Invitations extended to the nonprofit to provide expert advice or testimony

✔ Major grants received from other sources

Although you're not yet describing the project idea, the items you introduce here should back up your nonprofit's qualifications to do the proposed work. For example, suppose that an after-school program for teenagers offers multiple programs — athletics, arts, and youth-led volunteer work. If the grant proposal seeks money to expand the volunteer program, the writer can tell the story of how that volunteer work began and evolved, where the teens have provided services, and who has praised their contributions.

If your organization is brand new and you don't have accomplishments or accolades to describe in this section, tell the story of how and why the organization was created, its mission and purpose, and the qualifications of its founders.

If yours is the only organization that offers this program, mention it here. Funders like to know who else is addressing the same issues and how you differentiate yourself as an attractive source to receive financial support.

You may be tempted to write on and on (and on and on and on) (and on and on and on) about an organization's history or mission. Don't drag this section down by including too many details or by using too much eloquent verbiage. One or two paragraphs on these subjects are plenty.

Shaping the problem

A grant writer begins to shape the argument behind the proposal plan in a *statement of need* — sometimes called a *problem statement*.

This section brings forward the reasons behind the program for which your organization is seeking money. It does so by describing the needs of the constituents the project will serve. It should incorporate some data or statements from experts to back up the needs or problems it describes. And it should capture its reader's attention — making him want to read on.

You shouldn't describe your "need" as a lack of money but rather as a situation in the lives of the constituents, whether they're spruce trees, retired adults, or former race horses. Don't start to solve the problem in your statement of need.

Setting goals, objectives, and outcomes

After you've described a need, the next step is to introduce what the non-profit intends to achieve if it takes on the proposed project. You haven't yet described the project activities, but this section jumps ahead to show what can be accomplished if the project is a success. Why? First you pique the reader's interest and concern (in the statement of need), next you show him the possibility of a better future (in goals, objectives, and outcomes), and then you explain how to achieve that vision (in the methods section).

Goals, objectives, and outcomes are related but different terms. You can find out more about them in Chapter 7, which discusses planning. The following points give a brief overview of these terms:

- *Goals* are broad, general results. They may be somewhat lofty.

- *Objectives* should be measurable results. What degree of change do you want to achieve in what time frame, involving how many people (or trees or race horses)?

- *Outcomes* relate to your objectives, answering the question "So what?" So what if you provide anti-smoking classes to high-school students, reaching every teen in four school districts? The outcome isn't the number of teens attending a stated number of workshops, but it may be that a lower-than-average percentage of those students begins smoking in high school.

You want the outcomes to be significant, but you also have to be careful not to overstate how much the project can claim or measure. If a grant proposal says a nonprofit intends to achieve a long-term outcome, for example, the organization had better be prepared to follow up with participants in the future.

Presenting (ta-da!) your project idea

At last it's time to explain the project idea. Who will do what to whom over what period of time? If you're writing your proposal for a research project, generally this section is called *procedures*. For most other types of projects, it's called *methods* or *methodology*.

Although this section contains the idea that inspired the organization to seek funding, sometimes the writing is dull. The content is similar to writing a list of instructions, and writers often get wrapped up in describing each step in minute detail.

To avoid the dullness trap, think about constructing an argument from beginning to end. A good methods section opens with an overview of the approach and then leads the reader through key phases in the project's development. It includes enough detail so that the reader can imagine the project clearly but not so much that she sinks into the daily grind. Other techniques to preserve vitality include the use of charts or graphs to break up and complement the descriptive text.

Many projects require a few months of preparation before they can be launched. Factor in time for hiring and training staff, purchasing and installing equipment, identifying research subjects, or performing other necessary preliminary steps.

Because this section contains all the project details, you may accidentally leave out or forget important information. These two topics are often overlooked:

- ✔ **Hiring:** If you need to hire new staff to do the project work, be sure to discuss the hiring process, job descriptions, and qualifications. See Chapter 10 for ideas on hiring paid staff.

- ✔ **Marketing:** Just because you create something great doesn't mean that anyone will show up to take advantage of it. Your proposal must explain how your organization plans to spread the word about this new project and entice the target population into becoming involved. Chapter 12 provides tips on marketing your program to the public.

The proposal must explain what the organization will do and why the organization is taking that approach — the rationale. The reason may be that nobody has ever done it this way before. The reason may be that the organization has tested the approach through a pilot program and knows that it works. The reason may be that another organization in another part of the country has tested this method.

Some funding sources ask you to fill out a table with columns in which you describe your goals, the *inputs* (resources you'll put into the project), short-term objectives, long-term outcomes, activities, and intended results. These tables go by several names. Often they're called *logic models*.

Take a look at File1707 to see an example of a logic model. If you want additional information, look for the link to the W.H. Kellogg Foundation's website in File1712. The foundation offers a free report about logic models and program evaluation.

In an effort to raise as much money as possible, you may be tempted to change your programs to match a particular foundation's interests. Your board and management should carefully assess new project ideas to make sure they fit the organization's mission. Otherwise, the nonprofit may drift away from addressing its purpose.

Explaining how results will be measured

If you've carefully shaped the goals, objectives, and outcomes section of the proposal, the desired project results are clear. The *evaluation* section, then, explains how the organization will measure whether it met those goals, objectives, and outcomes.

This section says who will conduct the evaluation and why that person or consulting group is right for the job; what information is already known about the situation or population served; what instrument(s) will be used to measure the project's results; and how the finished report will be used.

Different kinds of evaluation are appropriate at different stages of a project. In a project's first year, the most important question may be, "How can we make it run better?" A nonprofit with a brand-new effort may want to spend the first year analyzing its internal efficiency, balance of responsibilities, and general productivity before beginning an in-depth study of whether outcomes are being achieved.

Some organizations evaluate all their projects with project staff. Who's better suited to understand the details and nuances of the work? Who else can grasp the purpose and objectives of the project so quickly? Of course, the opposing view is that you get biased results by asking staff members whose ideas may have shaped the programs and whose livelihoods may depend on continuation of the project. Yet, outside consultants are more expensive, and they, too, are employed by the nonprofit organization and may bring some biases to the evaluation.

Here are some common questions addressed in evaluations (progressing from basic to complex):

- ✔ What activities did you complete? Were project funds spent according to the proposal plan?

- ✔ How many people are being served and by how many units of service (hours of counseling, copies of publications, and so on)?

- ✔ How do consumers of the organization's services rate the quality of those services?

> ✔ How does this organization's work compare to industry standards for effective work of this type?
>
> ✔ What changes have been effected in the lives of the constituents served?

Often a nonprofit can discover a lot about the effectiveness of its work by analyzing information that it already gathers. For example, an organization may have on file intake and exit interviews with staff and clients, videotapes of activities, or comments submitted to the website.

If your organization plans to gather data from new sources (such as surveys, interviews, and focus groups), the proposal should explain what those sources are, who will design the instruments to be used, who will gather the information, and who will analyze the results.

Talking about the budget

It's time for your proposal to present information about project costs and the other funding that's available. If your organization offers only one service for which it's seeking money, the organization's budget is the same as the *project budget.* If the proposal seeks funds for an activity that is one of many things the nonprofit does, it's presented as a smaller piece of the overall budget.

Chapter 11 discusses how to compute the indirect costs that all programs within an organization share. Different foundations have different attitudes about covering the indirect costs associated with projects. Check with the foundation to which you're applying to see whether it limits how much can be charged to indirect costs or to management and fundraising expenses.

The project budget should be clear, reasonable, and well considered. Keep a worksheet of budget assumptions with the grant file in case anyone asks months later how you computed the numbers it contains. Foundations don't want to believe that an organization is inflating the budget, nor do they want to think that the applicant is trying to make his proposal more competitive by requesting less than he really needs. Either approach — budgeting too high or too low in relationship to the cost of a project — can raise a red flag for funders.

Unless the foundation is willing to consider a proposal for 100 percent of the project costs, the proposal budget should include both income and expenses. Some foundations ask for the information in a particular format. For those foundations that don't require a special budget format, here are some general standards that apply to the presentation:

- ✔ Income should head the budget, followed by expenses.

- ✔ If the organization has multiple income sources, contributed sources should be listed apart from earned sources. Within contributed sources, a writer usually lists grants first, followed by corporate gifts and contributions from individuals.

- ✔ All expenses related to personnel costs — salaries, benefits, and consulting fees — come first in the expense half of the budget. Usually personnel costs are subtotaled.

- ✔ Non-personnel costs — rent, materials and supplies, printing, and so on — follow the personnel costs and are also subtotaled.

- ✔ Some kinds of project budgets allow for contingency funds of a certain percentage of the project's projected costs. These funds are usually listed last among expenses.

- ✔ Budget footnotes can explain anything that may be difficult for a reader to understand.

The budget is like a spine for the rest of the proposal and supports every aspect of the plan. The costs of every activity in the methods and evaluation sections should be included.

Keep in mind that some project budgets seem simple and straightforward when they really are more complex. Say, for example, an agency wants to purchase a piece of equipment. It researches the cost and writes it down as the one and only budget item. This approach may be foolhardy: Other costs may include shipping and installation, insurance, training of staff, maintenance, and supplies.

You can find sample foundation budget forms in File1708. You can also find a sample proposal and its accompanying budget at File1704 and File1705.

Showing where the rest of the money comes from: The sustainability section

Willingness to cover the full cost of a project varies from foundation to foundation and agency to agency. Some like to "own" a project and have their name strongly associated with it; therefore, they may be willing to cover full costs. Many like to be one of several supporters so the nonprofit isn't entirely dependent on them. That way, the project can go on even if the funder can't continue to support it in a future year.

In Chapter 13, we introduce the age-old concept of not putting all your eggs in one basket. Between many foundations' reluctance to pay for 100 percent of a project's costs and their preference for offering short-term project support, if you seek a grant for a new project, you want to know how you can cover the balance of the costs in the present and all the costs when the initial project grants have been spent. Foundations reviewing your grant proposals want to know the same information.

Your *sustainability plan* — addressing these needs for additional and future funding — should be clear and reasonable. Because a nonprofit can't assume it will receive every grant for which it applies, a foundation understands if a nonprofit has applied for more grant funding than the full cost of the program. If a nonprofit lists another foundation as a possible source of income for a project, it doesn't necessarily have to have received that grant, but the prospect should be plausible. The size of the grant should be appropriate to others awarded by the agency, and the focus of the foundation should be aligned with the project request.

When listing sources of potential funding, note whether the funding is *proposed* (application has been submitted), *committed* (proposal has been accepted but funds have not been received), or *received* (money is in hand). Funders like to have a general idea of where you are in the fundraising process.

Foundation staff members talk with colleagues at other foundations. Never lie about having submitted a proposal or having received a grant from another foundation. That lie can undermine your request (and future requests, too)!

Generally, foundations hope to see nonprofit organizations growing less dependent on grants over time and are happy to see proposals projecting future increases in earned revenue or individual contributions. Here are some possible sustaining sources you may describe in your proposal:

- ✔ A government contract to continue a valuable service after it has been developed and tested
- ✔ The sale of publications, recordings, or services based on the project
- ✔ A membership drive
- ✔ A major donor campaign

Some proposals don't need to address these concerns. They seek support for projects that begin and end in short periods of time. For example, a grant proposal may support the publication of a study of an agency's work. After the agency edits, designs, and posts the report on its website, future funding isn't needed. For other projects, future funding is very important. For example, you wouldn't want to start a recreation center for low-income youths and have to close it after a few years. The lack of program continuity can have a negative effect on clients.

Writing the P.S.: The appendix

A proposal usually needs an appendix or attachments. Four key items that are routinely included in the appendix (and often identified by foundations as required enclosures) are:

- ✔ Proof of nonprofit status from the IRS (in the form of a determination letter)
- ✔ List of the board of directors (and of any advisory boards)
- ✔ Current year's organization budget
- ✔ Prior year's financial statement

Other common appendix items include the following:

- ✔ A list of major grants received in recent years
- ✔ An organizational chart outlining staff and board roles
- ✔ Copies of media clippings about the agency
- ✔ Job descriptions and/or résumés of key staff
- ✔ Samples of evaluations or reports
- ✔ A copy of a long-range plan
- ✔ Agency brochures and program announcements
- ✔ Letters of support

In File1709, we include a checklist for finishing and submitting your proposal.

Don't include attachments unless the grant instructions clearly ask for them. Funders receive many applications at a time and don't want to sort through information that isn't relevant to the proposal.

Throwing Special Pitches for Special Situations

If you prepare a grant proposal following the format we describe in the previous sections, you'll have in hand a very useful document, suitable for submission to many foundations. However, grantwriting isn't a field in which one size fits all or even one approach fits all. So in the next sections, we describe some common situations that call for variations on your basic proposal.

Tips for online applications

More and more foundations are inviting or requiring applicants to apply online. Online application systems vary widely, but a few things to keep in mind are:

✔ Well before any deadlines, check the funder's website to see if you need to create an account prior to submitting a proposal. This procedure can take a few days.

✔ Plan ahead by gathering documents you want to include with your proposal and by setting up your electronic signature if one is requested on the application.

✔ In the foundation's instructions for applicants, pay attention to whether you can save your work in the online system and come back to finish it later. If you can't, draft your proposal and edit it before you start working on the foundation's online form.

✔ Check to see whether the funder specifies a word count or character count. Track the length of any drafts you write so you don't have difficulty fitting your sections into the online form.

✔ Some online applications consist of a series of questions that aren't revealed until you've logged into the system and begun filling out the form. When writing such a proposal, set aside a generous amount of time to concentrate on each answer.

✔ If the funder's online system allows you to upload a PDF of your proposal, we recommend that you do so. We've had problems with using the Track Changes function in Microsoft Word to mark edits, and — even if we've saved a final, clean version of the proposal — having those edits reappear when the document is uploaded.

✔ Always look back over your drafted proposal before pushing the "upload" or "send" button. If possible, save it for a day to read with fresh eyes.

✔ Submit the proposal at least 24 hours before it's due to allow time to address any technical difficulties. Online applications can be tricky. Some don't work on certain web browsers. Others get overloaded and time out your submission. It's best to prepare ahead so if you encounter difficulties, you still have time to try other approaches or contact the funder for more information.

Trolling for corporate grants or sponsors

Proposals addressed to corporations and company-sponsored foundations are generally brief. A two-page letter or e-mail is an excellent approach.

Here's what to do in your proposal:

✔ Ask for a specific contribution early in the letter. If you've had prior contact with the funder, mention it.

✔ If applicable, mention the involvement of any company employees on your board or volunteer committees.

- ✔ Describe the need or problem to be addressed.

- ✔ Explain what your organization plans to do if the grant is awarded.

- ✔ Provide information about your nonprofit organization and its strengths and accomplishments.

- ✔ Include appropriate budget data. If the budget is more than half a page long, include it as an attachment.

- ✔ Discuss how the project will be sustained in the future.

- ✔ Describe how your organization can acknowledge the gift publicly and provide visibility to the corporation.

- ✔ Make a strong, compelling closing statement.

Some nonprofits seek sponsorships from corporations to help underwrite special programs, such as marathons, museum exhibitions, or beach clean-ups. Approaching a corporation about a sponsorship resembles proposing a business agreement.

Your organization may, for example, suggest to a local business that if it sponsors your charity's annual walk-a-thon, its name will be printed on banners and t-shirts that will be seen by 50,000 people.

A sponsorship pitch usually starts with a phone call that is followed by a brief, confirming e-mail. You can attach to that e-mail a list of possible sponsorship benefits and the level of contribution expected for each.

On the CD accompanying this book and through the link in the table of contents, you'll find sample company foundation guidelines (File1710) and a sample letter proposal to a corporation (File1711).

Seeking general operating support

If you're seeking funds for general operating support, your proposal needs to make an argument for the work of the entire nonprofit rather than for a specific project. In this type of request, some of the information about current activities, which is often included in the introduction or background information sections, should be moved to the methods section. The grantmaking organization judges the application based on overall organizational strength and the nonprofit's role in its field.

If you're tailoring a proposal for general operating support, we recommend the following:

- ✔ Prepare an introduction that covers the agency's purpose, goals, and current programs. Describe its leadership (board and staff) and its history.

✔ In the statement of need, describe current challenges the organization faces as it works to fulfill its mission.

✔ When preparing the section on goals, objectives, and outcomes, address the external goals (how the nonprofit plans to serve its constituents) and internal goals (such as training the board of directors to fundraise).

✔ Use the methods section to describe the agency's planned activities for the year ahead.

✔ In the evaluation section, describe various means the agency uses to assess and improve its programs.

✔ Include the entire annual budget for the organization in lieu of a project budget.

✔ In the sustainability section, briefly describe fundraising or earned income areas the organization is working to increase.

We include a sample grant proposal for general operating support in File1706.

Seed money: Proposing to form a new nonprofit

Some foundations specialize in "seed funding" for new projects and new organizations. A seed proposal has two key ingredients: careful assessment of the problem to be addressed and special qualifications its founders bring to its creation. Here's a quick outline of a proposal for a new endeavor:

✔ Background information introduces the people who are creating the organization, their vision, how they identified the idea, and steps they've taken to realize their vision.

✔ The problem statement thoughtfully presents what the founders have observed and learned about the needs to be addressed.

✔ Although the goals may be lofty, stated objectives and outcomes should be reasonable considering the developing state of the organization.

✔ Methods present plans for the first year or two of activities. They include discussion of how the organization will be structured and how services will be offered.

✔ Evaluation plans may "go easy" during the organization's initial phases. Founders may be testing basic ideas for their feasibility and efficiency for a year or two before studying a program in depth.

- The budget is likely to be the entire organizational budget. Some seed grant funders are willing to cover such start-up costs as equipment purchases or deposits for renting an office.

- The sustainability section should outline basic plans for supporting the nonprofit in the future (unless it addresses a discrete problem that may be solved within a few years).

The foundation may be willing to support a feasibility study that tests the viability of the seed project — how distinctive it is and who its likeliest sources of support might be.

The Homerun: Following Through after You Receive Funding

As is true with any good fundraising, your grant proposal is part of a relationship that you want to develop and maintain over time. If a funder doesn't want to be bothered, he or she will generally tell you. In most cases, we recommend:

- **Thank them.** Thank the foundation at the time the grant is awarded and acknowledge arrival of the check or wire transfer when the money arrives.

- **Recognize the gift.** For most kinds of grant awards, list the funder in your printed materials. It's always a good practice to check with funders about whether and how they want to be listed by sending them a brief letter or e-mail with the text you plan to use. Some foundations tell you in their award letters how to acknowledge them.

- **Keep them informed.** Your funder should hear from you at times when you're not requesting money. Don't overwhelm your funder, but sending her a copy of good media coverage or inviting her to see your program in action are good ways to build a relationship.

- **Let them hear bad news from you first.** If your organization is forced to move, a key staff member decides to leave, or you lose a contract you need to do the project you proposed, make certain that your funder hears the bad news from you, not as a rumor. Let the funder know the steps you're taking to resolve the situation. Your organization's integrity is one of its most important assets.

Chapter 18

Capital Campaigns: Finding Lasting Resources

*A*s nonprofit organizations mature, their staff and board may grow ambitious to develop resources that can stabilize them. One option is to raise *capital* — money to make specific, usually long-term, financial investments.

Some organizations raise capital funds for *ventures* — money they put aside for major program innovations. Some raise capital for cash reserves (funds available to grow and adapt in the future) or *endowments* — money they permanently invest, with the investment returns providing a source of annual income. Still others focus their capital fundraising on buying property or building facilities.

If you're the director of a nonprofit that's taking on a capital campaign, imagine yourself as suddenly having two jobs: leading your organization and its programs and leading its capital project. Can you picture yourself in those two hats? Exhausting thought, isn't it? However, if the campaign project goes well, it can attract new donors and attention to your nonprofit. That benefit, combined with new resources to invest in your work, can make those two hats worth wearing.

As varied as their purposes are, most capital campaigns share a set of fundraising activities. Not every organization is positioned to make those strategies work. Read ahead and proceed cautiously before stepping onto the capital campaign trail.

Beginning the Funding Plan

Suppose your adult literacy program wants to share its innovative teaching materials broadly through a series of books, but setting up an online publication and distribution program requires a substantial initial investment. Maybe your nonprofit school for children with hearing impairments balances its budget each year, but it depends heavily on a small number of income sources. Having annual investment returns from an endowment may allow it to provide scholarships for children who can't pay full tuition rates. Or say you've found the building of your organization's dreams. It's just around the corner from where you currently serve clients, and it's bigger and better than your current building. Better yet, it's for sale at a reasonable price. You need money to buy it and money to make repairs.

In each of these cases, you need to raise a significant amount of money that's above and beyond your normal annual fundraising. Where do you begin? Capital fundraising, of course! However, keep in mind that it requires you to analyze your organization's situation and plan carefully and thoroughly. Not every organization is positioned to succeed at capital fundraising. You need to do the following:

- ✔ **Preplan** by gathering information about technical assistance available to you, reviewing your donor records, and creating a rough campaign budget.

- ✔ **Develop** your case by brainstorming with staff and board members.

- ✔ **Test** the project's feasibility by meeting with a select group of potential contributors and gauging their possible interest. Consider the timing of your campaign: Will you be competing with other campaigns? How generous are donors in the current economic climate?

- ✔ **Analyze** what you find out from the interviews against your initial goal and then refine your goal and plan.

An unsuccessful capital campaign can cost your organization money, hurt its reputation, and exhaust and demoralize your staff and board. If your research suggests that you won't succeed, do *not* be foolhardy and forge ahead anyway.

Preplanning your campaign

After your board decides it may want to raise funds for a capital project, seek outside assistance in the form of workshops, classes, or consulting. Convincing yourself that your capital campaign can work is easy, so testing your vision on others is important. Possible resources include the following:

✔ A program officer at a local foundation or staff in your city's economic-development office or regional community loan fund may be able to suggest other nearby resources.

✔ The Nonprofit Finance Fund (www.nonprofitfinancefund.org) may offer programs in your area, including low-cost consultations, tools to analyze your financial position, workshops about raising capital, and loans for capital projects.

✔ Colleagues who have conducted capital campaigns may be able to guide you to resources they used. Your board may contain members with professional experience in financial lending and investing, architecture, construction, real estate, city government, and law; all can provide valuable assistance. If your board doesn't include such professional skills, its members may know professionals who do.

You need to begin raising funds from individuals and institutions that know your organization and care deeply about its work. Assess your organization's primary sources of contributed income. How detailed and accurate are your donor records? Who's been donating money to your cause and at what level? Critically important in this scan of supporters is identifying a person or a small team of people with resources, dedication, and good connections who would be willing to lead your campaign.

Begin identifying sources beyond your current supporters. Gather information about major capital resources in your area. For example, which individual donors' names appear on the walls of many nonprofits' buildings? Which foundations and corporations?

When identifying possible resources for your capital campaign, don't overlook loans, which often play an important role in facility projects, both as standard mortgages and in helping organizations complete projects on time. Often donors of large gifts don't write checks for the full amount of their pledges immediately, so organizations borrow some of the money they need to finish construction while waiting to receive those gifts.

If you're interested in loans, find out the following information first: Is your region eligible for federal community development investment funds? (Visit the Coalition of Community Development Financial Institutions at www.cdfi.org to find out more.) Does your area have a community loan fund? Do any local foundations make program-related investments (low-interest loans) to nonprofits? Do any local foundations guarantee bank loans for nonprofits?

Developing a rough budget

Before you test your project to find out whether it's feasible, you need assistance figuring out what it will cost. A common mistake organizations make is forgetting that raising money costs money. They need to dedicate staff time and invest in marketing materials and events. Often they hire outside consultants or new fundraising staff to assist them.

For example, if you want revenues from an endowment to cover five $10,000 scholarships, you need to raise at least $1 million. Your board may set a different policy, but most nonprofit organizations figure they can expect to earn 5 percent on their endowments and spend at that rate each year without depleting the money they've put aside. At times when interest rates are very low, the board may decide to spend a smaller percentage earned on the endowment, which requires you to increase your fundraising goal, but we're going to stick with the $1 million goal for this example. If you estimate that meeting that goal will take you a year and a half, you may want to budget for

- A skilled fundraising consultant who will spend an average of ten hours per week on your project

- Printed materials and a project web page describing your organization and the fundraising campaign

- Funds to cover the cost of meeting with prospective donors — travel and meals

- Money to invest in recognizing and thanking donors, including a celebratory event at the culmination of the campaign

Budgeting for building projects is complex. If you identify a plot of land or an existing building you want to renovate, you need to begin with rough estimates and develop a specific budget later — after you secure architectural drawings, construction permits from your city or county, and bids from contractors.

As you begin developing a budget, find out about the construction rules you need to follow. A local architect or city appraiser/inspector should be able to tell you what enhancements you're required to include in your building. For example, the Americans with Disabilities Act (ADA) establishes an important set of requirements. Buildings for public use must offer ramps and elevators for wheelchair users; appropriately placed plumbing, railings, and equipment; and large-print signs or audible signals. You may think to budget for the obvious, more-visible modifications that are needed, but an experienced professional can point out more subtle requirements that you may overlook.

Just because a building is currently in use doesn't mean you can move right in and begin operating your programs there. Building codes are closely tied to the building's function. Rules for classrooms, for example, sometimes change according to the age of the children. And rooms in which large numbers of people may gather are likely to have stricter safety requirements than those rooms used by individuals as offices. Building codes often change over time, so whenever a building changes hands or its use changes, it must then comply with the most recent requirements.

The CD and the link in the table of contents include "Capital: Hard and Soft Costs," a checklist from the Nonprofit Finance Fund (File1801), and three sample capital project budgets (File1802, File1803, and File1804).

Testing feasibility

Remember that tried-and-true method for buying a used car? The one where you circle the vehicle, kicking all the tires? An organization's capital campaign starts with that kind of tire kicking, except that it's called a *feasibility study,* which is research that tests the hypothesis that you can raise the amount of money you need. Four feasibility study test points are

- ✔ **Tire One:** How much money does this organization have the capacity to raise?
- ✔ **Tire Two:** For this particular need?
- ✔ **Tire Three:** At this location and at this time?
- ✔ **Tire Four:** Is that enough money to pay for what the campaign plans to do?

The accuracy of the feasibility study is important to the capital campaign. Whoever conducts it has to have enthusiasm for the project, yet be able to speak honestly about the organization's position and listen carefully to the direct and indirect messages conveyed in the interviews. The person conducting the study must interview key leaders in the organization along with its current supporters and others whose involvement in supporting the project is critical to its success.

Nonprofits often use a consultant for feasibility studies for this reason: She's a step removed from the organization, and therefore interview subjects are more likely to be frank with her.

Leading the way with the board

Whether or not an organization's board includes wealthy individuals, all its members should contribute to the campaign. The board's willingness to support the campaign is an indication of its feasibility. Also important, potential donors who aren't board members are likely to ask whether you have 100 percent board participation. They're asking whether every board member has given a gift or made a pledge to the campaign.

Board members are expected to lead the way. Their contributions may not be the largest, but they should be made in the campaign's earliest phases.

Why is this step so important? A charismatic executive director may be able to stir up enthusiasm about a capital project, but to succeed, such a project usually requires broad-based support and the assistance of all levels of leadership in the organization. If every member of the board of directors hasn't given to the campaign, it suggests that only a few people really support the idea. Also, people asking other people to make contributions are in a much better position to ask if they, themselves, have given. Board members must be willing to be involved in the campaign fundraising.

In addition, the size of a donor's gift (in relation to what the donor can afford) is some indication of enthusiasm. If a penniless playwright who serves on the board gives $100 toward a capital campaign for a theater, he's making as clear a sign of enthusiasm as a wealthy banker on the board who makes a gift of $1 million. If the wealthy banker makes the $100 gift, it suggests either that the board has one malcontent or that the project is unsupportable.

Going through feasibility study interviews

A typical feasibility study interview opens with an overview of the proposed project, emphasizing why the nonprofit selected the project and how it can enhance the organization's programs and better serve its constituents. Next, the interviewer describes how much money the project needs and how, in general, the organization plans to raise it. If any major donors are already involved, the interviewer mentions their levels of support. Finally, the interviewer suggests a possible donation to the potential contributor and makes note of whether that person is likely to give to the campaign and how much the contribution may be.

The interview should be a conversation among the parties in the room rather than a one-sided presentation. The more the interviewer can engage the interview subjects in discussion, the more the interviewer finds out about how outsiders view the organization and about the fundraising potential.

In these conversations, most contributors aren't making promises, but they're suggesting their probable levels of support. The study, therefore, is important for two reasons:

- ✔ It gathers information that helps the organization estimate whether its capital campaign goal is feasible.
- ✔ It begins the process of "cultivating" contributions to and leadership for the campaign.

On the CD accompanying this book and through the link in the table of contents, you can find an outline of a feasibility study interview (File1805) and an overview of the parts of a finished study (File1806).

Analyzing the results of your study

To continue with the used-car metaphor, a feasibility study is like finding out — after talking to your parents, spouse, or the bank — how much you can afford to pay for a car. Your parents may say that they'll give you money for a small sedan but not for a red sports car, and the same is true for a feasibility study. Board members, community leaders, and potential donors may tell you that they would support the venture or endowment if it were smaller, or the building if it didn't need a new foundation.

If the feasibility study suggests that you can raise more than you planned, you may consider increasing your capital campaign goal to include more scholarships or a cash reserve for building maintenance.

If the feasibility study suggests that you can't afford a "Champagne" version of your plans, you may have to settle for a serviceable "house wine" edition. If your plans were already of the house-wine variety, you may want to break the campaign into phases. If yours is a building project, over the first two years you can make major safety and structural changes or renovate one of several floors. Then maybe three or four years later you can launch the second phase of a capital campaign to cover the balance of the costs.

You may also find out that you need to wait. Perhaps your potential major donors recently gave to another campaign, and although they like your project, they aren't currently in a position to make a major gift to your organization. You may be able to come back to them in two years and receive major contributions. Or maybe potential donors voiced concerns about your organization. Perhaps you don't have good records about past donors. Maybe your board has dwindled in size or your executive director just accepted another job. When you organize, recruit, and hire anew, your campaign can proceed.

And you may find out that undertaking the project isn't a good idea at all. Period. At that point, it's time to start over and plan to address your goals in a different way.

Developing a Case Statement

In Chapter 14 on raising money from individuals, we outline steps for writing a case statement. A capital campaign cries out for a *case statement* — a brief, eloquently stated argument on behalf of the capital project. Sometimes these case statements are fancy brochures with profiles of scholarship recipients, drawings of a planned building, or stories about clients of the future taking advantage of new opportunities. Sometimes they're simple word-processed statements.

A capital campaign case statement should incorporate the following elements:

- ✔ A mission statement and brief history of the organization
- ✔ A list of major accomplishments
- ✔ Compelling information about the constituents served
- ✔ A vision of how the mission can be served better as a result of the capital project
- ✔ A vision for the results of the capital investment
- ✔ The campaign's leadership and goals
- ✔ Naming and giving opportunities

We provide a link to an article about the anatomy of a case statement in File1808 if you want more direction about putting together this document.

After you've put together your case statement, you can show it to prospective donors and use it to build your pyramid of gifts (see the next section).

Building the Pyramid of Gifts

You've sketched out your budget. You've set your sights on a reasonable goal. Your next most important need is to identify *campaign leadership* — a team or committee of volunteers who are willing to cheerlead on behalf of the campaign, make personal visits and calls, and sign letters asking for contributions. These leaders may be board members, but we recommend including some people from outside the board if appropriate enthusiasts can be identified. Not only do their efforts ease your board's workload, but their contacts also expand the pool of possible donors, and their involvement illustrates broader community support for the campaign.

Each campaign develops its own strategies, and each organization has distinctive strengths to call upon, but most of them use the same diagram, which is based on conventional wisdom. It's called a gift table, and it looks like a pyramid (see Figure 18-1).

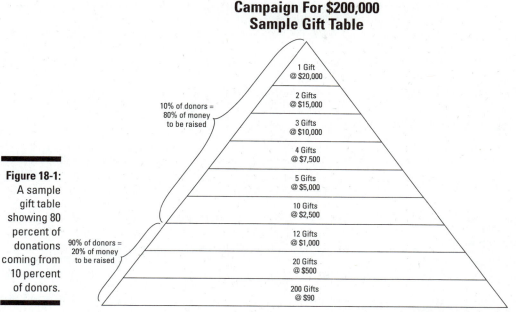

Campaign For $200,000
Sample Gift Table

1 Gift @ $20,000

2 Gifts @ $15,000

3 Gifts @ $10,000

10% of donors = 80% of money to be raised

4 Gifts @ $7,500

5 Gifts @ $5,000

10 Gifts @ $2,500

12 Gifts @ $1,000

90% of donors = 20% of money to be raised

20 Gifts @ $500

200 Gifts @ $90

Illustration by Wiley, Composition Services Graphics

Figure 18-1:
A sample gift table showing 80 percent of donations coming from 10 percent of donors.

Remember the old saying, "A handful of people do most of the work"? A capital campaign works that way. Only a few donors are able to contribute large gifts. They go at the top of the pyramid. Smaller gifts from many other donors fill in the lower levels as the campaign moves forward and the pyramid takes shape.

Starting at the top

We know you don't start at the top when building a pyramid, but that's where you begin with a capital campaign. Similarly, we structured the sample gift table in Figure 18-1 starting at the top, using the following scheme:

- ✔ Ten percent or more of the money comes from a single gift, known as the *lead gift*. This large donation crowns the tip of the pyramid.

- ✔ Fifteen percent of the money comes from the next two largest gifts.

- ✔ Fifteen percent of the money comes from the next three largest gifts.

- ✔ Overall, 80 percent of the money comes from 10 percent of the donors. In other words, if you receive 100 contributions, ten of those people will provide 80 percent of the money that you must raise.

Say you're driving across town and pass the Janice Knickerbocker Symphony Hall, the Engin Uralman Medical Center, and the Jerome Kestenberg Museum of Natural History. What do Janice, Engin, and Jerome have in common? Generally, those people whose names adorn buildings made the contribution of 10 percent or more of the campaign total. They're called the *lead donors*.

When you conduct your feasibility study, one thing you're trying to determine is the size of the campaign's largest gift and whether it totals 10 percent or more of the campaign total.

Your lead gift becomes one of your campaign's attractions. Some contributors may support a capital project because they like or admire the person after whom the scholarship fund or building is named, even if they have little connection to the cause or organization.

Many times the lead donors want to be part of something new and transformative and are looking for an opportunity for recognition. However, always clarify with your lead donor prospects if naming opportunities and public recognition are important to them. Sometimes a lead donor wants to be anonymous; you'll want to honor that request.

After the lead gift is in place, your organization begins seeking the other major gifts that make up the first one-third of the funds to be raised. (In our example in Figure 18-1, just six contributions make up 40 percent of the goal.) Individuals usually pledge these lead gifts during personal visits from nonprofit staff and board members. (See Chapter 14 for more about raising money from individuals.)

Continuing down the pyramid's structure to the widening middle, an organization usually moves beyond board members and major donors to seek grants from foundations and corporations.

Applying for grants as part of your capital campaign

Grant proposals for capital projects follow the general outline of a standard grant proposal (see Chapter 17) with some variations and additions. The grant writer needs to describe the organization's goals and activities and its constituents' needs, and convincingly describe how a stronger organization with stronger capital assets will better serve the organization's goals and clients. Although your proposal may focus on any kind of capital investment project, we discuss a standard building project in the following outline of a campaign grant proposal:

✔ The introduction includes general information about current facilities and leads up to a discussion of the need for a new or renovated building.

✔ The problem statement describes the needs of clients or potential clients and how the organization's current building (or lack of a building) hinders their satisfaction of those needs.

✔ The goals and outcomes section discusses aspirations that the organization holds for serving its clients and its goals for the capital project (the building's dimensions and amenities).

✔ The methods section briefly touches on how you're delivering services but primarily focuses on how you're conducting the capital campaign, how construction will proceed, and the activities you're undertaking to connect current and future clients to the building. Organizations often include a discussion of the results of the feasibility study in this section as a rationale for how they set goals and how they planned the campaign.

✔ The evaluation section focuses both on whether the building project will meet its goals (such as achieving all city fire and safety code standards) and on how the improved building serves clients.

✔ The budget usually includes two major sections: hard costs (for land or building purchase or construction) and soft costs (for financing, fundraising, promotion, and so on).

✔ The future and additional funding section discusses how the capital campaign is progressing and where the organization anticipates raising the necessary funds to complete it. This section also provides information about how the finished project will affect the organization's operating costs and how any additional expenses will be covered in the future.

Ending the quiet phase and moving into the public phase

Early on, when you're conducting the capital campaign among trustees, close friends of the nonprofit, past donors, and foundations, the campaign is in what's called the "quiet phase." When the organization has raised 75 percent to 80 percent of the money it needs, the fundraising style changes. The managers are growing confident that the campaign can succeed, and they announce it to the general public through a press conference, tour, gala party, or cornerstone-setting event.

This is the time to seek smaller donations from lots of people — neighbors, friends of friends, and grandparents. You can often raise these contributions through special events or through mailings to individuals, smaller foundations, and businesses.

Smaller gifts from many people construct the base of the pyramid. Don't discount these gifts. They're important financially to close out the campaign and also to build a feeling of participation among all your donors.

Annual campaigns and other focused fundraising drives are structured along the gift-table pattern. Whether you're raising money for your child's school, an election, or a community fair, a gift table can help shape your plans.

See File1807 for a sample capital campaign gift table.

Realizing the Benefits and Risks of Capital Campaigns

Although you may describe your request for capital support as a one-time need to potential supporters, many campaign donors continue to give after you finish the campaign project. They've been introduced to the agency, they've left their names in its lobby or attached to a scholarship fund, and they want to be sure that it succeeds over time. In the best situations, capital campaigns strengthen the nonprofit organization's programs both by enabling it to improve services and by broadening its donor base. A capital project can also be good for staff morale because it improves working conditions.

In recent years, some thoughtful foundations, service organizations, and consulting groups have advocated for better capitalization of nonprofit organizations. Their point is that donors — particularly foundations — have encouraged nonprofits to come up with break-even financial results year after year. Although breaking even is much better than going into debt, emphasizing it as a virtue means that nonprofit organizations rarely put money aside for an unexpected crisis or infrastructure investment.

No for-profit business would thrive under these circumstances. And nonprofit organizations, many of which are formed to tackle important social and environmental needs, should be just as innovative as businesses — maybe even more so. A campaign to "capitalize" your nonprofit with a cash reserve may be harder to explain to donors than a campaign to build a building, but it may be just as important to your organization's vitality.

We include links in File1808 to some key papers about capitalization that may help your nonprofit make the case for a capitalization campaign.

Although capital projects are meant to enhance your organization's programs and vitality, capital campaigns also have their drawbacks:

✔ Capital campaigns may detract from organizations' basic fundraising. If you ask a donor to your programs to contribute to a building project, he may not contribute to the organization's ongoing programs in the same year.

✔ Capital campaigns may double, triple, or quadruple an organization's fundraising needs while they're being conducted.

✔ Campaigns that don't succeed or that drag on for a long time can damage an organization's reputation. Because buildings tend to be visible entities, the public may be more aware of an organization's slow-moving construction project than of a problem with the programs or services.

✔ Organizations often have turnover in their fundraising staffs after a capital campaign. Employees may stick around to achieve the end of the project, but a heavy workload may cause burnout that leads to quitting soon after they finish the project.

In short, capital projects offer opportunities and pitfalls, buy-in and burnout, and new donor development and loss of current annual fund donors. But when completed, they often pay for concrete, lasting benefits and are worthy of celebration.

Part IV
The Part of Tens

Boost the number and size of donations you receive through your website. Check out the ten tips at www.dummies.com/extras/nonprofitkit.

In this part . . .

- Find out steps you can take if your organization runs into problems.

- Check out some proven ideas for increasing your fundraising dollars.

- Discover what risks your organization faces and get advice for protecting it.

Chapter 19

Ten Tips for Adapting in Hard Times

*I*t's likely that you'll come across problems in the course of managing your nonprofit organization. Everyone does. But sometimes those problems are so severe that you must change the way you do your work to address them.

You may face a catastrophe — a natural disaster, the destruction of a venue, or the serious illness or death of a staff or board member. Or shifts in legislation or foundation policies may cause you to lose important grants or contracts. Although some crises are sudden and fierce, others may build gradually. Several modest deficits may add up to significant debt. The needs of your constituents may change. A competitor may win away your clients or staff members.

The choices you make in challenging circumstances depend, in part, on how much time you have to plan. Is the change you're facing sudden, or has it been gradual? Is it long-term or temporary? Thinking about a crisis or dry spell when you're currently successful isn't fun, but it's necessary in order to survive. So, in this chapter, we provide ten tips to help you make it through those tough times.

Transforming or even closing a nonprofit in hard times draws on the same courage, leadership, and resourcefulness you used to create it. You need to be clear and decisive; include others in making and executing your plans; ask for help when needed; and base your decisions on clear, accurate information.

Recognize the Need for Change Before It's Too Late

Recognizing a sudden crisis is easy, but often the most difficult aspect of managing a nonprofit is seeing a gradual decline and the need to change. Likely, you work so hard and feel such dedication that you can't believe your organization is floundering.

Financial problems have clear consequences (so be on the lookout for them): When deficits exceed 10 percent of an operating budget, the organization will have trouble paying bills within 30 or 60 days. When the deficit exceeds 20 percent of the budget, the pressure intensifies. The inability to make payroll or timely tax payments signals severe problems.

A loan or emergency fundraising drive may solve a short-term problem, but an organization must consider whether its programs cost more money than its earned income and fundraising capacity can provide. It can't keep borrowing funds or crying out for help without alienating its friends and supporters.

Communicate When Making Hard Decisions

A colleague of ours once asked, "What do you mean by 'hard decisions'? Are they hard because they're unpopular? Or are they hard because we must choose among options and the best choice is unclear?" The answer is both.

If you're facing an unpopular decision — laying off staff, for example — it's better to communicate clearly and move forward decisively. The longer you delay, the greater harm you may do to your organization and to those employees.

Take a Break

Sometimes an appropriate first action when you recognize that your organization faces a crisis is to step back and take a breath. You might want to consider reducing the hours that a program operates or cutting back on the number of programs you offer. You may even consider suspending all your programs to give yourself time to plan your next move. Not every nonprofit can do so without harming constituents, but many can. Taking a hiatus can reduce operating costs and allow you to focus full attention on your options.

If you do take a break, communicate your reasons to your members, clients, and funders and keep everyone informed of your progress. Even if you suspend programs, don't stop publishing your online newsletter or quarterly status reports. It's critical to your long-term health as a nonprofit that your supporters know you care about them and — even more important — that you still exist.

Revisit Fiscal Sponsorship

We introduce the idea of fiscal sponsorship for new organizations in Chapter 2. If you're facing the need to downsize — even after you're established as a 501(c)(3) organization, a fiscal sponsor may be helpful to you. How? For a percentage of contributed revenues (often 10 percent to 20 percent), some sponsors provide check-writing and payroll services, access to human resources expertise and insurance, regular financial reports, grants management, and other back-office services — freeing you of those key administrative burdens. Your connection with a well-known fiscal sponsor may reassure a funder that your organization has the capacity to track and manage grant funds.

Collaborate with Others in Your Field

If the field in which you work has seen a decline in funding or an increase in competition for staff or clients, it may be time to identify others who provide similar programs and begin to work together. Who shares your organization's values and approach? Can you serve clients better by combining services?

Collaboration enables you to bring different strengths, resources, and knowledge to a task. It assumes that you can work with greater depth and understanding through a partnership. You also may save some money.

We recommend that you try a temporary, modest project with your partner before launching a large-scale combination of services. Shared goals and values and shared fields of interest matter, but personal compatibility is important, as well. Also, as you step into a partnership arrangement, make sure that more than one leader in each organization is participating in the conversations and negotiations. Collaborations often falter if the key contact person at one of the two organizations leaves. A team can ensure continuity.

Share a Back Office

Maybe program collaboration won't work for your organization, but other types of collaboration may be successful. For example, why not approach another nonprofit about sharing a staff member? By hiring together, you may be able to offer a stable, full-time job with a competitive salary rather than a part-time gig. In turn, your organizations can engage more experienced and qualified employees.

When sharing an employee, both organizations need to give that person clear direction about setting priorities and balancing attention between them.

Sharing things instead of people also can reduce your operating costs. Consider whether you can save money by purchasing equipment, securing office space, or combining supply orders with others. And don't assume that you can share these things only with organizations that resemble yours. In a study of nonprofits in the Puget Sound region, researchers found that some of the best shared-space experiences were among unlike nonprofit organizations, such as a theater school that operated in the late afternoons and evenings and a day-care center that operated early in the day.

Place a Program within Another Agency

One question you should continually ask is how to best meet the needs of the people you serve. Your clients are your reason for existence, after all. If your nonprofit is stretched too thin to achieve everything it's trying to do, why not spin off a program, placing it within another reputable organization that shares your values? You may find that another organization, operating at a different scale or involving people with different skills and knowledge, is positioned to do a better job of managing that program.

We understand that it's difficult to give up a piece of your agency's work, but making this choice is the responsible thing to do for your clients. Plus, it may enable you to focus on the services that best address your nonprofit's mission. Of course, placing a program with another agency also will likely reduce your costs.

Merge with Another Nonprofit

One challenging but responsible choice for your nonprofit may be to merge with another organization. Mergers in nonprofits are similar to those in the business world. Generally, in a merger, one organization dominates the other.

Mergers require thoughtful planning that involves teams of people from both nonprofits. Plan in two phases: First, thoroughly discuss your missions, goals, and program philosophies. If those aren't aligned, the merger won't work. Keep those goals foremost in mind as you move into the second phase of planning, which involves choosing a name, selecting staff, consolidating boards, and arranging a new structure. If problems arise in the second phase of planning, return to the primary conversation and ask whether your missions are aligned and your constituents will be well served by the merger.

We strongly recommend that, when executing a merger, you use a facilitator to lead you through the plans and decisions, and work with an attorney to draw up your final agreements. Also be open to the idea of bringing in new staff and board members who will be committed to the merged organization without loyalties to either of the original entities.

Close with Dignity If Necessary

Nonprofit organizations generally resist closure, maybe because they're usually founded by people with a vision and a desire to serve the public. Yet, sometimes closing is the right choice.

If your nonprofit's financial health fails and its program quality declines, it's best if you accept the idea of closure before it's a last-gasp necessity. Shutting down a nonprofit involves several stages — some of them formally defined and some of them merely good practices. We suggest you do the following:

- **Take care of your employees.** Warn them about the impending closure and, if possible, provide them with job counseling and severance pay.

- **Take care of your clients.** Work with other agencies to make sure that client needs will be met in the future. If you have subscribers or members, offer refunds or work with other nonprofits to honor their benefits.

- **Tell your donors and professional partners.** They should hear about your planned closure from you rather than through rumor or through the media. Clear communication of your story must be presented before rumors begin.

- **Pay your debts or negotiate settlements of your obligations before closing.** Doing so protects your reputation and the reputation of your board members and also engenders trust in nonprofits as good business partners.

- **Document your work.** What's your nonprofit's legacy of services to the field? What has it learned? How can your knowledge benefit others? We recommend gathering your information and placing it in a library, school, historical society, or online archive.

✔ **Celebrate and recognize your staff, board, and volunteers.** The people who have contributed their time, labor, and expertise to your nonprofit deserve applause and thanks.

Complete the Closing Paperwork

If you decide to close your nonprofit, it isn't enough to lock your doors and put up a Gone Fishin' sign. You also need to take a few formal steps. One of the first is to have a board meeting at which the board votes to dissolve the organization and records that decision in the board minutes. Another is to take an inventory of all your assets — money, furniture, client lists, web domains, costumes, fish tanks, and so on — and pass them on, sell them, or return them appropriately, honoring your donors' intentions if some things were contributed for specific purposes. If you have assets to distribute, you must pass them on to a nonprofit with a similar mission.

You'll likely want some technical assistance from a consultant or attorney to complete the paperwork, because you have certain state and federal requirements to meet:

✔ **State requirements:** You need to file a formal intent to close with your secretary of state or state licensing department. The form of this document varies by state. Check with the agency through which you incorporated on the appropriate steps to take.

✔ **Federal requirements:** Just as you turned to the Internal Revenue Service (IRS) to create your nonprofit, you return to the IRS to shut it down. You must file a final Form 990 tax return (see Chapter 5 for details about the 990) within four months and 15 days of your organization's termination. As you do so, check the Terminated box in Part B on the first page of the return. You'll also need to answer yes in Part IV about whether the organization is terminated, liquidated, or dissolved, and file Schedule N, which asks for a list of assets, their value, and where they were distributed.

Chapter 20

Ten Tips for Raising Money

. . . .

In This Chapter

▶ Using time-tested strategies to raise money for your organization

▶ Getting prepared to raise funds

. . . .

Raising money is essential to managing a successful nonprofit organization. In fact, nothing is easier than knowing you should be raising money — and nothing is more difficult than asking for it. This chapter contains our top ten tips for that all-important task of raising funds.

Ask

One of fundraising's oldest adages is, "If you don't ask, you won't get."

Developing fundraising plans, compiling lists of names and e-mail addresses for potential donors, and designing invitations to fundraising events are labor-intensive tasks. But those tasks aren't the things that slow you down in fundraising. Instead, many people pause when picking up the telephone or ringing the doorbell — in other words, when it comes to asking for money. Then, when it's a little too late for the prospective donor to make a decision, write a check, or forward a proposal to a board meeting, these fundraisers make their move and stumble over their own procrastination.

We repeat, "If you don't ask (and ask at the right time), you won't get."

Hit Up People You Know

Some fundraisers believe that the entire money-raising game is in knowing people with money and power and working those contacts — charming them to bend their wills and write those checks. To be honest, if yours is a good cause, that approach isn't bad.

But what if you don't know wealthy people? Does that mean you can't raise money? No, it doesn't. Begin with people you know. Don't be afraid to ask your friends and associates. From a donor's point of view, saying no to someone you know is more difficult than saying no to a stranger.

Tell Your Story

The best way to write an effective fundraising letter or make a successful presentation to potential donors is to tell a story. You don't have to explain how your organization was founded and everything it has done since then (although that history may be worth a brief mention). Instead, the best stories and presentations focus on the constituents you serve and how they benefit from your efforts. These stories are direct and free of jargon. They're hopeful stories that paint a picture of a better future and describe what "better" looks like in clear, specific terms.

Pace the story so it has a bit of drama (but don't stoop to melodrama or hyperbole). Include facts — clear evidence of your success. Recognize and discuss the complexity of the field in which you work, but don't drone on and on about technical matters that will cause your audience to zone out.

Show How You're Improving Lives

In grantwriting terms, this piece of advice would be worded as "clearly describe your outcomes." Keep in mind that outcomes are different from outputs. *Outputs* is the word used for the quantity of work a nonprofit organization produces — the number of meals served, shelter beds offered, workshops led, miles covered, or acres planted. *Outcomes* is the word used for the changes that occur as a result of those outputs. Well-defined outcomes are the hallmark of a good grant proposal, fundraising letter, web page, or pitch.

In other words, providing training about nutrition to a group of 50 seniors isn't enough if those seniors don't change their eating patterns and live longer, healthier lives. Removing toxins from a lake isn't enough if its fish population and ecosystem aren't revived. Exposing 500 children to formal music lessons isn't enough if none of them can read a simple score later. Don't leave potential donors thinking, "Sounds nice, but so what?"

Make the Numbers Sparklingly Clear

Effective requests for money include information about how much is needed to achieve change or test an idea. Make sure to present any data you cite in clear terms. In most cases, telling your reader or listener how much a needed change costs — the cost per child to participate in a special classroom for a year, the cost per injured sea mammal rescued, the cost per well in a remote village — helps to make your point.

Nothing undermines a well-written proposal or case statement faster or more thoroughly than a confusing budget or a muddled financial statement. Double-check your presentation to make sure every activity in your proposal is represented in the budget and that every item in your budget can be traced easily to the work outlined in your proposal. If some items may be confusing to your reader, include budget notes. In all cases, check your math.

Research, Research, Research

Earlier in this chapter, we tell you to ask people you know for money. We're not taking back that advice, but at some point you need to move beyond your immediate circle of acquaintances. That's where doing your homework pays off.

Before you send a fundraising letter, submit a proposal, or visit with a corporate giving director, find out as much as you can about the prospective contributor. Do you have anything in common on a personal level? Maybe the foundation director you're meeting recently published an article. If you read it, you have a conversation topic to break the ice. This advice holds true even when your approach is a membership mailing or e-mail appeal: You want to know as much as you can about the people whose names are on the lists you develop, borrow, or purchase.

More important, you want to find out as much as you can about your potential donor's giving behavior. Does this person give small amounts of money to a wide array of organizations or generous gifts to a few selected agencies? Does the foundation like to be the only contributor to a given project, or does it prefer to support an activity along with others? Does the corporate giving program prefer a low-key style, or does it like to have the company's involvement highlighted?

You can turn to many sources for this information; just be sure to make research a habit. For instance, you can do any of the following:

- Refer to the Foundation Center library and its published and online resources (www.foundationcenter.org). Don't overlook its Philanthropy News Digest ("PND" on its website), which announces research published and grants awarded by foundations and their grantees.

✔ Look up the foundation at the Council on Foundations' website (www.cof.org) to see whether it has recently issued a report or been featured in an article.

✔ For personal information about individuals, conduct an Internet search or check *Who's Who* directories, LinkedIn (www.linkedin.com), local newspapers, and college alumni associations.

✔ Follow business and social news along with obituaries to keep track of people's families, professional developments, and affiliations.

✔ Pay close attention to contributor lists when you attend events at other nonprofit organizations.

Know Your Donors' Point of View

Have you ever heard the old saying, "To catch a trout, think like a trout"? Well, this saying also applies to raising money for your nonprofit. The point of conducting research is to be able to talk or write about your organization in ways that are compelling to your listener or reader. You don't want to warp your message or change your mission, but you do want to think about it (and talk or write about it) in ways that respect your audience's point of view. To do so, you need to think about your organization as if you were a prospective donor yourself.

Donors have different personal giving styles, so you need to put yourself in donors' shoes when deciding how to raise money from particular individuals or companies. You don't want to offer to hold a tribute dinner in honor of someone who prefers to contribute anonymously, for instance. And you don't want to downplay a gift from a contributor who relishes public acknowledgment. Some donors prefer the sociability of supporting a cause through a special event, others respond to e-mail appeals, and still others like to see as much of their money as possible going directly to the service being provided. (If possible, let them see that service with their own eyes!)

Whenever possible, ask donors how they prefer to be recognized and also ask them why they donate to your organization. Their answers may surprise you and will help you craft your future message and approach.

Many people forget that foundations are nonprofit organizations with mission statements and that their job is to support proposals that further their missions. Your job as a grant seeker is to measure how your goals align with their purposes. For example, many corporate giving programs and company-sponsored foundations work to improve the communities in which their employees live and work. When these organizations discover that their employees are involved in or contribute to a given cause, they may be more inclined to support that cause.

Government grantmaking programs are created through legislation. If you find a program that seems well suited to your organization's work, reviewing the legislation or, when possible, attending public hearings about the program is worth your time. Doing so helps you fully understand the program's context and intentions.

Build a Donor Pyramid

Earlier in this chapter, we suggest starting by asking people you know. Imagine your fundraising approach as starting with those people at the peak of a pyramid and working your way down to the broader base. After asking people you know, try to enlist those donors in asking their contacts to support your organization as well. Some are likely to respond (in part because people they know also are contributors). Then ask those new donors to ask their friends. If each contributor leads you to two additional contributors, you steadily build your pyramid.

Make It Easy to Respond

You've written a brilliant appeal letter. You've created a compelling website. You've delivered a stirring speech to a roomful of prospective donors. You've got them hooked. They want to contribute. But they're glancing around the room with confused looks on their faces. You blew it. You didn't give them an easy way to respond.

Always suggest a specific amount for donors to consider contributing. Connect that amount to what you need and to their potential giving levels (which you can estimate from your research). And always make immediate giving easy for them: Distribute an addressed envelope and reply card with each mailing, enable a reader to click through your e-mail to the Donate Now button on your website, or set up a labeled box by the exit where donors can leave contributions. Give potential donors pens, stamps, e-mail addresses, pledge cards, and any other tools to help them respond when you have their attention.

Keep Good Records

After you begin attracting contributors, your donor records become your most valuable fundraising tools. Individuals who give to your organization once are likely to continue giving for three or more years. If you thank them, address them as if they're part of your organization, and generally treat them well, the size of their gifts is likely to increase over time.

Working with foundations, corporations, and government sources is a different story. In their case, you want to keep clear records of your original project goals and outcomes, project budget, and due dates for any required reports. Although these sources may not be willing or able to support your organization year after year, their future support is more likely if you're a conscientious grantee who submits reports on time and keeps clear records.

You can create a simple database on a set of index cards by recording names, addresses, phone numbers, e-mail addresses, patterns of giving, and personal information (such as whether a donor knows one of your board members or whether he or she is married and has children). Of course, these days we like to keep databases on computers. Consider investing in *donor management software*. Several good ones are available. Some are pricey, others are free. Find out more about donor software that's right for your organization by following articles in Idealware's e-newsletter (www.idealware.org).

However you keep it, guard your donor database carefully and invest the time necessary to keep it up to date. It's one of your organization's most valuable resources.

Chapter 21

Ten Tips for Protecting Your Nonprofit

In This Chapter

▶ Assessing risks and planning ahead

▶ Filing official paperwork and taxes

▶ Protecting your reputation

▶ Insuring your future

*P*rotecting your nonprofit organization encompasses tasks that can range from purchasing sandbags to filing government forms. These activities should be driven by an ongoing, thoughtful assessment of your organization's risks.

Some risks that nonprofits face vary according to where they're based and what they do. Is your office on the banks of a river or in earthquake country? Do you work with preschool-age children or with injured raptors? Other items are universal: protecting the safety of staff and clients, protecting the organization's assets, protecting its tax-exempt status, and protecting its reputation. Although no nonprofit manager can anticipate every problem that arises, it's wise to put systems and precautions in place.

Assessing Your Risks

Evaluating risks should be a routine part of your planning and operations. We recommend that you begin with a big-picture analysis of your nonprofit and its potential vulnerabilities. We recommend that your list include:

✔ Location and facility

✔ Activities and programs

✔ Beneficiaries of your programs

✔ Management and financial systems

✔ Employees

✔ Communications and reputation

You may note that your organization works with young children and uses organization-owned vans to transport them; its board has limited financial management knowledge; its employees and programs must be licensed; and its computer systems are old and prone to crashing. Each of these observations makes the organization vulnerable.

Planning for Emergencies

Blizzard belt, floodplain, earthquake fault line, hurricane path, gas leak: likely all the nation's nonprofits are vulnerable to some kind of natural or man-made disaster. Your emergency plan should have three elements:

✔ Preventing problems by eliminating as many potential risks as possible.

✔ Preparing for emergencies by devising procedures and assigning roles for enacting them.

✔ Training everyone on your staff to respond to several scenarios. Drill and practice your responses.

We recommend that your nonprofit put together an emergency planning team of three or four volunteers, staff, and board members. It's wise to include people on the committee who represent different kinds of expertise and who would be level-headed in an emergency. Sketch out different response scenarios. Three common options are evacuation, lockdown, and shelter-in-place.

Your emergency team should:

✔ Prepare to ensure the whereabouts and safety of staff members and their families. Phone lists that include information for staff members, their local family members, and an out-of-state contact should be kept up to date and in a safe place. The same kind of information should be kept current for clients.

✔ Plan evacuation routes, identifying nearby shelters, fire stations, or hazards.

✔ Collect and store emergency supplies — sufficient food and water for 72 hours along with flashlights, batteries, a radio, and a first-aid kit. Remember that cellphones may not work in an emergency. Encourage staff members to keep a few days' worth of prescription drugs (if you must stay in place) and a pair of comfortable shoes at work (if you must evacuate).

✔ Safeguard your records. Are your computers backed up regularly? If you depend on data collection, do you send it away regularly to a safe location? Also, if your accounting system is online, you may want to lock away some checks that can be handwritten in an emergency.

You can find useful tools for emergency planning at www.ready.gov (the federal government's all-hazards approach to planning). San Francisco CARD (www.sfcard.org) offers a template for an emergency plan that focuses on the San Francisco Bay Area but is adaptable to other settings.

Filing Annual Federal Forms

Each year, the federal government requires 501(c)(3) nonprofit organizations to submit a *Return of Organization Exempt from Income Tax,* commonly known as Form 990. The complexity of that document varies according to the size of your organization:

- ✔ The 990-N or e-postcard is for organizations with gross receipts of less than $50,000.

- ✔ The 990 Short Form or 990-EZ is for organizations with gross receipts of $50,000 or more but less than $200,000 and total assets of less than $500,000.

- ✔ The 990 is for organizations that are larger than those permitted to file the 990-N or the 990-EZ.

Your 990 tax form needs to be postmarked or filed electronically on the 15th day of the fifth month after the close of your financial year. You may request an extension if needed. Failing to file can jeopardize your nonprofit status.

Filing Annual State Forms

Each state has its own laws and regulations for how and when a nonprofit must report its activities. In some states, your nonprofit will receive a sales-tax exemption. To find your state laws, visit the directory of state offices in File0402.

If you change your articles of incorporation or bylaws during the year, you'll need to follow the laws of your state (in the case of articles of incorporation) or the rules described in your bylaws to register the change.

Furthermore, more than 30 states, the District of Columbia, and some local governments require nonprofits to register and pay an annual fee if they are fundraising in the state.

Paying Employment Taxes

Although nonprofit organizations don't need to pay taxes on revenue related to their exempt purpose, and — in some states and jurisdictions — don't need to pay local property taxes or sales taxes, they must pay employment taxes, including the employer's portion of employment and Social Security taxes and unemployment insurance. In most cases, these taxes are paid quarterly to state tax boards and the Internal Revenue Service. Not every state requires nonprofits to pay unemployment taxes but every nonprofit must pay federal unemployment taxes. Failing to pay these taxes leads to stiff penalties and interest charges. Unpaid employment taxes are one of the few nonprofit liabilities that may be seized from the bank accounts of an organization's board members. Check with your local state unemployment office or department of revenue for filing and payment requirements for your state.

Reporting Payments to Consultants

If your organization hires a consultant to design its website, conduct an evaluation, or manage other specialized tasks, and if that consultant is paid $600 or more during one year, your nonprofit must report these payments by filing the IRS Form 1099 shortly after the end of each calendar year. Some states also require that this information be reported. You can find more information at www.irs.gov and a link to your state information in File0402.

Maintaining Transparency

Transparency is a buzzword in the nonprofit arena these days, and although it may seem like jargon, it represents an important set of standards, namely: Nonprofits should be aboveboard and honest in their delivery of services, personnel matters, fundraising, and finances. One smart thing to do is to review IRS rules for public disclosure by visiting www.irs.gov. Also, it's useful to review the recommended principles and practices for nonprofits in 19 different states, compiled by the National Council of Nonprofits at www.councilofnonprofits.org. Transparency practices to consider are:

- Be honest with donors about how their contributions are used and offer them the opportunity to opt out of being identified as contributors.

- Have a conflict-of-interest policy for staff and board members.

- Post your most recent 990 or financial statement on your website.

- Adopt an internal complaint and whistle-blower policy in accordance with laws in your state.

Responding to Negative Press

Even good, conscientious nonprofit organizations can draw negative media attention. The negative coverage may be based on accurate or inaccurate information, but even untrue accusations can be damaging. When bad press arises:

- Don't speak to the media or members of the public until you've fully investigated the complaint or critique and are ready to give a clear statement. You don't want to delay a response for a long time because your silence can appear to be an admission of guilt, but you also don't want to retract an initial statement. It's fine to say, "We are issuing a statement on Friday morning" when asked to comment.

- Decide on a small number of people (perhaps your executive director and board chair) who are authorized to speak to the media. Don't permit others to comment. It's important to present a clear, consistent message.

- Answer the media's questions directly and truthfully, but also be sure to insert a positive message about how you're rectifying the situation or the value of your organization's work.

- Acknowledge and address the controversy on your website, in a press release, and — if it's a major concern — in a letter to your funders and donors. In all communications, indicate that you're taking the criticism seriously.

Protecting Your Online Reputation

Information reported online is important to your organization's reputation. Negative comments collected on your website or social media pages can be damaging because of how quickly and easily they can be transmitted to many people.

If someone is disappointed with your services, apologize (if appropriate) and invite them to try again, either for no charge or at a discounted fee. Sometimes people may offer what they consider to be constructive criticism. Treat these comments with respect and thank them for their advice. Generally, it's best to ignore angry, vengeful comments. Responding often makes it worse.

Determining Insurance Needs

A nonprofit's insurance needs vary according to, among other things, the following:

- Whether it offers services within its own (or a rented) piece of property
- Whether it has employees (we discuss employee benefits in Chapter 10)

- Whether it makes use of volunteers (see Chapter 9)
- Whether it has direct contact with clients, students, patients, or audiences and the nature of that direct contact

Most of the claims reported by nonprofit organizations are accidents and injuries related to falls at nonprofit locations or special events or are related to the use of automobiles. All nonprofit organizations should purchase general liability (sometimes called "slip and fall") insurance. You need to purchase specialized kinds of liability insurance if your organization has significant direct client contact that involves a potential risk. Health clinics and therapy programs need such insurance to protect them if a client is hurt or handled inappropriately. So do programs offering activities with possible physical dangers, such as rock climbing, sailing, or horseback riding.

If your organization occasionally produces events or conducts work in locations other than its central office or building, double-check to make sure you're covered for these off-site events. You may need to purchase a rider to your regular liability insurance policy to cover such situations.

You should also purchase "non-owned/hired" auto insurance in case an employee or volunteer is involved in an automobile accident.

In most states, workers' compensation insurance is required by law. If an employee is injured in the course of performing her job, this insurance helps protect both the employee and the employer. The cost of your workers' compensation insurance is calculated according to the number of employees, the number of hours they spend on the job, and the nature of the work they do.

Other kinds of insurance to consider are:

- Property insurance for damage to property and equipment owned or leased by the nonprofit
- Employee dishonesty insurance or fidelity bonds to protect against embezzlement
- Directors and officers insurance to protect directors' and officers' personal assets from lawsuits against the nonprofit organization. Corporate laws vary by state, but in most cases directors and officers are protected (even without insurance) if they're providing reasonable oversight of the nonprofit. That "reasonable" oversight involves attending meetings, asking questions, keeping well informed about the organization, and acting in good faith in the best interests of the organization. However, directors and officers insurance covers the cost of a legal defense against lawsuits.

Part V

The Appendixes

Go to www.dummies.com/extras/nonprofitkit for a list of some of our favorite books, magazines, and websites that can help you start and manage your nonprofit.

In this part . . .

- ✔ The nonprofit world has its own lingo. Flip to the glossary when you encounter an unfamiliar word.

- ✔ The CD that accompanies this book includes many helpful documents and links to useful websites. Appendix B lists what's available on the CD.

Appendix A

Glossary of Nonprofit Terms

• •

annual report: A voluntary report published by a nonprofit organization, foundation, or corporation describing its activities and providing an overview of its finances. A foundation's annual report generally lists the year's grants.

articles of incorporation: A document filed with an appropriate state office by persons establishing a corporation. Generally, this filing is the first legal step in forming a nonprofit corporation.

bylaws: Rules governing a nonprofit organization's operation. Bylaws often outline the methods for selecting directors, forming committees, and conducting meetings.

capacity building: A general term used to describe activities that help a nonprofit organization do its job better. Examples include staff and board training, computer and financial-management systems upgrades, and consultant assistance for organizational planning.

capital campaign: An organized drive to raise funds to finance an organization's capital needs — buildings, equipment, renovation projects, land acquisitions, or endowments.

capital support: Funds provided to a capital project.

case statement: A brief, compelling statement about an organization's projects, accomplishments, and vision.

challenge grant: A grant made on the condition that other funds must be secured before it will be paid — usually on a matching basis and within a defined time period.

charitable contribution: A gift of goods, money, property, or services to a nonprofit organization.

charity: The word encompasses religion, education, assistance to the government, promotion of health and the arts, relief from poverty, and other purposes benefiting the community. Nonprofit organizations formed to further one of these purposes generally are recognized as exempt from federal income taxes under Section 501(c)(3) of the Internal Revenue Code.

community foundation: A grantmaking organization receiving its funds from multiple public sources, focusing its giving on a defined geographic area, and being managed by an appointed, representative board of directors. Technically, it's classified by the Internal Revenue Service as a public charity, not a private foundation.

community fund: An organized community program making annual appeals to the general public for funds that are usually disbursed to charitable organizations rather than retained in an endowment. Sometimes called a federated giving program.

company-sponsored foundation: A private foundation that derives its grantmaking funds primarily from the contributions of a profit-making business.

corporate giving program: A grantmaking program established and managed by a profit-making company. Unlike with a company-sponsored foundation, gifts of money, goods, and services go directly from the company to grantees.

demonstration grant: A grant made to experiment with an innovative project or program that may serve as a model for others.

donor-advised fund: A fund held by a community foundation or other charitable organization for which the donor, or a committee appointed by the donor, may recommend charitable recipients for grants from the fund.

donor-designated fund: A restricted fund — often held at a community foundation — for which the donor has specified how the proceeds from the fund will be used.

endowment: Funds intended to be kept permanently and invested to provide income for continued support of an organization.

excise tax: An annual tax of net investment income that private foundations must pay to the Internal Revenue Service.

family foundation: Not a legal term, but commonly used to describe foundations that are managed by family members related to the person or persons from whom the foundation's funds were derived.

federated campaign or federated giving program: Raising funds for an organization that will redistribute them as grants to nonprofit organizations. This fundraising often is led by volunteer groups within clubs and workplaces. United Way and the Combined Federal Campaign are two examples.

fiscal sponsor: A nonprofit 501(c)(3) organization that formally agrees to sponsor a project led by an individual or group from outside the organization that may or may not have nonprofit status. If the outside individual or group receives grants or contributions to conduct an activity, those funds are accepted, approved, and managed on behalf of the project by the fiscal sponsor.

foundation: A nongovernmental, nonprofit organization with funds and a program managed by its own trustees and directors, established to further social, educational, religious, or charitable activities by making grants. A private foundation may receive its funds from an individual, family, corporation, or other group consisting of a limited number of members.

gift table: A structured plan for the number and size of contributions needed to meet a fundraising campaign's goals.

grantee: An individual or organization receiving a grant.

grantor: An individual or organization awarding a grant.

independent sector: The portion of the economy that includes all 501(c)(3) and 501(c)(4) tax-exempt organizations as defined by the Internal Revenue Service, all religious institutions, all social-responsibility programs of corporations, and all people who give time and money to serve charitable purposes. It's also called the voluntary sector, the charitable sector, the third sector, or the nonprofit sector.

in-kind contribution: A donation of goods or services (not of money).

lobbying: Efforts to influence legislation by shaping the opinions of legislators, legislative staff, and government administrators directly involved in drafting legislative policies. The Internal Revenue Code sets limits on lobbying by organizations that are exempt from tax under Section 501(c)(3).

logic model: A graphic illustration that outlines an organization's or program's resources, activities, outputs, and outcomes, and shows, thereby, how it intends to achieve change. Sometimes called a theory of change.

matching gifts program: A grant or contributions program that matches employees' or directors' gifts made to qualifying nonprofit organizations. Each employer or foundation sets specific guidelines.

matching grant: A grant or gift made with the specification that the amount contributed must be matched with revenues from another source on a one-for-one basis or according to another defined formula.

mission statement: A succinct statement of the purpose and key activities of a nonprofit organization.

nonprofit: A term describing the Internal Revenue Service's designation for organizations whose income isn't used for the benefit or private gain of stockholders, directors, or other owners. A nonprofit organization's income is used to support its operations and further its stated mission. It may sometimes be referred to as an NPO, or nonprofit organization.

outcome evaluation: An assessment of whether a project achieved the desired long-term results.

program officer: A staff member of a foundation or corporate giving program who may review grant requests, recommend policy, manage a budget, or process applications for review by a board or committee. Other titles, such as program director or program consultant, also are used.

program-related investment: A loan or other investment (not a grant) made by a foundation or corporate giving program to another organization for a project related to the grant maker's stated charitable interests.

proposal: A written application, often with supporting documents, submitted to a foundation or corporate giving program when requesting a grant.

public charity: A type of organization classified under Section 501(c)(3) of the Internal Revenue Code. A public charity normally receives a substantial part of its income from the general public or government. The public support of a public charity must be fairly broad, not limited to a few families or individuals.

restricted funds: Assets or income whose use is restricted by a donor for a specific purpose or activity.

tax exempt: A classification granted by the Internal Revenue Service to qualified nonprofit organizations that frees them from the requirement of paying taxes on their income. Private foundations, including endowed company foundations, are tax-exempt; however, they must pay a modest excise tax on net investment income. All 501(c)(3) and 501(c)(4) organizations are tax-exempt, but only contributions to a 501(c)(3) are tax-deductible to the donor.

unrelated business income: Income from an activity that's not within the scope of the organization's mission.

unsolicited proposal: A proposal sent to a foundation without the foundation's invitation or prior knowledge. Some foundations don't accept unsolicited proposals.

venture philanthropy: A style of grantmaking drawing on the business practices of venture capitalists.

Appendix B

About the CD

In This Appendix
▶ Finding out what tools you need to use the CD
▶ Using the CD with Windows and Mac
▶ Perusing a listing of the digital files
▶ Troubleshooting potential CD problems

*T*hroughout this book, we refer to specific files that help you set up and run your nonprofit organization. We've placed those files on a CD that accompanies this book. This appendix explains how to use the companion CD, what it contains, and what to do if you run into problems. *Note:* If you're reading an electronic format, go to `http://booksupport.wiley.com` for access to the additional content.

System Requirements

Make sure that your computer meets the minimum system requirements shown in the following list. If your computer doesn't match up to most of these requirements, you may have problems using the files on the CD.

- ✔ A PC running Microsoft Windows
- ✔ A Macintosh running Apple OS X or later
- ✔ An Internet connection
- ✔ A CD-ROM drive
- ✔ Microsoft Word
- ✔ Microsoft Excel
- ✔ Adobe Reader 7.0 or later

If you need more information on the basics, check out these books published by John Wiley & Sons, Inc.: *PCs For Dummies,* by Dan Gookin; *Macs For Dummies,* by Edward C. Baig; *iMac For Dummies,* by Mark L. Chambers; and

Windows XP For Dummies, Windows Vista For Dummies, and *Windows 8 For Dummies,* all by Andy Rathbone.

Using the CD

To use the CD, follow these steps:

1. **Insert the CD into your computer's CD-ROM drive. The license agreement appears.**

   Note to Windows users: The interface won't launch if you have autorun disabled. In that case, choose Start➪Run. (For Windows Vista, choose Start➪All Programs➪Accessories➪Run.) In the dialog box that appears, type **D:\Start.exe**. (Replace *D* with the proper letter if your CD drive uses a different letter. If you don't know the letter, see how your CD drive is listed under My Computer or Computer.) Click OK.

   Note for Mac users: When the CD icon appears on your desktop, double-click the icon to open the CD and double-click the Start icon. The content menus may not function as expected in newer versions of Safari and Firefox; however, the documents are available by navigating to the Contents folder.

2. **Read through the license agreement and then click the Accept button if you want to use the CD.**

   The CD interface appears. The interface enables you to browse the contents with just a click of a button (or two).

Software

The files on the CD are in Adobe PDF, Microsoft Word, and Microsoft Excel formats. In case you don't have Adobe Reader, Microsoft Word, or Microsoft Excel on your computer, we've added links to the following software so you can access all the files:

- ✔ **Adobe Reader:** Adobe Reader is a freeware program that enables you to view, but not edit, Adobe Portable Document Format files (PDFs).

- ✔ **OpenOffice.org:** OpenOffice.org is a multiplatform office productivity suite. It is similar to Microsoft Office and Lotus SmartSuite, but OpenOffice.org is absolutely free. It includes word processing, spreadsheet, presentation, and drawing applications that enable you to create professional documents, newsletters, reports, and presentations. It supports most file formats of other office software. You should be able to edit and view any files created with other office solutions.

The Digital Files that Accompany This Book

In nearly every chapter of the book, we refer to files that can help you create and run your nonprofit organization. The files include useful forms for tracking spending; examples of job descriptions, budgets, and grant applications; and lists of websites where you can turn for even more information. Poke around to your heart's content, but don't blame us when you lose track of time!

The following list summarizes the files that you'll find on the CD or through `http://booksupport.wiley.com` if you purchased the e-book.

File0101	Types of Nonprofit Organizations
File0102	Chapter 1 Web Resources
File0201	Sample Fiscal Sponsorship Contract
File0202	Chapter 2 Web Resources
File0301	Chapter 3 Web Resources
File0401	Checklist for Forming a Nonprofit Organization
File0402	Directory of State Offices with Websites
File0403	Writing Organizational Bylaws
File0404	Chapter 4 Web Resources
File0501	Chapter 5 Web Resources
File0601	Sample Grid for Planning Board Recruitment
File0602	Board Officer Position Descriptions
File0603	Sample Board Contract
File0604	Sample Outline of Board Meeting Minutes
File0605	Sample Simple Board Agenda
File0606	Sample Formal Board Agenda
File0607	Chapter 6 Web Resources
File0701	Sample Planning Retreat Agenda
File0702	Sample SWOT Analysis
File0703	Matrix Map: A Tool for Bottom-Line Decision Making (included with permission from Jeanne Bell, CEO, CompassPoint Nonprofit Services, `www.compasspoint.org`)
File0704	Sample Outline of an Organizational Plan
File0705	Sample Needs Assessment Questionnaire

File0706   List of Required Spaces (included with permission from the Nonprofit Finance Fund, © Nonprofit Finance Fund, `www.nonprofitfinancefund.org`. All rights reserved.)

File0707   Planned Change and Facilities (included with permission from the Nonprofit Finance Fund, © Nonprofit Finance Fund, `www.nonprofitfinancefund.org`. All rights reserved.)

File0708   Sample Planning Interview Protocol

File0709   Chapter 7 Web Resources

File0801   Chapter 8 Web Resources

File0901   Sample Volunteer Job Description, Food to the Table Delivery Volunteer

File0902   Sample Volunteer Job Description, Take My Hand Adult Mentor

File0903   Sample Internship/Volunteer Intake Form

File0904   Sample Volunteer Agreement Form

File0905   Chapter 9 Web Resources

File1001   Sample Job Description, Executive Director

File1002   Sample Job Description, Development Director

File1003   Sample Job Description, Office Administrator

File1004   Sample Reference-Checking Form

File1005   Sample Hire Letter

File1006   Chapter 10 Web Resources

File1101   Sample Organization Budget, Photography Workshops for Teenagers

File1102   Sample Organization Budget, Midsized Sheltered Workshop for Persons with Disabilities

File1103   Sample Organization Budget, Education and Recreation Center for Homeless Children

File1104   Total Project Costs for Tutoring Center, Including Indirect Costs

File1105   Tracking Actual Income and Expenses: Sample Organization Simple Budget and Monthly Report of Budget versus Actual Income and Expenses

File1106   Tracking Actual Income and Expenses: Sample Organization Budget and Monthly Report of Budget versus Actual Income and Expenses with Budget Variance Columns

File1107   Five-Year Financial Trend Line (included with permission from LarsonAllen Nonprofit and Government Group)

File1108	Monthly Information Every Nonprofit Board Needs to Know (included with permission from LarsonAllen Nonprofit and Government Group)
File1109	Sample Cash-Flow Projection
File1110	Blank Cash-Flow Projection Form from the Emergency Loan Fund (modified for general use) (included with permission from Colin Lacon, president and CEO, Northern California Grantmakers, www.ncg.org)
File1111	Advice for Reading an Audit
File1112	Sample Audited Financial Statement
File1113	Tips for Reading Financial Statements
File1114	Chapter 11 Web Resources
File1201	Sample Audience Survey, Neighborhood Historical Society
File1202	Sample Participant/Volunteer Survey
File1203	Sample News Release (included with permission from Carla Befera)
File1204	Sample Media Alert
File1205	Sample Calendar Release
File1206	Sample Photo Caption
File1207	Sample Photo Use Permission Form
File1208	Sample Public Service Announcement
File1209	Chapter 12 Web Resources
File1301	Sample Donor Information Record
File1302	Sample Fundraising Plan, High School Music Awards Program
File1303	Sample Fundraising Plan, Neighborhood Park Coalition
File1304	Sample Fundraising Budget, High School Music Awards Program
File1305	Sample Fundraising Budget, Neighborhood Park Coalition
File1306	Chapter 13 Web Resources
File1401	Acknowledgement Letter for Contribution over $250, No Good or Service Provided
File1402	Acknowledgement Letter for Contribution over $250, Good or Service Provided
File1403	Sample Solicitation Letter
File1404	Sample E-Solicitation Letter (reprinted with permission from Graywolf Press, Minneapolis, MN, www.graywolf press.org)

File1706   Sample General Operating Support Grant Proposal
                (included with permission from UCSF AIDS Health Project)

File1707   Sample Logic Model (included with permission from
                Harvard Family Resource Center. © 1999 President and
                Fellows of Harvard College. Published by Harvard Family
                Research Project, Harvard Graduate School of Education.
                All rights reserved. No part of this publication may be
                reproduced without permission of the publisher. Since
                1983, HFRP has helped stakeholders develop and evaluate
                strategies to promote the well-being of children, youth,
                families, and communities. HFRP's work focuses on early
                childhood education, out-of-school time programming,
                family and community support in education, comple-
                mentary learning, and evaluation. Visit www.hfrp.org to
                access hundreds of resources with practical information for
                evaluators, practitioners, researchers, and policymakers.)

File1708   Sample Foundation Budget Form

File1709   Steps to Take for Finishing and Submitting a Proposal

File1710   Sample Company-Sponsored Foundation Guidelines and
                Application Information

File1711   Sample Letter Proposal to a Company-Sponsored
                Foundation

File1712   Chapter 17 Web Resources

File1801   Capital: Hard and Soft Costs (included with permission
                from the Nonprofit Finance Fund, © Nonprofit Finance
                Fund, www.nonprofitfinancefund.org. All rights
                reserved.)

File1802   Sample Capital Campaign Budget, Constructing a Youth
                Center within an Existing Building

File1803   Sample Capital Campaign Budget, Constructing a Small
                Theater within an Existing Building

File1804   Sample Capital Campaign Budget, Constructing a Child
                Care Center within an Existing Building

File1805   Capital Campaign Feasibility Study Interview
                Questionnaire

File1806   Capital Campaign Feasibility Study Overview

File1807   Capital Campaign Gift Table (Pyramid of Gifts)

File1808   Chapter 18 Web Resources

File2101   Chapter 21 Web Resources

Troubleshooting and Customer Care

We tried our best to compile programs that work on most computers with the minimum system requirements. Alas, your computer may differ, and some programs may not work properly for some reason.

The two likeliest problems are that you don't have enough memory (RAM) for the programs you want to use or you have other programs running that are affecting how the program runs. If you get an error message such as "Not enough memory" or "Setup cannot continue," try one or more of the following suggestions and then try using the software again:

- **Turn off any antivirus software running on your computer.** External programs sometimes mimic virus activity and may make your computer incorrectly believe that it's being infected by a virus.

- **Close all running programs.** The more programs you have running, the less memory is available to other programs. If you have several programs running, try closing a couple and then starting the CD again.

- **Have your local computer store add more RAM to your computer.** This is a somewhat expensive step. However, adding more memory can really help the speed of your computer and allow more programs to run at the same time.

If you have trouble with the CD or website, please call the Wiley Product Technical Support phone number at 877-762-2974. Outside the United States, call 317-572-3993. You can also contact Wiley Product Technical Support at http://support.wiley.com. John Wiley & Sons, Inc., provides technical support only for installation and other general quality-control items. For technical support on the applications themselves, consult the program's vendor or author.

To place additional orders or to request information about other Wiley products, please call 877-762-2974.

Index

• B •

background checks on volunteers, 139
background information, grant proposals, 288–289
background materials, for new board members, 89–90
backing up records, 330
bake sales, 259
balance sheets, 190
beneficiaries of nonprofits, 35
Benefit Corporations (B-Corps), 28
benefits, including in budget, 172
bequests, 13, 14, 223, 230
Better Business Bureau's Wise Giving Alliance, 217
bills, falling behind in payments, 183
biweekly schedule for paychecks, 148
B-Labs, 28
blogs, 250, 279
board books, 52, 65
board contracts, 91
board meetings
  effective, 92–94
  frequency of, 93
  holding first, 52
  keeping minutes of, 65
boards of directors
  borrowing money for debts from members, 183
  bylaws, 43
  commitment from members, encouraging, 91–92
  committees, 88–89
  continuously recruiting members, 86
  delegating to staff, 83–84
  duties of, 81
  evaluation results, sharing with, 127–128
  general discussion, 79–80
  input on mission statements, 38
  lists of contacts from, 241–242
  meetings, holding effective, 92–94
  meetings, holding first, 52
  new members, introducing, 89–90
  number of members, 86–87
  officer positions, selecting, 87–88
  overview, 79

persuading people to join, 85
planning, hiring, and other tasks, 81–83
preserving public trust, 80–81
reporting on Form 990-EZ, 71
reporting on long Form 990, 74–75
staff members on, 90–91
stating in articles of incorporation, 48
support for capital campaigns, 305–306
thanking, 94
traits and skills of members, 84–85
as volunteers, 12–13, 135
BoardSource, 67, 81, 85
bookkeeping
  accounting software, 186–187
  accounting systems, 185–186
  overview, 185
borrowing money for debts, 183–184, 318
brainstorming possible donors, 226–227, 239–242
brochures, 197
budgets. *See also* cash-flow projections; financial statements
  based on past years, 174
  bookkeeping, 185–187
  for capital campaigns, 304–305
  expenses section, 172–173
  financial systems, managing, 193–194
  fundraising costs, 175
  general administration costs, 175
  general discussion, 169–170
  good, defining, 173–174
  income section, 170–172
  in-kind contributions, 175–176
  overseen by board of directors, 82–83
  overview, 169
  program planning, 111
  for programs and departments, 176–178
  project, in grant proposals, 293–294
  for special events, 258–262
  starting nonprofit organizations, 18–19
  working with, 178–180
buildings
  capital projects, 116
  free spaces, 115
  leasing, 115
  maintenance, 114
  owning, 114–115
bulk-mail permits, 246

Notes

John Wiley & Sons, Inc.
End-User License Agreement

5. **Limited Warranty.**

   (a) WILEY warrants that the Software and Software Media are free from defects in materials and workmanship under normal use for a period of sixty (60) days from the date of purchase of this Book. If WILEY receives notification within the warranty period of defects in materials or workmanship, WILEY will replace the defective Software Media.

   (b) WILEY AND THE AUTHOR(S) OF THE BOOK DISCLAIM ALL OTHER WARRANTIES, EXPRESS OR IMPLIED, INCLUDING WITHOUT LIMITATION IMPLIED WARRANTIES OF MERCHANTABILITY AND FITNESS FOR A PARTICULAR PURPOSE, WITH RESPECT TO THE SOFTWARE, THE PROGRAMS, THE SOURCE CODE CONTAINED THEREIN, AND/OR THE TECHNIQUES DESCRIBED IN THIS BOOK. WILEY DOES NOT WARRANT THAT THE FUNCTIONS CONTAINED IN THE SOFTWARE WILL MEET YOUR REQUIREMENTS OR THAT THE OPERATION OF THE SOFTWARE WILL BE ERROR FREE.

   (c) This limited warranty gives you specific legal rights, and you may have other rights that vary from jurisdiction to jurisdiction.

6. **Remedies.**

   (a) WILEY's entire liability and your exclusive remedy for defects in materials and workmanship shall be limited to replacement of the Software Media, which may be returned to WILEY with a copy of your receipt at the following address: Software Media Fulfillment Department, Attn.: *Nonprofit Kit For Dummies,* 4th Edition, John Wiley & Sons, Inc., 10475 Crosspoint Blvd., Indianapolis, IN 46256, or call 1-800-762-2974. Please allow four to six weeks for delivery. This Limited Warranty is void if failure of the Software Media has resulted from accident, abuse, or misapplication. Any replacement Software Media will be warranted for the remainder of the original warranty period or thirty (30) days, whichever is longer.

   (b) In no event shall WILEY or the author be liable for any damages whatsoever (including without limitation damages for loss of business profits, business interruption, loss of business information, or any other pecuniary loss) arising from the use of or inability to use the Book or the Software, even if WILEY has been advised of the possibility of such damages.

   (c) Because some jurisdictions do not allow the exclusion or limitation of liability for consequential or incidental damages, the above limitation or exclusion may not apply to you.

7. **U.S. Government Restricted Rights.** Use, duplication, or disclosure of the Software for or on behalf of the United States of America, its agencies and/or instrumentalities "U.S. Government" is subject to restrictions as stated in paragraph (c)(1)(ii) of the Rights in Technical Data and Computer Software clause of DFARS 252.227-7013, or subparagraphs (c) (1) and (2) of the Commercial Computer Software - Restricted Rights clause at FAR 52.227-19, and in similar clauses in the NASA FAR supplement, as applicable.

8. **General.** This Agreement constitutes the entire understanding of the parties and revokes and supersedes all prior agreements, oral or written, between them and may not be modified or amended except in a writing signed by both parties hereto that specifically refers to this Agreement. This Agreement shall take precedence over any other documents that may be in conflict herewith. If any one or more provisions contained in this Agreement are held by any court or tribunal to be invalid, illegal, or otherwise unenforceable, each and every other provision shall remain in full force and effect.

About the Authors

Stan Hutton became involved in the nonprofit world after co-founding a nonprofit organization in San Francisco. Since that time, he has worked as a nonprofit manager, fundraiser, consultant, and writer. He served as executive director of the Easter Seals Society of San Francisco and a fundraiser for Cogswell College. For five years, he wrote for and managed a website about nonprofits for About.com. He has worked at the San Francisco Study Center and the Executive Service Corps of San Francisco. He currently is a senior program officer at the Clarence E. Heller Charitable Foundation.

Frances N. Phillips is program director for the Arts and the Creative Work Fund at the Walter and Elise Haas Fund in San Francisco. She also teaches grantwriting and creative writing at San Francisco State University. Previously, Frances worked as executive director of Intersection for the Arts and of the Poetry Center and American Poetry Archives at San Francisco State University, and as a partner in the public relations and fundraising firm Horne, McClatchy & Associates. Frances is current board chair of Community Initiatives, a board member for GreatNonprofits and Kelsey Street Press, and a policy council member for the California Alliance for Arts Education. She also is co-editor of the Grantmakers in the Arts *Reader*.

Dedication

To Alice and Tristan, who are about to embark on a great adventure.

Authors' Acknowledgments

This book started with our agent, Maureen Watts, who had the idea and approached us to write it. Many thanks to her and to project editor Vicki Adang, copy editors Amanda Langferman and Ashley Petry, acquisitions editor Stacy Kennedy, and technical editor Sally Bindley, who guided us through shaping and revising our manuscript for this edition. We also thank our colleagues who gave us permission to include examples of their work on the CD that accompanies this book. Finally, we are grateful to Marcelle Hinand of Helicon Collaborative, Julie Taylor of Chitresh Das Dance Company, and Jennifer Wong of the California Alliance for Arts Education for their advice.

We owe much of our knowledge of the nonprofit sector to a remarkable array of professionals with whom we have worked. It is impossible to list everyone who has helped and inspired us, but we would be remiss if we didn't name a few. Lori Horne, Jean McClatchy, and Ginny Rubin showed Frances the satisfaction of raising money for good causes. She is grateful to the boards of the Poetry Center at San Francisco State and Intersection for the Arts for giving her a chance to be a nonprofit executive director, and to her current and past colleagues at the Walter and Elise Haas Fund — particularly Bruce Sievers and Pamela David. Stan wants to add his thanks to Arthur Compton, Louise Brown, Neil Housewright, John Darby, Jan Masaoka, and Bruce Hirsch, all of whom have given him opportunities to work in the nonprofit sector and provided guidance along the way.

Publisher's Acknowledgments

Acquisitions Editor: Stacy Kennedy

Senior Project Editor: Victoria M. Adang

Copy Editors: Ashley Petry,
    Amanda Langferman

Technical Editor: Sally Bindley

Project Coordinator: Sheree Montgomery

Cover Image: © iStockphoto.com/cienpies